Malcolm Walles gained his B.A. at Reading and his Ph.D. at London University. He has lectured in Politics at Monash University Australia, and has held a post as Visiting Professor of Government at the City University, New York. He is at present Lecturer in Politics at the University of Leeds. The late A. H. Hanson was Professor of Politics at the same university. He wrote extensively on parliamentary government and administration, and also edited *The Commons in Transition* with Bernard Crick.

Governing Britain

A Guide-Book to Political Institutions

Malcolm Walles
Lecturer in Politics, University of Leeds

and A. H. Hanson
Formerly Professor of Politics, University of Leeds

Fontana/Collins

First published 1970
Reprinted 1970, 1971, 1972 (twice), 1973, 1974
Revised Edition October 1975
Sixth Impression May 1979

Made and printed in Great Britain by
William Collins Sons & Co Ltd, Glasgow

Contents

Preface to the First Edition

This is a book about the institutions through which Britain is governed, and the way they work. Although introductory, it tries to avoid the merely descriptive, which can be deadly dull. Description has been confined to what we hope is the minimum necessary for intelligibility, so as to permit concentration on the interesting problems of institutional change. Our approach, therefore, is 'problem-oriented', and our main purpose to define challenges and examine responses.

As it is the fashion prefatorially to declare value-premises, we will do so by expressing our agreement with the following statement by Mr Michael Shanks:

> I believe that the greatest challenge facing the world today is the growing failure to adjust our ideas and institutions to the frighteningly accelerating pace of change—and a major contributing factor is the tendency of institutions themselves to ossify.

For reasons of space, we have limited ourselves to the political and administrative institutions of central government. The judicial system receives only passing mention, and there is no attempt to deal systematically with local government, although some of its problems are necessarily referred to, particularly in the chapter on regionalism and decentralization.

In labelling our two main sections with the titles 'New Wine in Old Bottles' and 'New Bottles' we shall perhaps offend some purists. The distinction, although obviously inexact, is intended to emphasize the contrast, which obviously exists, between adaptation and innovation. We also owe the reader an explanation of the rather unusual position occupied by our chapter on group activities. Although this subject would appear to be naturally associated with political parties, we felt that, to be fully intelligible, it should follow rather than precede our account of Parliament, the Cabinet and the central administration.

Of special concern to us are those readers whose interest in British government has led them to undertake a systematic study of the subject. In particular, we hope that what we have written will be found useful by first-year students in universities and other institutes of higher education.

Leeds, March 1969 A.H.H.
M.J.W.

Preface to the Second Edition

In this second edition of *Governing Britain* most of the original text remains but the opportunity has been taken to revise facts and figures where necessary. However, while recording changes it has not been possible in several important instances to offer comment on those changes in operation. For instance, the reforms in the Civil Service which followed on from the publication of the Fulton Report have yet to work their way through, while the new Local Government system only started to operate on 1 April 1974. Some readers may well feel that a failure to discuss the implications of membership of the European Economic Community represents a serious omission but at this point, in the relatively early days of the transitional period, it would be premature to attempt an assessment of that membership upon the nature and style of British Government. (The purely 'political' arguments have, of course, been entirely eschewed.) The position in Northern Ireland is so troubled that it has been thought best to leave the general comments from the first edition unaltered and to await a resolution of that unhappy situation before updating the section.

Finally, I must record with deep personal regret the death in 1971 of 'Harry' Hanson. His knowledge, advice and, above all, his friendship are still sorely missed.

Leeds, January 1975 M.J.W.

Part I

The Heritage

Chapter 1

Royal and Ancient, Democratic and Modern

Politically and administratively, Britain is a highly developed country. For the performance of governmental functions, she has well-established, clearly-defined and widely-respected institutions, run by men and women who are familiar with the roles they are expected to play. Moreover, despite the recent upsurge of Scottish and Welsh nationalism and the growth of tensions between white and coloured people, the political community is highly integrated. Political values do not differ radically as between different social groups, and the degree of political stability that has been achieved, which tends to be taken for granted by Britons, is a matter for envious admiration by many other countries.

That Britain is politically 'modernized', however, by no means sets her apart in the world. What distinguishes her most sharply from most other 'modern' countries is the slowness and gradualness of the evolutionary process by which she has achieved her modernization. This process displays few sharp breaks and provides evidence of considerable capacity – which some would rather tautologically attribute to 'national character' – for adapting old institutions to new requirements.

It is this continuity that has been so heavily emphasized by the classical commentators on the British constitution. It can nevertheless be over-stressed. Violence has played a prominent part in Britain's constitutional evolution, particularly during some of its more decisive phases. For instance, the Tudor monarchy, under which England reached a new level of national integration, essential for her futher economic and political development, was preceded and – in a sense – made possible by the extremely destructive Wars of the Roses, which sounded the death-knell of the medieval baronage. The following century saw a civil war, a royal decapitation, an abdication, and an 'Interregnum' generally regarded by our European neighbours as a radical horror, much as the Bolshevist regime in Russia was regarded by the other European powers in the 1920s and 1930s. Throughout the sixteenth and seventeenth centuries, moreover, riots and rebellions were so frequent that England acquired a reputation for political violence as widespread as her reputation for peace and stability during the two following centuries, when the new landowning-mercantile classes consolidated their political power and then, under pressure, gradually allowed 'the people' to come within the pale of the constitution, through the extension of the franchise.

Continuity, therefore, is relative rather than absolute – and the same applies to the Englishman's far-famed conservatism and respect for the past. These qualities have proved quite compatible with a fierce radicalism in defence of what he has regarded as his ancient rights, whether embodied in Magna Carta, the Common Law or the Revolution Settlement of 1688. Indeed, in the history of England, resistance to despotism and assertion of 'the rights of free-born Englishmen', said to be based on immemorial tradition, have tended to be closely associated, particularly since the sixteenth century – so much so that the English have been seen by others as a people peculiarly resistant to being governed, if willingness to be governed is equated with acceptance of or acquiescence in tight centralized control.

Despite these important qualifications, however, continuity remains a striking feature, in that Britain has made far fewer (and also far less successful) efforts than most others to rub out the political past and start again *ab ovo*. Gradual institutional adaptation has been the rule; and one of the results of this process is Britain's unique lack of a written constitution. As is well known, the institutional essence of the British system is not to be found in any single legal instrument protected from 'rash' or ill-considered' changes by arrangements designed to make amendment difficult and infrequent, but in ordinary laws, judicial decisions, conventions and customs. Another consequence is the existence of a large number of political, legal and conventional survivals from past ages, liable to cause almost as much confusion among native students of the British political system as among foreign ones.

In a sense, the monarchy itself is an anachronism – although it may well be a useful one. That this most ornamental and least functional of all parts of the constitution satisfies a psychological need is suggested by prevalent attitudes towards the Queen and the Royal Family. One should note, however, that this need, which is subject to discreet exploitation by politicians of both the major parties, has become significant only with the advent of mass democracy. Until Disraeli undertook the popularization of the monarchy, overt republicanism was far more common and respectable than it is today, and a monarch tended to be judged by reference to personality and performance rather than in terms of constitutional symbolism. George IV and William IV were deservedly unpopular, and even Queen Victoria was strongly criticized for her retreat into the somewhat self-conscious isolation of apparently perpetual mourning after the death of her husband, Prince Albert, in 1861. Today, even marginal criticisms of the monarch's behaviour provoke hostile reactions, except among 'intellectuals'. Although the quality and content of the monarchical symbol is subtly changing, its political importance as an outward and visible sign of a national unity that transcends party controversies, is by no means declining.

Indeed, as the actual powers of the monarchy have decreased almost to the vanishing point, its symbolic significance has increased. Whether these powers have suffered total atrophy is a question that cannot be answered with complete confidence. The last remaining power that, in recent years, has involved some measure of real personal choice is the selection of a Prime Minister. Normally, the choice is predetermined by constitutional convention, like all the other 'decisions' the Queen is called upon to make; she appoints the leader of the party with a majority in the House of Commons. Now that the Conservative Party has adopted a formal process for the election of a leader, even the decision whether Mr A or Mr B should be 'sent for', in the event of a Conservative Prime Minister dying or retiring, is out of her hands. Hence it is unlikely that she or her successors will ever again be confronted with the problem of choice that faced her in 1957, when she took advice from the elder statesmen, Churchill and Salisbury, before deciding to send for Mr Macmillan to replace Sir Anthony Eden, or in 1963, when she visited the bedridden Macmillan before summoning Lord Home. If, however, there were no clear party majority in the House, and no arrangements already made between the parties collectively enjoying majority support, the last royal prerogative to be personally exercised could again acquire importance. It is also not impossible that a future monarch – or even the present one – might play a role similar to that played by George V in the formation of the 'National' Government of 1931.

There are even some who still think of the monarch as the ultimate 'guardian of the constitution', equipped with powers which, although normally dormant, might be revived in circumstances of serious constitutional crisis or incipient revolution.

Such a view, although recently expressed in a *Times* leader,[1] is of doubtful validity: for intervention in the circumstances as envisaged, which would involve the monarchy in political decisions inevitably unacceptable to substantial sections of the British people, could hardly fail to destroy its symbolic value and might even result in its abolition.

For the present, however, this 'medieval anachronism' remains securely established, and it can be taken for granted that the strange and imperfectly-defined collection of powers known as the Royal Prerogative will in fact be exercised on the Queen's behalf by her loyal ministers. On the other hand, 'secure' is by no means the adjective that anyone would be likely to apply to that other major constitutional survival from medieval times, the House of Lords. A relic of the medieval Kings' Great Council, and still consisting overwhelmingly of hereditary peers, this most anomalous of all Second Chambers is – unlike the monarchy – *seen* to be at variance with a modern, democratic political culture. Recent attempts to bring it up to date will be discussed in Chapter 4.

As for other medieval survivals, most of them are 'quaint' rather than important – although one should remember that the House of Commons, the very name of which reflects its medieval origins, still operates procedures which, in their tortuous complexities and ambiguities, can be explained only by reference to its former struggle with the Crown to assert rights, such as 'redress of grievances before granting of supply', which today have ceased to possess more than formal significance. Of recent years, however, these curious methods of doing business have been considerably rationalized, as we shall see.

At the really trivial level, there is the retention of titles of office which have ceased to bear any relationship to the duties which the offices carry with them. The 'Speaker' (i.e. the presiding officer) of the House of Commons is known as such only because in late medieval times, when the House was still regarded by the Crown as a body of humble supplicants, he was the elected official who spoke for his fellow-members, by conveying to the King the requests that resulted from their deliberations. Among ministers of the Crown are to be found a Lord President of the Council, a Lord Privy Seal and a Chancellor of the Duchy of Lancaster, all of whom once had duties denoted by their titles but whose responsibilities are now allocated at the discretion of the

1. *The Times*, 21 September 1968.

Prime Minister. It might be added that the parliament building itself is still in theory, a royal residence – the Palace of Westminster.

All these and many other apparent anomalies are the product of a gradual adaptation of ancient institutional forms to the new political needs that have emerged from changing social and economic conditions. A few major features of this process of adaptation will now be briefly examined.

An important clue to British constitutional history is the failure of the monarchy, in contrast with many of the Continental monarchies, to establish a despotism, benevolent or otherwise, on the ruins of medieval feudal institutions. To elucidate the reasons for this failure would involve writing a social history of England from late medieval times up to the 'Glorious Revolution' of 1688 – and even then, in our present state of knowledge, a whole number of important questions would remain unanswered. Briefly, the smashing of the medieval baronage by the Tudors (a comparatively easy task in view of the fact that, in the Wars of the Roses, it had already almost committed *felo de se*) was followed by a development of royal bureaucracy which proved abortive. The work of Thomas Cromwell in the 1530s was thoroughly undone, never to be revived, by Oliver Cromwell and his associates just over a century later. The effort by the Stuart kings to consolidate the still fairly embryonic bureaucratic institutions created by their Tudor predecessors, and to use these to cramp the style, both economic and political, of the new landowning and mercantile classes, was brought to an end by the Long Parliament and never seriously resumed when Charles II was brought back to enjoy what was rather inappropriately called 'his own' again. How far the abortiveness of this attempt at bureaucratization was due to socio-economic factors and how far to the personal deficiencies of the Stuarts is still a controversial question. Whatever answer may be given to this particular 'if' of history, the fact is that the issue was decided by the Civil War, which pronounced a judgment subsequently confirmed by the 'Revolution' of 1688. As a result, Britain embarked on a course of political development very different from that taken by many other European countries, such as France and Prussia, where monarchs defeated parliamentarians, extinguished local 'liberties', and established highly centralized forms of administration.

Although, even after 1688, the British monarchy still had great resources of political patronage at its disposal, the ultimate reality of political power, for more than a century and a half, was in the hands of the greater landlords and merchants, acting centrally through Parliament and locally through unpaid and virtually 'independent' Justices of the Peace. The 'liberties' claimed and won by these classes might have provided the foundation for an oligarchic as distinct from a monarchical form of government. Indeed, 'equality before the law' was a bad joke, not only in the eighteenth century but well into the nineteenth, for the vast majority of Englishmen, who were politically impotent except to the extent that they could frighten the 'establishment' by riot or the threat of riot. As things turned out, however, these liberties proved to be extensible. That this was so may be attributed to two factors: first, the almost unique flexibility and adaptability displayed by a ruling class which depended for its living, to a much greater extent than its contemporaries in most other European countries, on its preparedness to innovate and experiment, or at least to seize the opportunities held out to it by the innovations and experiments of others; secondly, the inability or unwillingness of this class (as 1832 proved) to resist the powerful forces of political change emanating from a changing social structure and from the clamant demand for wider 'participation' created by the Industrial Revolution.

The major adaptive achievements of the seventeenth and eighteenth centuries were the establishment of parliamentary 'sovereignty', the creation of an independent judiciary and the consolidation of the 'rule of law'. These victories, having been won by the upper classes of English society in struggle with the Crown, were of little immediate significance to the politically-submerged mass of Englishmen, but nevertheless provided the launching pad from which the masses were later to take off for full participation in the nation's political life.

These same centuries also saw the beginnings of that organizing principle without which real mass participation is virtually inconceivable: the party system. Here again we are confronted by that remarkable interpenetration of tradition and modernity that is characteristic of Britain. The essentially two-party system of the present day can trace its origins to the period of the Restoration, or even – according to some – to that of the Civil War. One of the major parties, the Conservative, has a continuous if somewhat chequered history dating from the 1670s, and is still familiarly known as the Tory Party, the name, originally opprobrious, which it received at that time. Similarly, the Liberal Party is the lineal descendant of the equally opprobriously-named Whigs; and although it is now a small third party with little prospect of achieving office, much of the reforming ethos characteristic of it has become transferred to the Labour Party, which in some senses may be regarded as its twentieth-century successor.

Sometimes it is claimed that a two-party system is 'natural' to Britain, and that the alternation in office of a party of preservation and a party of change constitutes the machinery through which old institutions have been simultaneously retained and adapted to modern needs. Certainly, the existence of a third party, particularly when strong enough to hold the political balance, would nowadays seem to be a source of discomfort to those (whom recent public opinion polls would appear to show to be a majority) who admire 'strong' government. But such pseudo-psychological explanations should be treated with great reserve, particularly when other, more likely and more provable, explanations seem to be available. What explains the secular tendency of British politics to gravitate towards a two-party rather than towards a multiparty structure is more probably the nature of the cleavages in British society, particularly since the Industrial Revolution. If these cleavages had been more complicated – if, for instance, the advent of toleration had not taken the sting out of religious conflict, and if geographical mobility had not reduced regional particularism and Celtic nationalism to forces of comparative insignificance – it might have been much less easy for the two parties to play their 'aggregative' roles. We must, however, recognize that should the recent growth in support for nationalist parties in Wales and Scotland continue, we may well see a dramatic move away from that old 'natural' order and the emergence of multi-party-ism and coalition governments.

Originally, the struggle between King and Parliament produced two major groups of opinion rather than parties in the modern sense. Until that struggle was finally resolved in 1688, Whigs and Tories were distinct if fluctuating political entities. During the eighteenth century, however, as a result of the victory and consolidation of the upper classes, the faction as distinct from the party tended to predominate, particularly since 'Toryism' became partly identified with a failing cause, that of the Stuarts. The revival of party organization, towards the end of the century, was due to George III's attempt to reassert, as a form of personal property, those prerogatives that his predecessors had allowed to be exercised by their ministerial 'servants', and was later reinforced by the new struggle for parliamentary reform, itself a reflection of the advent of a new kind of class conflict. The rise of an industrial capitalist class and the beginnings of independent political activity on the part of the masses (the latter dateable from the French Revolution) gave fresh significance to the Whig–Tory dichotomy. The transformation of Whigs into Liberals and Tories into Conservatives, each of them still dominated by aristocratic factions but possessing increasingly distinct class identifications, dates from the great Reform Act of 1832, which rationalized the system of representation to the extent of bringing into the parliamentary area the growing urban concentrations, hitherto unrepresented or under-represented, where the new manufacturing classes predominated.

Later in the nineteenth century, with the growth of the urban working-class population and successive extensions of the franchise, further transformations in party affiliations became evident. As a result of a series of partly accidental circumstances (in which the perennial Irish issue played a prominent role), the Conservatives became the party favoured by the great majority of the upper classes (although then, as now, dependent on working-class votes for the achievement of office), while the Liberals became more closely identified with the 'progressive' middle classes and won the support of important sections of the organized working-class movement. Religious differences, although no longer as politically significant as in earlier years, were also reflected in this political cleavage. Generally speaking, the Conservative Party could be identified with the Established Church, while the Liberal Party drew much of its support from 'non-conformist' ranks. The issue of 'Church–versus–Chapel', which dated from the seventeenth-century revolt of the sects against the establishment, could still provide more than a little political liveliness.

In the twentieth century, the Liberals, unable to hold together the somewhat miscellaneous social groups upon whom they depended for the achievement of office, became replaced as the 'second' party by the Socialists. To a considerable extent, this last transformation of the party structure reflected the democratization of the franchise (a process in which 1918 was the decisive date), and the growth of a desire and capacity among working people for independent political representation. The Liberals might conceivably have adapted themselves to these democratic stirrings among the masses – as, indeed, they have belatedly attempted to do – but in the first three decades of the present century, when the effort to adapt might have produced favourable results, they failed to make it with sufficient vigour, partly because they underestimated the seriousness of the Labour challenge and partly because their own leadership was predominantly upper-class – and even aristocratic – in origin.

Yet even the class-oriented politics which the two-party system now reflects (and which, to some extent, it has always reflected in various forms) has failed to undermine the essential political homogeneity of the British people, which is the despair of the 'radical' minority. This homogeneity finds its expression in an agreement, implicit rather than explicit, to conduct political disputes through established constitutional forms and to accept the verdict of the majority, as expressed in the results of elections, on the questions at issue, which are usually more marginal and less fundamental than the political disputants would pretend. Such consensus is possible because class conflict, although real and occasionally (as in 1909–14, 1918–21 and 1926) reaching a high level of intensity, has never become *sufficiently* intense to break the barriers of constitutional rule and political convention, both of which have acquired the respect normally given in Britain to ancient monuments. Such respect is reinforced by the fact that both major political parties, although class-based, have been compelled in order to maximize the likelihood of being returned to office, to appeal to the nation as a whole as well as to the classes with which they have specific affinities. (This applies particularly to the Conservative Party, which could never achieve office unless it could rely on the one-third of the working class vote that it normally receives.)

Thus, once again, a remarkable degree of continuity has been preserved, which is conventionally attributable to the British 'genius for compromise'. 'We are,' said Lord Balfour, 'a people so fundamentally at one that we can afford to bicker.' These attributions are certainly founded in reality, but that reality, one may suggest, is primarily historical and has nothing to do with a mysterious 'national character' independent of the events that have gone to create it.

The gradual 'constitutionalization' of the monarchy, as we have seen, involved the extension of Parliament's authority which, initially established by the Revolution Settlement of 1688, became further consolidated with the expansion of the electorate. Simultaneously, political parties developed as organizing entities essential to the coherent functioning of the new collegiate 'sovereign' and to the confrontation of the expanded electorate with intelligible alternatives. Both processes demanded that there should be a centre of political initiative, sufficiently small in size to reach clear, and if necessary rapid decisions, yet legitimized by direct responsibility to the legislature and indirect responsibility to the electorate. This need was met by the gradual evolution, out of the King's Privy Council, of the modern Cabinet, 'the keystone of the constitutional arch'.

Here again, the process of change was gradual, with the new emerging from the old so imperceptibly that the use of dates to mark stages in the evolution of cabinet government is almost impossible. In the late seventeenth and early eighteenth centuries, those bodies of Ministers which, with the help of hindsight, we term 'cabinets' were by no means always politically homogeneous, while the convention of collective responsibility, whether to King or Parliament, was unknown. Despite the growing significance of party, the King could still select, within the limits set by the current political situation, those whom he wished to be his ministerial 'servants', appointing and dismissing them individually. The modern convention of cabinet solidarity had not yet been developed, and neither collectively nor individually were Ministers really responsible to the House of Commons, since the King could use his extensive patronage to ensure that the government of his choice obtained adequate support in the legislature. Even the office of Prime Minister, which until recently, like the Cabinet itself, was unknown to the law of the constitution, can be dated only very doubtfully from the long 'reign' of Sir Robert Walpole (1721–42).

As we can now see, the decisive changes that brought into being the modern cabinet occurred towards the end of the eighteenth century, being provoked by the attempt made by George III to resume the patronage that had been *de facto* exercised, during the reigns of his two predecessors, by the dominant Whig politicians. The failure of George's efforts to retain the American colonies stimulated the view, expressed in a Commons' resolution, that the power of the crown 'had increased, was increasing and ought to be diminished', and compelled the monarch, for the first time, to accept a Government which was in reality chosen *for* him by 'the country'. It was the leader of this Government, the younger Pitt, who created for himself the position of Prime Minister in the modern sense, and it was during his ministry that the modern convention of the collective responsibility of the Cabinet to the House of Commons became, if not firmly established, at least widely accepted. This change of emphasis was materially assisted by measures which reduced the power of the monarch to influence the results of general elections. Even so, it was not until after the Reform Act of 1832 that the constitutional predominance of the House of Commons was finally assured and with it the leading political role of a Prime Minister and Cabinet made unmistakably dependent upon the maintenance of their majority in the House. This, of course, was by no means the end of the evolutionary process, which, indeed, still continues. With the advent of mass parties and the tightening of party discipline, the meaning of 'collective responsibility' underwent a change of emphasis, and today the suggestion is frequently made – although just as frequently denied – that the modern constitution has become a virtual prime ministerial dictatorship, tempered only by public opinion, group pressures, and the prospect of the next election.

Here then is another well-known example of the characteristic British habit of pouring new wine into old bottles. By the development of custom and convention – and it must be remembered that the Cabinet and the Prime Ministership were themselves in origin purely conventional – the old system of government became subtly but fundamentally transformed without any perceptible break in constitutional continuity.

However, important as it is, the record of gradual change from the royal and ancient to the democratic and modern is by no means the whole story. The British constitution is based on parliamentary statute as well as on convention and judicial decision. Even in the earlier stages of its evolution, changes in the law played an important part in registering and consolidating the new political balances that had been achieved. One need mention only the abolition of the 'prerogative courts', Habeas Corpus, the so-called Mutiny Act, and the Septennial Act of 1715. In these and other instances, the passing of a law represented a constitutional innovation clearly recognized as such and providing a new starting point for the development of custom and convention.

Since the period of the Industrial Revolution, such deliberate innovation, by way of statutory enactment (or, in some cases, the use by the Government of 'prerogative' powers) has become immensely more important. The mounting impact of technological change, with its accompanying social problems, induced, in the nineteenth century, a more rational and consciously innovatory approach to 'machinery of government' questions, originally pioneered by the Utilitarians.

Such innovation might be the subject of virtually endless illustration. Here we will use as our main example the creation of the modern bureaucracy, as this topic is of peculiar importance for an understanding of contemporary politics, with which we are primarily concerned.

This development involved much more deliberate forms of innovation than in many Continental countries, where the new bureaucracy, necessary to cope with the rapidly increasing needs of civil and military administration, could grow 'naturally' (despite revolutions) out of the pre-established royal bureaucracy. In Britain, as a result of the Parliamentary victory over the King, the bureaucratic institutions available to the Government in the late eighteenth century were so embryonic and poorly organized that virtually a new beginning had to be made. Between 1780 and 1830 the groundwork of the modern civil service was being laid – not consciously but bit by bit, in response to specific political and administrative requirements. By 1830, writes Dr Henry Parris, 'from being one strand in the unified executive, the civil service had become a distinct entity, at the service of each successive cabinet. Ministers found themselves obliged by the bulk and complexity of departmental business, and by parliamentary pressure, to devolve much of their administrative responsibility. They also renounced any serious hope of longer periods of office for themselves, accepting the idea of a political career as one in which spells of office would alternate with spells of opposition. The continuity which Ministers no longer provided was supplied by a new group of senior officials, the permanent secretaries. They were at the head of an administrative machine manned by officers who can be styled, without anachronism, permanent civil servants. They were civil servants as distinct from the political servants of the Crown – a distinction not yet drawn in 1780. In withdrawing from politics they became permanent, not liable to have their careers interrupted by ministerial or parliamentary crises. As the monarchy rose above party, so the civil service settled below party. Constitutional bureaucracy was the counterpart of constitutional monarchy.'[2]

Obviously, there is an enormous gap between the tiny bureau-

2. 'The Origins of the Permanent Civil Service' in *Public Administration* Vol. 46, Summer 1968, p. 164.

cracy of 1830, haphazardly organized and predominantly recruited by patronage, and the massive bureaucracy of today, the managerial apparatus through which the Government exercises the powers it has acquired during the intervening 140 years. How that gap was filled will be one of the subjects dealt with in our chapter on the Civil Service. The only points we would make here are (*a*) that the process by which the modern civil service came into existence was one involving a series of deliberate innovations, and (*b*) that the creation of this body affected the ancient constitution in ways that called for mutual adjustment between the old and new of a more deliberate and conscious kind than had hitherto been characteristic of Britain's constitutional evolution. Our second point is of particular importance; for 'big government', in which a highly-organized civil service not only implements political decisions but plays an important part in determining what these decisions are to be, is not easy to reconcile with the maintenance of those principles traditionally regarded as fundamental to the British constitution, the sovereignty of Parliament and the rule of law. Indeed, there have been some critics of the modern civil service, of whom the most famous was a former Lord Chief Justice, Lord Hewart, who have claimed that the 'ancient constitution' was being undermined – even deliberately – by the new bureaucracy. Although few believe this nowadays, the British have found it necessary to establish novel institutions to try to ensure that, by publicity and control, the behaviour of the bureaucracy is kept within constitutionally acceptable bounds and that 'arbitrariness', the characteristic disease of the bureaucrat, is reduced to tolerable limits. Of these institutions, such as the various parliamentary select committees, the apparatus of administrative tribunals, and the recently established Council on Tribunals and Parliamentary Commissioner, we shall have something to say later in this book. Here it is sufficient to note that innovations in the machinery of government have been sufficiently extensive to provoke a series of corresponding constitutional innovations, of which we have perhaps as yet seen only the beginnings.

Another field of government where the nineteenth century saw radical innovation was local, as distinct from central administration. This again represented a response, somewhat belated, to the unprecedented need for positive government action if society was to be provided with the infrastructural services required for economic progress and civilized living in an increasingly technological age, and if the more and more clamant demands of an expanding electorate for collectively-organized and collectively-financed benefits were to be adequately met. It was also related, perhaps even more obviously, to the fact that, as a result of the development of industry and the expansion of foreign trade, Britain had ceased to be a predominantly rural society and had become a predominantly urban one. With the ratio of town-dwellers to country-dwellers rising to 5:1 by the end of the century, Britain became the most thoroughly urbanized country the world had ever seen. Services appropriate for a village were inappropriate for a small town and disastrously inappropriate for a large one. It was necessary, therefore, to develop a series of administrative authorities with both the strength and the will to tackle qualitatively new – and very urgent – problems.

The old local authorities, i.e. the Justices of the Peace and the corporations of the ancient towns, had become obsolete as administrative agencies as early as the latter half of the eighteenth century. Some reforms of these elements in the traditional structure were possible, such as those actually made by the Municipal Corporations Act of 1835. But the main immediate response to such new needs (as were sufficiently obvious to be generally recognized) was to by-pass the established authorities and to set up a series of unco-ordinated ad hoc agencies, or 'statutory authorities for special purposes' as Sidney and Beatrice Webb called them – Turnpike Trusts, Highway Boards, 'Improvement' Commissioners, Boards of Health, and the never-to-be-forgotten Poor Law Commissioners of 1834. These were successful in staving off what could have been administrative disaster, but offered no permanent or even reasonably long-term solution to problems which were becoming increasingly urgent. Hence, towards the end of the nineteenth century, a more modern structure of local authorities was created: county councils, district councils, county borough councils, municipal councils and parish councils – all of them, except for some of the municipal councils, brand new and all of them, as seemed appropriate in an age when representative rather than democratic government had become fully accepted, elected by those who contributed towards their finances, through the local 'rate'. Thus, far from being one of those ancient features of the Constitution that gradually adapted to changing views and evolving needs, British local government is a political invention of the nineteenth century severely modified, in the 1972 Local Government Act, by the exigencies of the twentieth.

While the contemporary pace of change makes traditional policies of gradual adaptation less and less realistic, the force of tradition continues to inhibit British innovatory capacities.

Only once has the attempt been made to look at British government as a whole, with the object of elucidating certain general principles to guide the hands of those anxious to bring it fully 'up-to-date'. This attempt, recorded in the Report of the 'Haldane' Committee of 1918, failed to produce a fully practicable scheme of politico-administrative reform, with the result that today it tends to be regarded as something of an historical curiosity. Improvisation, with a bias towards the minimum rather than the maximum amount of institutional change, has been the favoured method of adaptation. Ministerial departments have been perpetually re-vamped, by division, amalgamation and transfer of powers, in response to immediate pressures and to the multiplication of governmental responsibilities; an immense and rather chaotic multiplication of 'administrative jurisdictions' has taken place; new regulatory agencies, such as the Monopolies Commission, the Industrial Reorganization Commission, the Prices and Incomes Board, the Pay Board, the Price Commission and the Industrial Relations Court (to name but a few examples) have been created (and often rapidly killed off); and, above all, large chunks of the Government's newer-type administrative responsibilities, particularly those of a commercial or quasi-commercial character, have been hived off to ad hoc agencies, of which the most important and best known are the boards of the nationalized industries. The result is an immense complication of the governmental apparatus and a correspondingly great variety of relationship between administrative institutions and political authorities.

Some have said that this disorderly process of innovation is analogous with what happened during the Tudor period and in the late eighteenth and early nineteenth centuries, which were also characterized by an institutional creativity provoked by the appearance of new governmental needs. It has been argued, furthermore, that just as the plethora of early-nineteenth-century ad hoc agencies became largely absorbed by general-purpose authorities, fully responsible, either through the national Parliament to the national electorate or through local councils to the local one, so the new miscellany will eventually fit itself into the established political framework. This seems to us highly unlikely. It is much more probable that Britain will be faced, as far ahead as one can foresee, with the problem of continuous institutional creation and that this will compel politicians to look more seriously at the 'machinery of government' question as a whole, in order to evolve patterns capable of accommodating, within a political system that remains both responsible and democratic, the dynamic forces which threaten disruption of those traditional features of the constitution which most British people still hold to be of paramount value. As a recent writer on the British system of government has said:

> In the 1970s, the durability of the system is likely to be severely tested, as means are sought of dealing with the problem of maintaining the democratic bases of the system, while at the same time overcoming the practical factors that limit the ability of British governments to take speedy and decisive actions that are required in the modern world.[3]

Administratively, the British face the prospect of still further variety, complexity and ubiquity, as the centre of political gravity shifts, not only from Westminster to Whitehall, but from Whitehall to 'outstations', decentralized either in the geographical sense or in the sense of constituting separate power centres, and sometimes in both senses. Both regionalism and ad hoc-ism may well be major features of the future development of the machinery of government, while simultaneously the size, power and *expertise* of the bureaucracy continues to grow. Already the long-established chain of responsibility, from civil servants to ministers, from ministers to Parliament and from Parliament to the electorate is being presented, by some writers, as a fiction rather than as a convention of the constitution. Already there is an inchoate but nevertheless deeply-felt demand for greater openness in government, and greater *participation* on the part of the governed, to make responsibility more 'real' by providing a popular counterweight to the ponderous politico-bureaucratic 'establishment'.

How far can these demands be reconciled with the paramount need for governmental efficiency and coherence? How far can both requirements be satisfied by drawing upon and adapting Britain's traditional political resources? Simply to jettison these resources and to attempt a radical reconstruction of the system of government would offer a possible solution only in the event of complete political breakdown, of which, fortunately, there is no sign. But a vigorous creativity rather than a passive worship of

3. R. M. Punnett, *British Government and Politics*, (Heinemann 1968), p. 422.

tradition would seem to be what is needed in the later twentieth century. Britain, for all the ancient political wisdom she possesses, cannot evade the massive and unprecedented challenge of our times, thus summarized in a broadcast talk by Sir Geoffrey Vickers:

> The man-made environment in which the industrial epoch is enclosing us – created as it now is largely by the unintended results of what everyone does – is becoming too unpredictable to live in and may soon become too unacceptable to live with; so if it is to survive, it will have to be controlled – that is, governed – on a scale and to a depth which we have as yet neither the political institutions to achieve nor the cultural attitudes to accept.

The British system of government, the modern and democratic has emerged from and interpenetrated with the royal and ancient. This amalgam represents a remarkable and indeed unique political achievement. But, whereas one may admire it, there is less and less cause to regard it with self-satisfaction. If, however, it is to be changed fast enough to meet the demands that are crowding in upon it, the first requirement is that it should be *understood*. Towards such an understanding the following chapters are dedicated.

Part II

New Wine in Old Bottles

Chapter 2

The Electoral System

Elections in democratic societies are concerned with the question 'who shall govern?' They represent what Theodore Sedgwick has called 'a democratic substitute for the barbarous system whereby executive power is transmitted through the organs of generation'. They are now a widely, though by no means universally, accepted means for conferring legitimacy and authority upon governments, and for securing peaceful transition from one government to another. Elections in states where more than one party has a role in the political system represent a formalized conflict in which certain rules are laid down, in which certain conventions are observed. These rules and conventions may differ from state to state and may be more, or less, fair according to our points of view, but the common overriding factor is that, by and large, the parties to the conflict accept the outcome, and those who lose seek to reverse the result only through the constitutional channels. This is a situation quite different from that in one-party states where elections are required, not to resolve conflict, or to determine succession, but to register legitimacy: hence the importance attached to very high turn-out at the polls. Such turn-out is pointed to as being indicative of political consensus within the state.

The British do not claim so much for their elections. They grant them their legitimizing power – even though a government may have come to office on a minority of the votes cast – but they do not (at least they should not) claim that the result of a general election represents the emergence of a consensus throughout the nation, or is a statement of something like a 'general will'. In normal circumstances an election vests the authority for governing the country in the leaders of one of the major political parties for a period of not more than five years, and is the outcome, not of some dramatic overwhelming surge in favour of one party or in revulsion against another, but of relatively small changes in party support. Thus, since the Second World War the swing at general elections has been:

1950	2.9 per cent to Conservative
1951	1.1 per cent to Conservative
1955	1.8 per cent to Conservative
1959	1.1 per cent to Conservative
1964	3.1 per cent to Labour
1966	2.7 per cent to Labour
1970	4.8 per cent to Conservative
1974 (Feb.)	2.0 per cent to Labour
1974 (Oct.)	2.0 per cent to Labour

and only once in the post-war years has the gap between the two major parties exceeded 7 per cent. The large bulk of British voters are creatures of habit, upon whose allegiance the major parties can count from one election to the next, almost it would seem without regard to policies or leaders. C. O. Jones, in a study of 453 constituencies that experienced little or no boundary changes during the four elections of the 1950s, found that 87.2 per cent did not change party hands at all, that only 7 changed twice, and another 51 changed once. This in fact represented only 4.8 per cent of the potential changes.[1] Jorgen Ramussen, in a study of these same constituencies after the 1966 election, found that 77 per cent had been won by the same party at every election held during the preceding 16 years. However, he did not accept this simple figure as indicating the percentage of 'safe' seats but went on to use more elaborate techniques which led him to conclude that 76 per cent of the seats in the Commons could be regarded as safe.[2] The British, it would seem, still continue to display a bifurcation of the type Gilbert offers in Iolanthe, and if consensus exists it is concerned not with the policies or programmes of a victorious or dominant party but rather with the constitutional framework within which British politics operate.

But acceptance of a framework does not necessarily involve passive acceptance of the various institutions functioning within that framework, and the electoral process has not escaped the perennial calls that have gone up for reform of this or that part of the political system.

The development of the modern British electoral system has

1. C. O. Jones, 'Inter-Party Competition in Britain 1950–1959' in *Parliamentary Affairs*, Vol. XVII, Winter 1963–64.

2. See 'The Implication of Safe Seats for British Democracy' in *Western Political Quarterly*, 1966: reprinted in R. Rose (ed.), *Policy-Making in Britain* Macmillan 1969).

been slow, spread over more than a century, with 1948 perhaps representing the terminal date of a process begun in 1832. The Representation of the People Act of 1832, usually referred to as the Great Reform Act, is often, with much reason, cited as opening a new era of representative government in Britain; yet, in itself, it did little either to extend the franchise or to abolish the many abuses that existed. 'Nomination' boroughs continued in being, while the opportunities for corruption may even have increased as a result of the multiplication of marketable votes. The real importance of the Act was to make reform a respectable if not always acceptable topic, and to pave the way for the 1867 Representation of the People Act, which came close to doubling the electorate. However it was not until the Corrupt and Illegal Practices Act of 1883, the Franchise Act 1884,[3] the Redistribution Act and the Registration Act of 1885, that the worst anomalies in seat distribution were abolished, and election corruption almost eliminated. While several questions were left untouched by these Acts, most notably that of women's suffrage, D. E. Butler has suggested that 1885 can claim to be regarded as the climax of that evolution begun in 1832.[4] The Acts that were to follow could be classed in large part as Acts of consolidation rather than of principle, save perhaps for the granting of the vote to women, which was to come partially in 1918 and completely in 1928. The electorate was more than doubled by the Representation of the People Act of 1918, which provided universal suffrage for men on the basis of residence and accorded the vote to women over the age of 30 if they or their husbands were local government electors. The Act also reduced significantly the cost to candidates of contesting elections, but at the same time sought to discourage frivolous candidatures by introducing a deposit of £150 which was forfeit if a candidate failed to secure one-eighth of the total votes cast in the constituency.

This Act further concerned itself with the question of redistribution, accepting in theory the principle that constituencies should be approximately equal in numbers of electors. But it was only with the 1944 House of Commons (Redistribution of Seats) Act and the establishment of permanent boundary commissioners

3. Important more for the fact that it moved representation from communities to numerical constituencies, than for the increased numbers to whom it gave the vote. Indeed 40 per cent of the male population were not enfranchised until 1918.

4. D. E. Butler, *The Electoral System in Britain, 1918–1951* (Oxford 1935), p. 1.

that redistribution came to receive more or less continuous attention. The principle of numerical equality was also subject to certain exceptions. The first of these is derived from the old principle that parliamentary constituencies should be identified with communities; in the light of it, attempts are made, whenever practicable, to avoid conflict between local government and parliamentary boundaries. The second exception relates to Wales, Scotland and Ireland: the first two receive greater representation than is their numerical due as acknowledgement of the existence of national sentiments; the third, as a result of having its own parliament in Belfast, is numerically under-represented. Again 'it has been generally accepted that the more remote rural areas cannot be treated on just the same basis as the rest of the country and 'that the Boundary Commissioners might depart from their instructions "if special geographical considerations including, in particular, the area, shape and accessibility of a constituency" appeared to render this desirable'.[5]

The 1928 Representation of the People Act having given full voting equality to women, there remained few exceptions to the general principle of 'one man one vote' when the Labour Party came to power in 1945. Even so, the business vote and the university seats still existed, vestiges of privilege to many in the Labour Party, and by the Representation of the People Act of 1948, passed in the face of the considerable Conservative Opposition, these were swept away. Finally, in 1970 under the terms of the 1969 Representation of the People Act, the voting age was lowered to 18.

Thus today the British have an electoral system based on the principle of adult suffrage – all citizens over the age of 18 have the vote although this privilege is not extended to peers, felons or lunatics. The vote is cast in single-member constituencies – constituencies that return one member to Parliament – and in normal circumstances is exercised at least once in every five years. The principle that the votes are of equal value is somewhat modified by the fact of constituencies of unequal size. For instance, Antrim South has an electorate of 118,483 while Newcastle upon Tyne Central has a mere 25,023. Even if we omit Northern Ireland from this comparison we still find that at the time of the 1974 general elections Meriden, with 96,966, had nearly four times as many voters as the Newcastle constituency. Furthermore, the British do not indulge in the electoral sophistications of other countries that seek to ensure, through the use of schemes of proportional

5. ibid. p. 216.

representation, that representation in the legislature closely reflects the votes cast by the electorate. They do not even seek to ensure that the man elected secures 50 per cent of the votes cast in his constituency. Theirs is a simple majority system, which means that when more than two candidates stand in a constituency there is a strong chance that the victor will emerge with only a minority of the votes cast. Indeed, 408 of the 635 Members elected to parliament in February 1974 received fewer than 50 per cent of the votes cast in their constituencies, and 41 in fact failed to poll even 40 per cent. (In 1945 it proved possible for the Conservative Member for Dumbartonshire East to be elected by only 33.4 per cent of the votes cast, and in October 1974 for the Scottish Nationalist candidate to take Dumbartonshire East with 31.2 per cent of the vote.)[6] This possibility of 'minority' victories at the constituency level can, when transferred to the national scene, involve the election of governments by a minority of the votes cast. On only two occasions since 1929 has the government with a parliamentary majority also won more than 50 per cent of the votes cast – 1931 and 1935. In 1929, 1951 and February 1974 the party with the largest number of popular votes did not even win the most parliamentary seats. One must bear in mind, however, that even if a system were introduced that ensured that every elected representative had to secure a majority of the votes cast in his constituency – through some alternative vote scheme – this would not in itself necessarily ensure that governments supported by a majority of votes would emerge. So long as the phenomenon of the so-called 'wasted' vote continues to exist – as in some constituencies where a party's strength is such that it always wins by a massive majority – the possibility of a party receiving a minority of the total national vote cast, yet winning a majority of the seats in the House of Commons, remains.

Recent election figures give some idea of what can happen with single-member constituencies of uneven size and with the simple-majority method of counting.

The tables on page 36 illustrate admirably the vagaries of the electoral system. First there is the fact that in 1951 the Labour Party received the largest percentage of the votes while the Conservative Party won the most seats, while in 1974 the Conservative Party received more votes than the Labour Party but fewer seats in the House of Commons. Or take the record of the

6. P. G. J. Pulzer, *Political Representation and Elections in Britain* (Allen & Unwin 1967), p. 55 n.

Liberal Party. Although between 1951 and 1959 it more than doubled its share of the popular vote, the number of seats it received in the House of Commons remained the same. Again, between 1959 and 1964 it increased its share of the popular vote by 5.3 per cent but its share of the seats in the House by only 0.4

	Votes '000	*Seats*	*% votes*	*% seats*
1951				
Conservatives	13,718	321	48.0	51.4
Labour	14,019	295	48.8	47.3
Liberal	731	6	2.5	1.0
1959				
Conservatives	13,750	365	49.4	57.9
Labour	12,216	258	43.8	41.0
Liberal	1,639	6	5.9	1.0
1964				
Conservatives	12,001	304	43.4	48.3
Labour	12,206	317	44.1	50.3
Liberal	3,093	9	11.2	1.4
1966				
Conservatives	11,418	253	41.9	40.1
Labour	13,065	363	47.9	57.6
Liberal	2,328	12	8.5	1.9
1970				
Conservatives	13,144	330	46.4	52.4
Labour	12,179	287	42.9	45.6
Liberal	2,117	6	7.5	0.9
1974 (Feb.)				
Conservatives	11,963	296	38.2	46.6
Labour	11,655	301	37.2	47.4
Liberal	6,063	14	19.3	2.2
Others	1,652	24	5.3	3.8
1974 (Oct.)				
Conservatives	10,459	276	35.8	43.4
Labour	11,459	319	39.3	50.25
Liberal	5,348	13	18.3	2.05
Plaid Cymru & Scot. Nationalist	1,006	14	3.5	2.2
Others	886	13	3.0	2.05

per cent. But, as though to confuse the Liberals, the 1966 election brought a drop of 25 per cent in their vote and an increase of more than 33 per cent in their parliamentary seats. The table also illustrates the wide divergence that can occur between votes and seats for the two major parties. But it would also appear that as between the two 'giants' these divergencies tend to balance each other out over the years, while the minor party suffers continuously.

If we translate the above figures into a popular vote-per-parliamentary-seat table, we can see again how the Liberal Party has, by these criteria, been grossly under-represented in recent years.

	Votes per Seat ('000)						
	1951	*1959*	*1964*	*1966*	*1970*	*1974 (Feb.)*	*1974 (Oct.)*
Conservatives	42.7	37.7	39.5	41.2	39.8	40.4	38.0
Labour	47.5	47.4	38.3	36.0	42.4	38.7	35.9
Liberal	121.8	273.2	343.7	194.0	352.8	433.1	411.4
Plaid Cymru & Scot. Nationalist							71.8

All votes may be equal but some votes are patently more equal than others. This inequality has led to demands for reform of the voting system in order that 'justice' may prevail, or at least be more closely approached.

That the call for reform comes principally from the Liberals, who suffer most from the present system, is hardly surprising: that the major parties, which gain most from it, are opposed to change is not to be wondered at. Nevertheless, in fairly recent years the leader of one of the two major parties was induced to raise the question of electoral reform. After the 1950 General Election Winston Churchill said:

We must not be blind to the anomaly which has brought to this House of Commons 186 representatives who are returned only by a minority of those who voted in their constituencies. Nor can we . . . overlook the constitutional injustice done to 2,600,000 voters who . . . have been able to return only nine members. . . . I therefore . . . [propose] that we should set up a select committee to inquire into the whole question of electoral reform . . . I am well aware that it has several times been examined before, but we have never examined it in the light of a practical situation of major importance such as has now been brought about.[7]

But Churchill's position was not that of his party. The majority of Conservatives were quite happy with a situation which effectively resolved the electoral contest into a battle between the

7. Debate on the Address, 7 March 1950, quoted in *Parliamentary Reform 1933–1960* (published for the Hansard Society), p. 14.

two giants. Thus, when in 1954 a request for a Royal Commission on Voting Systems was presented to the Conservative Government, led by Churchill, it was rejected.

What the reformers seek is a closer relation between votes cast and parliamentary seats won, and in this search the methods most commonly advocated have been the single transferable vote and the alternative vote.

Using multi-member constituencies and a quota system the single transferable vote (STV) introduces some element of proportionality into the electoral process. Thus, in a five member constituency voters would be required to indicate their preferences among the 12 or 13 candidates who might be standing. In a constituency where 120,000 votes were cast, a candidate would require 20,001 votes to be elected. (This figure, the Droop quota, is determined by dividing the number of votes cast by the number of seats to be filled plus one, and by then adding one to the dividend i.e. $\frac{120{,}000}{5+1} + 1 = 20{,}001$. This represents the minimum number of votes required per candidate to fill the five seats.) When a candidate receives more than the quota his surplus votes are distributed among the other candidates according to the expressed second preferences. If, then, a candidate receives 23,000 votes, there are 2,999 to be distributed. This is done by counting the second preferences on all 23,000 papers and by allocating to each candidate $\frac{2{,}999}{23{,}000}$ of the extra votes he thus receives. If no candidate succeeds in reaching the quota, the bottom candidate is eliminated and his second preferences distributed. Eventually, through this process of distribution and redistribution, five candidates will receive the quota and be elected.[8]

While the use of the single transferable vote significantly reduces the inconsistencies of single-member constituencies and simple majorities, the arguments for its introduction are not limited to its mitigation of the capriciousness of the present voting system. Questions of voter choice, quality of candidates, party caucus control over the constituencies, and apathy among the electorate are also involved.

There is certainly some concern in the country about the manner in which parliamentary candidates are selected. After all, when something like two-thirds of the seats in the House of Commons

8. For a thorough discussion of STV and other electoral systems see W. J. M. Mackenzie, *Free Elections* (Allen & Unwin 1958), pp. 61–9.

never change party hands, the selection process becomes in effect the electoral process. The voter is presented with the choice of voting for the candidate his local party has picked, no matter what his qualities, or of 'bolting' the party, either through abstention or through voting for a rival candidate. And although most voters would not go so far as to subscribe to the sentiment that if their party selected a pig they would vote for it,[9] few are prepared to desert their party because of the manifest deficiencies of the candidate. This means that the local party 'bosses' have a fairly free hand, subject to the approval of the national party headquarters, in the selection process. If a voting system were introduced that involved the use of multi-member constituencies, it is argued, voters would then be able to make some kind of choice between candidates through the use of their preferences. And this, so the argument continues, would probably lead to the emergence of better quality candidates, for a candidate would now be seen to be worth more than those mythical 500 votes that have often been calculated his maximum potential contribution to the vote-gathering process. In addition, it seems likely that the individual Members of Parliament would become less dependent upon party machines, and more inclined to use their own judgment rather than jump to the crack of the party whips. Finally, the supporters of the introduction of some form of proportional representation would argue that the system, by giving the voters an opportunity to exercise effective choices among a numbe rof candidates, would do much to lessen the widespread apathy that, it is claimed, exists. This is an apathy felt not only by many of those who abstain at election time, but also by the large numbers who continue to vote but at the same time feel 'alienated' from the political process, i.e. who do not see their contribution, through the vote, as having significance in that process. Rose and Mossawir, for instance, in a study of voters in Stockport,[10] found that 35 per cent of the respondents believed that voters did not have much influence on government and that 23 per cent of them believed that there was nothing to choose between the parties. While the introduction of proportional representation would not necessarily induce voters to believe that they could now influence governments, it would certainly permit them a more effective choice among candidates.

9. D. E. Butler, *The British General Election 1951* (Macmillan 1952), p. 173.

10. R. Rose and H. Mossawir, 'Voting and Elections: A Functional Analysis' in *Political Studies*, Vol. XV, No. 2, June 1967.

However, the use of systems of proportional representation to secure greater arithmetical consistency or to give the voters greater choice of candidates has not had widespread appeal in Britain. The arithmetical anomalies that spring from the present system are regarded by many as a small price to pay for the major benefit it is thought to offer: namely the production of decisive majorities in the House of Commons – majorities that can govern without recourse to the coalitions which are considered to be the natural and undesired outcome of any form of PR. According to this line of argument, the purpose of elections is not to 'mirror' the views of the electorate, but rather to provide strong, single-party governments which can be held directly responsible at the next election. Government should be representative but it should also be responsible. Coalition governments involve a sharing of power that entails diffusion of responsibility. Thus, while a system of proportional representation might increase the representative character of the British legislature, at the same time, if it led to coalition, it would tend to weaken the element of responsibility which has an equally vital role to play in the political process. A first-past-the-post system, then, may be easier to defend in practice than by logic.

Most of the arguments of the anti-PR school rest on the fundamental assumption that if, say, the single transferable vote system were introduced into the United Kingdom weak coalition governments would follow as a matter of course. Such arguments may conceivably ascribe to electoral systems more than is warranted by the available evidence; for, as Pulzer writes,[11] it is 'more likely that the desire for sectional representation inspires the demand for proportional justice, not that the proportional system causes the proliferation of parties'. Indeed, Pulzer goes even further and suggests that the introducing of STV into Great Britain might actually be disadvantageous to the smaller parties. After all, if the widely held belief that the British vote for a government rather than for an ideology or an interest is true, then it seems likely that those parties seen to be capable of forming a government will be those most likely to benefit from the change. It would appear from electoral statistics, as analysed by Michael Steed in the Butler and King election study of 1966, that a large part of the increased Liberal vote since the early 1950s has been a protest vote, gained in safe seats and largely at the expense of the weaker of the major parties. Acceptance of this analysis renders invalid any simple

11. Pulzer, *Political Representation and Elections in Britain*, p. 49.

summation of Liberal votes across the country and their translation into potential seats under a PR scheme.

The alternative vote, which also has its supporters, represents, in effect, merely a modification of the first-past-the-post system: no constituency boundary changes are required, and the constituency still returns only one member to Westminster. The differences are to be found on the ballot sheet and in the requirement for election. The voter indicates his preferences among the candidates, and to succeed a candidate must secure an absolute majority of the votes cast. Should no candidate receive such a majority on the first count, the weakest candidate is eliminated and his second preferences are distributed among the remainder. Should this fail to produce an absolute majority for one candidate the process is repeated until at last one emerges with more than 50 per cent of the votes. The alternative vote has been attacked for many reasons: for failing to give the mirror-like reflection of the vote claimed for STV; for forcing parties to pay undue attention to minorities; for allowing the decision to be determined, in Churchill's now famous words, 'by the most worthless votes given for the most worthless candidates'.[12] But perhaps the greatest criticism that can be levelled against the system is that it would probably fail to achieve what it seeks, namely fairer shares all round. Studies by David Butler and by Michael Steed indicate that while the alternative vote would probably have given fairer representation to all three parties in 1966, this would not necessarily have been so in other elections. Indeed, in 1929 and 1951, two years when the party winning the most votes failed to win the most parliamentary seats, it seems likely that, under AV, the distortion would have been even greater.

The dispute about the nature of the electoral system is, in effect, a dispute about the objects of the system. Professor Mackenzie has suggested that an appraisal of an electoral system should be concerned with the quality of the members who get elected; the effectiveness of the legislature produced; the 'fairness' of the result, and the public confidence it inspires.[13]

Few would argue that the British electoral system guarantees anything about the quality of the candidates who present themselves or of the representatives who emerge. The process of candidate selection is not in fact known to British electoral law. Any

12. HC Debates, 2 June 1931: quoted in *Parliamentary Reform 1933–1960*, p. 12.
13. W. J. M. Mackenzie, *Free Elections*, pp. 69–71.

person may become a parliamentary candidate who is over 21, eligible to vote, can secure the support of ten local citizens, and can afford the £150 deposit. In fact, however, the vast majority of the candidates in any election are limited to the selected representatives of the three major parties — the products of limited competitions with other potential candidates conducted before committees of constituency party stalwarts. The parties dominate the electoral process. It is the parties which determine who shall reach Westminster. If good Members of Parliament emerge, it is less because the voters have approved them than because the local parties have been astute or lucky in their choices. Indeed, one could argue that good men are returned despite the defects in the process by which they are selected.

Does the electoral system facilitate the performance by the legislature of its tasks? To answer this question is difficult, as one can hardly isolate the effect of the electoral system from that of all other factors. The House of Commons, as we shall see, is expected by public opinion to produce and maintain a government capable of running the country, preferably without recourse to coalitions. Generally speaking, the majorities to meet this requirement do emerge from general elections; but there is little to suggest that this satisfactory outcome may be directly attributed to the nature of the electoral system itself. Other factors, such as the comparative homogeneity of British political culture, widespread agreement about the purposes that elections are intended to serve, and a general preference for coherent party-based government, would seem to play a more important role.

As for the fairness of the system, while the large majority of voters would appear to be quite content with the present arrangements, there is that sizable minority of Liberal voters which feels that it suffers gross under-representation by the use of 'first-past-the-post'. Thus confidence in the system is far from complete.

We are left, then, with the conclusion that Professor MacKenzie's major criteria are not met. If we couple this with the widespread alienation we discuss elsewhere, and the low esteem in which Members of Parliament are apparently held,[14] it would appear that now might be an appropriate time to consider the adoption of some other method of electing our representatives.

14. See the report in the *Sunday Times* of 8 July 1973.

Chapter 3

Political Parties

The vote, as we have seen, is cast in the main for a representative of one of the three major parties in the country, and on only three occasions this century have the Conservative, Liberal and Labour Parties failed to secure at least 94 per cent of the votes. Twice, 1918 and 1931, coalition governments were involved, and the third time, 1922, the Liberal Party had split in two. In fact the position is even more extreme than this, for at thirteen of the twenty-one general elections since 1900 two major parties have received between them a minimum of 87.5 per cent of the vote (1964) and a maximum of 96.8 per cent (1951). The exceptions to this are to be found in the period between the coalition elections of 1918 and 1931 – a transitional period in which the Labour Party consolidated itself as the second party of the nation at the expense of the Liberals – and in both 1974 elections when there was a sharp increase in the votes cast for the Liberals and the nationalist parties.

Year	1900	1906	1910	1910	1918	
2-party vote	95.7	92.6	90.1	90.1	coa-lition	
Parties	C/L	C/L	C/L	C/L		
Year	1922	1923	1924	1929	1931	
2-party vote	67.7	68.6	81.3	75.3	Nat.	
Parties	C/Lab.	C/Lab.	C/Lab.	C/Lab.	Gov.	
Year	1935	1945	1950	1951	1955	
2-party vote	91.6	87.6	89.6	96.8	96.1	
Parties	C/Lab.	C/Lab.	C/Lab.	C/Lab.	C/Lab.	
Year	1959	1964	1966	1970	1974 (*Feb.*)	1974 (*Oct.*)
2-party vote	93.2	87.5	89.6	89.3	75.4	74.5
Parties	C/Lab.	C/Lab.	C/Lab.	C/Lab.	C/Lab.	C/Lab.

In the light of this record we would appear to be justified in describing the British system as a *two-party* system, meaning by this that at any particular time the voter is presented with a choice between two possible Governments: before 1918 Conservative or Liberal; since 1931 Conservative or Labour. Indeed, one might go further and suggest that party history this century has generally displayed a general desire on the part of the electorate to have an either/or choice at the polls: a desire to vote for a potential Government. Quite obviously, as the events of the 1920s indicate, it is possible for a minor party to become a major force. But the significant fact about these events is not the rise of the Labour Party but rather that the three parties did not long continue as more less equal contenders for power. The Labour Party did not join the other two parties as a potential governing party: rather it displaced one of them. We must, however, recognize, as we suggested on page 17, that recent voting behaviour may indicate the onset of a new era in party competition in Britain.

Modern British party organization finds its origins in the period immediately following the Reform Act of 1832, and its continued growth in the subsequent legislation which further extended the franchise. Prior to this there existed no country-wide organization of parties; indeed there was no parliamentary party organization as we know it today. Parties in Parliament were essentially informal groups of like-minded men, coalitions that were forever forming, breaking and re-forming. In the country, candidates ran as individuals, not as party members. In fact 'run' may well be the wrong verb here, for with a small electorate and widespread corruption, and with many seats being in the gift of a local 'notable', the tasks of the aspiring Member of Parliament were somewhat different from those which face candidates today – although perhaps not as different as many would believe.

The 1832 Act, while not wildly radical in terms of the numbers it enfranchised, did nevertheless lead to the establishment of registration societies or associations which were concerned to see that all potential supporters in a constituency were duly registered and thus eligible to vote. Among those quick to appreciate the new situation that had arisen was Sir Robert Peel, who wrote in 1838 that 'there is a perfectly new element of political power – namely the registration of votes. . . . That party is the strongest in point of fact which has the existing registration in its favour. . . . The registration will govern the disposal of offices, and determine the policy of party attacks.'[1] These registration societies were the forerunners of modern constituency party organizations.

1. C. S. Parker, *Sir Robert Peel*: quoted Ivor Bulmer-Thomas in *The Party System in Great Britain* (Phoenix House 1953), pp. 13–14.

They were, however, neither representative bodies nor part of a nation-wide organization. Further, no national party headquarters as yet existed, although an early approach to it was to be found in the Carlton Club for the Tories, and the Reform Club for the Whig/Liberals.

While the occasional registration society had adopted democratic practices earlier, it was not until after the 1867 Reform Act that real progress was made towards representative associations. The impetus came from the Birmingham Liberal Association, which realized that with careful directions to its supporters as to how they should vote it could thwart the intentions of the framers of the 1867 Act and secure all three Parliamentary seats recently given in the city. But such control of the voters demanded confidence in the would-be controllers; and such confidence required the existence of a representative body whose officers and committee were elected by the members. The Association was transformed into a representative body, and proved highly successful. Gradually other associations, Liberal and Conservative, followed this example, and eventually all the constituency associations were organized on a representative basis.

In the same year that the Liberals of Birmingham led the way towards representative associations the Conservatives instituted the first national union of associations. This body, the National Union of Conservative and Constitutional Associations,[2] was to 'afford a centre of communication and action between local associations supporting constitutional views'.[3] It was also concerned to strengthen local associations, and to encourage the establishment of associations in areas where they were lacking. It made no claim to determine party policy. Four years later, at Disraeli's instigation, a Conservative Central Office – a national party headquarters – was established, and the success of the Conservatives in the 1874 election has been attributed in large part to this development of a strong party organization throughout the country.

The Liberals had themselves established a party headquarters back in 1861. Indeed, this body, the Liberal Registration Association, was the first British party headquarters in the modern sense of the term. But the party had not then proceeded to the stage of

2. In 1912 the name was changed to the National Unionist Association of Conservative and Liberal Unionist Organizations, and in 1924 to the National Union of Conservative and Unionist Associations.

3. Bulmer-Thomas, *Party System*, p. 22.

developing an equivalent of the National Union. In this respect they were to follow the lead of the Conservatives – the National Liberal Federation came into being in 1877. But while the Liberal body was similar to the National Union in composition and in holding an annual conference, it had a different conception of its role *vis-à-vis* the party leaders. In contrast to the Conservative Union, which was prepared to leave policy decisions to the party leadership, the Liberal Federation considered that it had a major role to play in policy formulation – a view that was not acceptable to the Liberal leadership in Parliament.

Thus, before the end of the nineteenth century, all the ingredients of the modern party system were in existence in Britain: representative constituency associations with a national organization; an annual conference; a party headquarters which would become more and more powerful; an acceptance of the need for party election manifestoes; and a recognition of the special role to be played by the leader of the party.

All these developments took place before the third member of the 'big three' of modern British party history had come into being. The Labour Party was not born until around the turn of the century – its birth date is usually given as 1900, when the Labour Representation Committee was formed, although it did not adopt its present name until 1906, when it first appeared as a substantial party in the House of Commons with 30 seats – and its growth offers interesting contrast with that of the other two parties. The latter, as we have seen, had their origins within Parliament, and grew through building up an extra-parliamentary organization to capture the support of the newly-enfranchised. The Labour Party, on the other hand, grew from the grass roots. Parliamentary representation was an extension of an extra-parliamentary movement aimed at improving the condition of the working classes. The extension of the franchise to many less-skilled workers in the 1880s, and their influx into the Trade Union movement in the 1890s, led first to the establishment by Keir Hardie of the Independent Labour Party in 1893, and then in 1900 to the Labour Representation Committee itself, in which a number of trade unions joined with socialist societies with the aim of securing the election of working-class representatives to Parliament. This was Conservative/Liberal Party development stood on its head, though it is important to bear in mind that even if the thrust came from below there was still nothing like a nation-wide party organization at that time. Indeed, until Arthur Henderson's reorganization plan was accepted by the 1918 party conference the party was still essentially a loose federation of trade unions and socialist societies. The majority of constituencies were without local organizations, as the party had never fought more than a small minority of the seats, and, perhaps significantly for later developments, individual membership did not as yet exist. Henderson's plan was aimed at making the Labour Party a truly national party, by opening up membership to all, whether or not they were members of trade unions or other affiliated societies, and by creating local parties in almost every constituency with the aim of fighting every possible seat at the first post-war election. In fact in the election of December 1918 there were 406 Labour candidates in the field compared with the 59 of eight years earlier.

The general election of 1918 marked the full-scale entrance of the Labour Party on to the political stage and foreshadowed the demise of the Liberal Party as a major political force. For a few years the picture remained a little blurred, but it was soon apparent (after the general election of 1924 when the Labour vote was almost twice that of the Liberals) that the Liberal Party was unable to compete with Labour or with the Conservatives as a feasible alternative government. Split by dissensions within their own ranks, and with the Labour Party pre-empting much of the working-class vote upon which they depended, the Liberals slipped rapidly towards a minor, now very minor, role.

The organizational structures of the Conservative and Labour parties, while in many respects similar, do nevertheless display significant differences which are in large part directly traceable to their respective origins. The Conservative organization came into being, as we have seen, as a result of impetus from the top. It was created in order to aid the parliamentary leaders. The growth of the Labour Party, on the other hand, was the result of a thrust from below, from groups of voters, the Parliamentary Labour Party being created to further the goals of extra-parliamentary bodies. The former development involves a conception of the party that is hierarchical, the latter one that is egalitarian. As Robert McKenzie points out, the terminology used by the parties is of interest here. 'The term "The Conservative Party" applies strictly only to the party *in* Parliament; it is supported outside Parliament by its creation, "The National Union of Conservative and Unionist Associations". The term "The Labour Party" is properly applied only to the mass organization of the party *out-*

side Parliament; it supports in Parliament a distinct and separate organization, "The Parliamentary Labour Party".'[4]

The parties as national entities are most readily observed at their annual conferences. The presence of representatives of the constituencies, of areas, central associations and other organizations, and of Members of Parliament and prospective candidates, brings attendance at the Conservative Conference to between 3,000 and 4,000. The Labour Party Conference similarly comprises representatives of the constituency and central parties, affiliated organizations (most notably the trade unions), and the Parliamentary Party and prospective candidates. Total attendance is much smaller than at the Conservative Conference, usually numbering about 1,200, but of more significance is the special position of the trade union representatives in the Labour Party organization. While in the Conservative Party the constituency association representatives provide the bulk of those attending conference, in the Labour Party the trade unions are entitled to more than 50 per cent of the delegates and, although they do not take up all their places, being in fact in a minority when the conference meets, they control some five-sixths of the votes. Representation and voting at the Labour Conference are based on membership, of which the unions provide the bulk. The constituency parties account for something over 800,000, but the affiliated membership (in 79 trade unions, 5 small socialist societies and 1 co-operative society) is approximately seven times as large.

In theory the annual conference is the ruling body of the Labour Party. The constitution of the party states that 'the work of the party shall be under the direction and control of the party conference', and there has long been a tendency on the part of the rank and file members to argue that the Parliamentary Labour Party should accept the instructions of the Annual Conference and of its National Executive Committee. This claimed pre-eminence for the extra-parliamentary organization finds its origins in the history of the party – in the fact that the parliamentary party was a product of political activity that originated outside Parliament. It was therefore natural that the representatives of the Labour movement in Parliament should be regarded as subservient to the wishes of their extra-parliamentary masters. Such a theory enabled Winston Churchill in the 1945 general election campaign to raise the spectre of extra-parliamentary forces, led by

4. R. T. McKenzie, *British Political Parties* (Heinemann 1963), p. 12, n. 2.

Harold Laski, chairman of the NEC that year, wielding undue influence over a Labour Government. Further, Churchill did not have to go back to the Labour Party constitution to substantiate his charge. He could point to the words of the man challenging him for the prime ministership, Clement Attlee, who, in 1937, had declared that 'the Labour Party Conference . . . issues instructions which must be carried out by . . . its representatives in Parliament'.[5]

Both Churchill and Attlee were, however, wrong. A party constitution might declare the parliamentary party subservient to its extra-parliamentary organization but such a claim could not be reconciled with the traditional and accepted practices of government in Britain. Representatives in Parliament are, constitutionally, representatives of the nation as a whole, and they cannot be bound by any extraparliamentary body. Delegates to the Conference may still feel that ultimate sovereignty rests in their hands, but that this is not the case is indicated by the position of the party leader. Originally it was intended that the leader of the Parliamentary Labour Party and the chairman of the National Executive Committee should be co-equals as leaders of the Party. This intention was, however, unfulfilled almost from the start. The chairman of the NEC could not aim at the target of the Parliamentary leader, namely the Prime Ministership. Consequently the leader of the Parliamentary Labour Party has come to be accepted as the national leader of the party, even though the party outside Parliament, which claims supremacy over the parliamentary party, plays no part in his election.

Nevertheless, the authority of the Conference to 'decide from time to time what specific proposals of legislative, financial or administrative reform shall be included in the Party programme' if 'adopted by a majority of not less than two-thirds of the votes recorded on a card vote',[6] remains unchallenged. In addition, the Parliamentary Committee of the Parliamentary Labour Party is required by the same clause of the party constitution to meet with the National Executive Committee to decide which items shall be included in the election manifesto. This is a consultative process and the NEC certainly cannot dictate to the Parliamentary leadership what items shall be included in the manifesto. Indeed, when the NEC sought to do just that in 1973 over the question of the nationalization of twenty-five leading companies, it received a

5. ibid. p. 10.
6. Labour Party Constitution, Clause V.

sharp rebuke from Mr Wilson who declared that he would veto any attempt to bind the leadership. (The expected clash over the issue at the Party Conference of that year did not materialize as the Party, shifted to the Left in its agreed policy statements, adopted a unified front in anticipation of the next general election.)

On 27 November 1968, the NEC also decided that, when Government policy differs from resolutions passed by the Annual Conference, the responsible Ministers would be asked to appear before the relevant sub-committee to explain the Government's position. This was not a new development but rather a formal extension to the home policy sub-committee of practices already adopted by Mr Walter Padley, chairman of the overseas policy sub-committee, who made a practice of summoning Foreign Office Ministers to explain policies which were a cause of intra-party friction.[7] No shades of Churchill and the Laski bogey need to be raised here. Calls for explanation are far removed from binding instructions.

While, then, there are certain limits upon the parliamentary leadership in its policy-making role, they should not be exaggerated. Several factors are at work to mitigate conference influence and to minimize the conflicts that might well have been more in evidence between the parliamentary and the extra-parliamentary wings of the party.

The most conspicuous of these factors has been the support formerly accorded the parliamentary leadership at conference by several of the larger trade unions. This was particularly the case during Clement Attlee's leadership of the party. Since then, however, some of the larger unions have taken significant steps to the 'left', and their support has no longer been automatically guaranteed. Thus, in 1960 the leadership suffered Conference defeat over its defence policies, largely as a result of the stand taken by the Transport and General Workers' Union, the Amalgamated Engineering Union, the National Union of Railwaymen and the Union of Shop, Distributive and Allied Workers. The votes of 1960 were reversed the following year, with the AEU, the NUR, and USDAW changing their stand, but the result was less important as a victory for the party leader, Gaitskell, and his announced determination to 'fight, fight, and fight again', than as an indication that *in opposition* the support of the unions could no longer be exacted but rather had to be won through negotiation and compromise.

7. See article by David Wood, *The Times*, 2 December 1968.

An observation of events during the first few years of Harold Wilson's Prime Ministership would seem to indicate that, when in power, the parliamentary leadership can usually but not always rely upon Conference support for its major policies. The opposition to the Government's stand over American policy in Vietnam, that led to an adverse resolution being carried at the 1967 Conference, was insignificant in the Government's view when put alongside the support it received for its economic policies. On the other hand, the continued failure of those policies to provide even a glimpse of the 'promised land' eventually resulted in such disenchantment that, at the 1968 Conference, a Transport and General Workers' Union resolution calling for the repeal of the prices and incomes legislation was carried by a majority of nearly 4,000,000 out of the total of just over 7,000,000 votes cast. Paradoxically, the available evidence points to Government support on this occasion having come largely from the constituency representatives. Thus, whereas at the Trades Union Congress, four weeks earlier, a similar motion was carried by more than seven to one, the majority at the Conference was less than five to one. Most of the resolutions submitted by the constituency associations appeared to accept the legislation and sought only to make it more effective so far as prices were concerned. It should also not go unnoticed that Mrs Barbara Castle, the Minister most closely associated with the prices and incomes policy, came top in the constituency-section elections to the National Executive Committee.

Conflict is further reduced by the fact that MPs usually constitute a majority on the NEC: in 1973 seventeen of the twenty-nine members were MPs. While the views of those Members of Parliament elected to the NEC do not always correspond with those of the parliamentary leadership (indeed, as the examples on pp. 99–100 indicate, even members of the government on the NEC may take stands contrary to announced government policy) their presence on that body has certainly enabled the dialogue between the two wings of the party to take place in more moderate tones than might otherwise have been the case. Again, it is probably the case that conference influence is, in most instances, largely an antenatal influence, 'exercised', as Beer has written, 'largely by anticipation, as the moderate leadership [makes] such adjustments in its views as [are] necessary to avoid defeats at Conference'.[8] Finally, the role of the leader of the party as an important initiator of policy must not be overlooked, for in those areas where he is not

8. S. H. Beer, *Modern British Politics* (Faber 1965), p. 233.

bound by Conference pronouncements he has considerable latitude in offering policy leads, although even here he will still be concerned to minimize opposition from the extra-parliamentary organization.

Such concerns are not generally uppermost in the mind of a Conservative leader. Confusion about the location of the centres of power does not exist within the Conservative Party. Conflict and tension seldom arise between the parliamentary and extra-parliamentary wings. The conference of the National Union occupies a recognizably inferior place as the servant of the parliamentary party, and rarely displays an ambition to dictate to Conservative MPs. Balfour's remark, that he would as soon take advice from his valet as from the Conservative Conference,[9] still finds much sympathy among Conservative leaders. Indeed, the terminology employed by Balfour does provide an appropriate analogy here, with the National Union playing Jeeves to the Parliamentary Wooster, offering advice when the aster appears too ready to don clothes of undue liberal hue, and yet acknowledging his final authority to decide in what raiment he shall appear before the public. This is an approach fundamentally different from that to be found in the Labour Party. Here can be seen the hierarchical attitude of the Conservatives. Conference may now and then affect Conservative policy, with party leaders temporizing to avoid conference votes that run counter to announced party policy, or, as in 1950, accepting Conference direction with regard to the number of houses to be built – an oft-quoted example which in fact reflects the paucity of such examples – but the position of the conference is nevertheless quite clear: it exists to advance the cause, to debate the issues, and to offer advice and warning. It does not exist to issue directives binding upon the party leadership. The Conservative Associations and the National Union may regard themselves as keepers of the Conservative conscience, but it is the elected representatives in Parliament who are the keepers of the party's electoral fortunes. It is an opportunist party that would prefer to compromise its way into power rather than maintain ideological purity in opposition; and this has meant that power has always resided in the hands of those capable of producing electoral victories. Ultimately for Conservatives the greater sin is not compromise of principles but failure to attain office. This then helps to explain the relationship between the leaders of the party and the extra-parliamentary

9. Quoted McKenzie, *British Political Parties*, p. 82.

organizations: a relationship highlighted by the interesting convention, breached by Mr Heath in 1965, that the Conservative leader did not even attend the annual conference of the National Union. Instead he appeared after the formal adjournment, his ex cathedra address to the faithful being thus beyond debate or challenge. Mr Heath's decision to attend the Conference and to participate in debate was perhaps a gesture towards greater democracy within the party, in keeping with the recently introduced method of electing the leader;[10] but there has been no fundamental change in the relationship between the leader and the rank and file.

Neither party conference is of a size for vigorous and detailed discussion, whether in debating the reports of its executive committee, or of the parliamentary party (in the Labour case), or the resolutions submitted from the floor. Nevertheless they do both have a useful role in keeping the leadership informed of the changing moods of the membership throughout the country. In general, the Conservatives also use the occasions for demonstrations of their solidarity and of their confidence in the leader, while their opposite numbers in the Labour Party seem to welcome the chance to assert their independence of the leadership, and to publicize the differences that exist.[11]

The governing body of the National Union is not, in fact or even in theory, the Annual Conference but the Central Council, 'a smaller and briefer version of the Annual Conference'[12] although smallness is relative here, as the Central Council has a potential membership of more than three and a half thousand. It is the Central Council that elects the officers of the National Union – the president, chairman, and three vice-chairmen – and has the power to make amendments to the constitution of the National Union. However, the major function of the Council is to provide an additional occasion for the airing of views by the representatives of the constituency associations. The National Union also has an executive committee of approximately 150 members, made up of representatives of the provincial areas, and of officers of the Parliamentary Party, the National Union Central Office, and associated organizations. The committee deals with resolu-

10. Discussed below, pp. 64–5.

11. Indeed, too often, not only at Conference, it would seem that the Labour Party prefers the launderette to the laundry as the appropriate means of dealing with its dirty linen.

12. McKenzie, *British Political Parties*.

tions submitted by the local branches, and has the right to approve or reject the affiliation of constituency associations to the National Union. Through its general purposes sub-committee the executive has the important task of preparing the agendas of the annual conference and of the meetings of the Central Council.

The powers of the National Union do not extend to control of the Central Office, the party's civil service. The bureaucracy of the Conservative Party is under the direct control of the leader. It is he who appoints all the principal officers of the party machine: the chairman, the deputy chairman, the vice-chairman, and the treasurers are all his appointees, and as such are directly responsible to him. The work of Central Office is done through a number of departments concerned with such topics as constituency organization, publicity, local government, the trade unions, and the Young Conservatives. In addition, close links are maintained with two other central agencies which, while not technically part of Central Office, come within the general framework of the party headquarters. The first of these is the Conservative Political Centre, which is concerned with the more active party members throughout the country, providing special publications for study groups and lecture courses in the constituencies, and generally strengthening the party organization at the grass roots. The second is the Research Department which, working in close association with the party's Advisory Committee on Policy,[13] has an important role in the preparation and shaping of policy. This is particularly the case when the party is in opposition. In addition the Department provides official secretaries for the party's parliamentary committees, and briefs Conservative MPs on issues before Parliament. The chairman is appointed by the leader and is responsible to him. This, in addition to the fact that the chairman and vice-chairman of the Advisory Committee on Policy are also appointees of the leader, minimizes the possibility of clashes between the leader and those responsible for policy formulation.

13. The committee is intended to provide liaison between the Parliamentary Party, the National Union, and the Leader on policy matters. It has 21 members – 5 backbenchers elected annually by the 1922 Committee; 2 Conservative peers; 8 members of the executive committee of the National Union; up to 4 co-opted members, and a chairman and vice-chairman appointed by the leader. It has sometimes been described as the most important committee in the party, although David Hennessy, in the *Political Quarterly*, July–Sept. 1961, Vol. 32, No. 3, wrote that it was little more than 'a useful opinion panel from which all types of party reaction could be got'.

As we have already noted, in contrast with the Annual Conference of the National Union, the Labour Party conference is the formally sovereign body of the party. However, its executive, the NEC, while the servant of the Conference, has, as Herbert Morrison put it,[14] 'a duty to lead the Conference, to advise the Conference in the way it ought to go'. Indeed, his view was 'that every Executive that has responsibility will never hesitate to give the Conference firm advice as to what it ought to do'. The composition of the National Executive Committee reflects the different strands that make up the party. Of the twenty-six members elected annually by the Conference – the leader and deputy leader of the Parliamentary Party are ex-officio members – twelve are elected by the trade union delegates (these are usually second or third-rank union leaders, as the General Council of the TUC precludes its members from standing for the NEC); seven are elected by the constituency party and Federation delegates (these usually include several prominent parliamentary figures); five women and one treasurer are elected by the Conference as a whole; and one member is elected by the delegates of the socialist, co-operative and professional associations. In addition, in 1972 a representative of the Young Socialists was added, having been elected (in anticipation of the Annual Conference approving his appointment) at the 11th National Conference of the Young Socialists held at Scarborough that year.

The NEC has an important role to play in policy-making. Working through sub-committees, it produces policy statements that are submitted to the Annual Conference for approval, and, acting jointly with the executive committee of the Parliamentary Party, it decides what items from the party programme shall be included in the election manifesto. It is the NEC that is charged with the maintenance of discipline within the party, having the power to withdraw or refuse the endorsement of candidates, to expel individuals from the party, and to disaffiliate organizations. Again in contrast to the position in the Conservative Party, the Labour Party bureaucracy, Transport House, is under the control of the National Executive, and is not responsible to the leader of the party.

The National Executive Committee is then quite obviously a most powerful part of the Labour Party organization – powerful enough to offer serious challenge to the parliamentary leadership. The fact that such a challenge rarely materializes can be ascribed

14. Quoted McKenzie, *British Political Parties*, p. 523.

to the composition of the committee. The twelve union members have been described as 'safe and silent', while the other places have, in recent years, been mainly occupied by Ministers. Thus, in 1974, five of the seven constituency representatives, three of the five women, and one of the 'silent' unionists, were members of the Government. This, plus the ex-officio presence of the leader and the deputy leader, has meant that while, constitutionally, the extra-parliamentary organization of the party is formally autonomous the parliamentary leadership is usually in a position to dominate and direct much of its work. The key power of Transport House has become, rather, one of obstruction in such areas as spending money or appointments to jobs within the party.

The work of Transport House, as of the Central Office, is done through a series of departments – organization; Press and Publicity; Research; Finance; the Women's Department, and the International Department. It does not play a major role in policy making, which is left to a large extent to the National Executive, although the Research Department does much preparatory work for the party programme and for the policy reports of the executive. The principal task of Transport House is that of organizing and co-ordinating Labour Party activities throughout the country.

The rank and file membership of the political parties is organized in constituency associations which provide the local centres of political activity throughout the country. Is is these associations, with their branches in the wards and polling districts, which conduct the main work of the parties both between and during the elections. Theirs is the arduous task of canvassing, of compiling registers of voters' political inclinations, or raising the money necessary for the election campaign, and of getting the voters out on the day. Membership is open to all who accept the objectives of the parties and who are prepared to pay an annual subscription.

The governing bodies of the Conservative local associations are generally known as Executive Councils, and those of the local Labour parties as General Management committees. They comprise delegates from the wards and from associated groups, such as the Young Conservatives and local Conservative clubs; or the trade unions and co-operative societies. Both the Executive Councils and the General Management Committees do their work through 'inner' executive committees, and through various sub-committees concerned with such areas as political education, Trade union affairs, local government, and publicity.

Probably the most important task undertaken by the constituency associations is that of selecting the parliamentary candidates. In a situation where such a small proportion of seats changes hands at election time the selection of the candidates is obviously a vital process. The election of 1966, for instance, gave the Labour Party a commanding majority in the House of Commons, but only fifty-four constituencies changed hands, while in 1970, when the Conservatives came to power, only 88 seats changed. Even in 1945, a year of landslide victory for Labour, little more than a third of the seats changed. The position is thus that a high percentage of the seats in the House of Commons is essentially in the gift of the local constituency parties. This usually means that a parliamentary seat is at the disposal of a few active party workers in the constituency. To adapt an analogy employed by Mark Abrams in 1951,[15] the 'state of affairs *is* not unlike the era of rotten boroughs before 1832', but now the great Whig and Tory families that disposed of so many seats are replaced by small selection committees, or, in many Labour-held constituencies, by the trade unions.

The theory and practice of candidate selection in the major parties are basically very similar. It is accepted in both that in the exercise of this choice the local associations are autonomous, subject only to the requirement of Central Office or National Executive approval of the candidates. Further, the broad procedural lines followed, while exhibiting certain differences, are in essence much the same. The Executive Council or the General Management Committee appoints a sub-committee to sift through the list of nominations and to produce a short list for consideration by the full executive. The short-listed candidates, usually some three to six, are then invited to address the executive for fifteen minutes or so and to answer questions put to them from the floor. A ballot follows, and normally a parliamentary candidate emerges. In the Conservative Party the selection must be ratified at a general meeting of the constituency association, while in the Labour Party the choice of the General Management Committee is final, subject to National Executive approval.

The lists with which the selection committees have to deal are usually significantly different in length. That which faces a

15. In *Parliamentary Affairs*, Vol. 1, Winter 1951: quoted McKenzie, *British Political Parties*, p. 553.

Conservative association may well contain more than 100 names. A local Labour Party on the other hand is unlikely to receive more than 15 nominations. While this may in part be due to greater eagerness on the part of Conservatives to exercise their talents in the House of Commons, the major reason for the discrepancy can be found in the different procedures for nomination in the two parties. In the Conservative Party any individual may submit his name for consideration, but in the Labour Party nomination may only be made by affiliated organizations. Thus a would-be Labour candidate must persuade a ward or local party, or a trade union branch, or a local co-operative society, for instance, to put his name forward. The initial vetting process, therefore, differs between the two parties in that in the Conservative Party it takes place within the local association while in the Labour Party it takes place outside the formal machinery of the constituency party. Hence Labour selection committees are not beset by the problems with which their Conservative counterparts have to deal. For example, following the announcement by Sir William Teeling, Conservative Member of Parliament for Brighton Pavilion (1966 majority 6,354), that he would retire at the next general election, the Constituency Association received 124 applications for this safe seat. This represented a formidable task for the selection committee of 27. Six syndicates were set up, and each was given 20 or so names to sift. After four meetings the 124 had been reduced to 39, and these were then pared to a 'short list' of 17 from which eventually emerged the 5 names forwarded to the executive council.[16] No constituency Labour Party has ever had to face such a formidable problem.

There have at times been deviations from the usual pattern, and certain constituency associations have adopted procedures similar in approach to the American primary. Thus in 1949 Henry Brooke was selected as the candidate of the Hampstead Constituency Association at a primary held in the Embassy Theatre, Swiss Cottage. A circular was sent to the 7,500 subscribing members, and in the event, by a vote of 714 to 449, Brooke was selected in preference to Charles Challen. In 1959, as an outcome of the dispute between Nigel Nicolson and his constituency association in Bournemouth East, ballots were mailed to 9,724 members of the association asking them to indicate

16. For an interesting account of the Brighton selection process see 'How Amery and Brighton got each other' by Julian Critchley in the *Sunday Times*, 5 November 1967.

whether they favoured Nicolson's re-adoption. Of the 7,433 valid votes, 3,671 were pro-Nicolson, 3,762 against him.[17] In June 1968, the Reigate Association, having whittled down an initial 267 applicants to 2, required its finalists, Geoffrey Howe and Christopher Chataway, to appear before 600 (1 in 25) of the membership to speak and answer questions. The meeting was open to the Press and TV, and was therefore the first public primary in this country. In May and July 1969, the South East Leeds and Wimbledon Associations respectively adopted a 'primary' system for the selection of their parliamentary candidates, although on neither of these occasions were television cameras present. Primaries, as Julian Critchley has written, have 'the merit both of widening the area of choice and of casting light on procedures that are hidden from the public'.[18] In our view processes that illuminate the darker corners of politics and encourage greater participation by the electorate in the political process are to be welcomed.

Both parties keep lists of potential candidates which the constituency parties may consult if they wish, although there is no compulsion upon them to adopt a candidate who is so listed. The Labour Party keeps two lists, segregating the sponsored from the unsponsored candidates, that is, those who have the backing of a trade union or the Co-operative Party from those who do not have such support. Sponsorship in the Labour Party means that the sponsoring body will undertake to contribute a large part of a candidate's election expenses, up to a maximum of 80 per cent of the legally permitted amount. Usually it also means a generous contribution to the constituency party funds. Not unexpectedly, many constituency parties welcome sponsored candidates as a way around their financial difficulties: in some constituencies seats are regarded as being in the gift of particular unions, while in others, not committed to one union, the practice prevails of short-listing only sponsored candidates. Sponsored candidates usually account for over one-fifth of the party's candidacies, and occupy more than two-fifths of its parliamentary seats. The system does at times smack of the buying of seats which used to go on in the Conservative Party before the Maxwell Fyfe reforms became operative in 1949. Prior to these reforms Conservative candidacies had a tendency to go to the highest bidder. Indeed, it is reported that one of Harold Macmillan's stories to the younger members of

17. For an account of the difficulties Nicolson had with his constituency association see his *People and Parliament* (Weidenfeld & Nicolson 1958).
18. *Sunday Times*, 23 June 1968.

the Carlton concerned a selection committee in the twenties 'at which the chairman simply asked each applicant to write his name on a piece of paper together with the amount he was prepared to donate to the Association's funds. The highest bidder was adopted forthwith.'[19] The 1945 election, however, gave the Tories reason to question the 'rich man's party' image that prevailed. Four years later, an end was put to the purchase of candidatures when the Maxwell Fyfe reforms were adopted. Under the new rules, no candidate or MP could make any contribution to his election expenses, and annual contributions to the association's general fund were limited to £25 by prospective candidates and £50 by MPs. Furthermore, the associations were forbidden to raise the question of contributions until after the candidate had been selected. The party image has probably been improved by these changes, even though there is no great difference in the type of men selected. Certainly many constituency associations, thrown back upon their own fund-raising activities, have been greatly revitalized.

A concomitant of these new rules, and one that has not been universally welcomed, has been the increased dependence of candidates and MPs upon their local associations. Indeed, it would appear that the vital relationship in the Conservative Party is that which exists between the MP and his constituency association rather than that which prevails between the MP and his national leaders. The central organs of the party are loth to impose sanctions upon rebellious members, and since 1942 no Tory MP has been denied the party whip. The position of members who have resigned the Whip or who have failed to support the party leadership in Parliament has been regarded as a matter not for national interference but for local discretion. When Oliver Poole, as party chairman, was asked in 1957 what action Central Office would take if the 'Suez' rebels were supported by their local associations, he replied: 'It is a matter for each Association, which is entirely autonomous, to deal with.'[20] Central Office has in fact directly vetoed only one parliamentary candidate since 1945.[21] Thus it would appear, as Ranney has said, that 'for a Conservative MP, the first law of political survival is to cultivate

19. From David Watt, 'Picking and Choosing', in the *Spectator*, 1 May 1964: quoted Austin Ranney, *Pathways to Parliament* (Macmillan 1965), p. 52, n. 52.

20. Quoted Ranney, *Pathways to Parliament*, p. 51.

21. Mr Andrew Fountaine, 1949.

and maintain the support of his association'.[22] The guardians of the Conservative conscience are found less in Westminster than in the constituencies where local activists, '*plus royaliste que le roi*', stand ready to demand party orthodoxy from those who represent them, and are eager to punish those who stray. But it should be noted that mere failure to obey the party whip does not in itself incur this displeasure. For example, at the time of the 'Suez' incident, the Conservative Party in Parliament was subject to defection from both the left and the right wings. Four of the seven left-wing rebels subsequently failed to secure readoption by their constituencies, while all eight right-wing rebels were readopted, and without criticism. It would seem that the latter were regarded as being closer to Conservative Orthodoxy than the party leaders themselves.

The powers of the national leadership of the Labour Party *vis-à-vis* MPs and the constituency organizations have been used more frequently than have those of the Conservative Party leadership. For instance, since 1945 six MPs have been expelled from the Labour Party, the latest being Desmond Donnelly on 27 March 1968. In addition at least five candidates proposed by constituencies have been vetoed by the National Executive. Again when left-wing constituency parties tried to sack right-wing MPs for following the national leadership (Liverpool Exchange and Bessie Braddock 1955; Coventry South and Elaine Burton 1955) Transport House, through the threat of disaffiliation of the local party, intervened to ensure that both were readopted. Certain Labour MPs have also had the whip withdrawn for various periods without suffering expulsion from the party,[23] although in these cases the party leadership was careful to restore the whip before the next general election. At by-elections Transport House is given more formal power to intervene in the selection process, and this has enabled it at times to find places for leading members of the party who may have been defeated at a general election or who may be entering Parliament for the first time. Recent examples of this are to be found in 1964/1965, in the persons of Frank Cousins and Patrick Gordon Walker. The former, who had never been in Parliament, but who had been given a post in the Cabinet, was placed in Nuneaton by the NEC which persuaded the incumbent Member, Frank Bowles, to accept a life peerage. The latter, who

22. *Pathways to Parliament*, p. 87.
23. As in 1954 when the whip was withdrawn from eight Labour MPs including Aneurin Bevan, or in 1961 when withdrawn from five left-wingers.

had lost Smethwick at the general election, was placed in Leyton on the elevation of Reginald Sorenson to the House of Lords. Cousins was elected, but Gordon Walker lost the seat – a loss in part attributable to the disgruntlement of many Labour voters in Leyton about the way their former Member had been treated. Thus in one case the placement power was successful, while in the other it backfired. In yet other instances, as when the NEC tried to foist Creech Jones on Bristol South East, or Tom Driberg on St Helens, it failed altogether – the constituency parties rejected the suggestions and selected their own candidates.

However, even though the central powers of the party may have been used more by Labour than by the Conservatives, the difference is still only marginal, and it is fair to say that 'even in the Labour Party the final word in the selection of most parliamentary candidates rests, in party law and political fact, in the Constituency Labour Parties, not in Transport House'.[24] This autonomy of the local parties and associations, while no doubt of importance in offering greater opportunities for citizen participation in the nation's political life, does have certain disadvantages for the national leadership. It may be recognized at party headquarters in London that there is a need for a better balance in the composition of the parliamentary parties, but this need is not generally recognized at a local level. The leadership of the Conservative Party may well utter pious cries for greater working class representation in the House of Commons but Conservative associations have steadfastly declined to nominate such candidates in any numbers. Thus, while the Conservatives regularly depend upon the working class for practically half of their vote at election time, less than 1 per cent of Conservative MPs can be classed as workers. In this, the local associations may be displaying a certain political acumen, in that they recognize the attitude of social deference characteristic of many working class Tory voters – a deference which demands a candidate of solid middle class qualities. A working class candidate might well lose working class votes. In similar manner it has been suggested that much of the prejudice against women in politics stems from women.[25] That such prejudice does exist generally would seem evident from the October 1974 election, which is fairly typical in this respect. Of the 2,252 candidates only some 11% were women and they fared worse than the male candidates

24. Ranney, *Pathways to Parliament*, p. 166.
25. See R. E. Leonard, *Elections in Britain* (Van Nostrand 1968), pp. 75–6.

with only 21% elected as opposed to 28%. In that particular election the Labour women were more successful than their Conservative counterparts, with more than half their candidates being elected while only 7 of the 23 Tories were returned. The Liberals, as in the previous election failed completely in their bid to send a woman to Westminster.

Generally speaking, the outcome of the selection and election process in the United Kingdom is not unlike that of similar processes in other countries, in that the professional and managerial classes are greatly 'over-represented'. Thus, in 1970, 47 per cent of Conservative and 51 per cent of Labour Party candidates were drawn from the professional classes, although the similarities between the parties are not as great as these blanket figures might suggest, for 54 per cent of the Labour candidates were to be found in the ranks of the teaching profession, while only 16 per cent of the Conservatives were so classed. Businessmen constituted a further 34 per cent of the Conservatives and 12 per cent of the Labour candidates. Again the figures disguise even greater differences between the parties, for 68 per cent of the Conservative businessmen ranked as Company directors while only 24 per cent of their Labour counterparts held such positions. In general the latter were concerned with small businesses or were junior employees of larger companies.[26] The number of working class candidates in the Conservative Party was, as already mentioned, minimal, representing less than 1 per cent of the total, but even in the Labour Party the figure was only 17 per cent, although as this group had the greatest relative success in the election (70 per cent elected) they in fact comprised 26 per cent of Labour MPs.

A consideration of educational background also reveals the 'un-representative' nature of Members of Parliament, and highlights the differences that exist between the Conservative and Labour Parties. 79 per cent of the Labour MPs had attended a state elementary or a secondary school, while only 25 per cent of the Conservative MPs had been so educated. 75 per cent of the Tories had been to a Public School – 18 per cent of them to Eton. Again, while in both parties a majority of MPs had been to university (Conservatives 63 per cent, Labour 54 per cent) Oxbridge claimed the bulk of the former (82 per cent), Redbrick the majority of the latter (53 per cent).

In Parliament the two parties display marked similarities in

26. ibid. pp. 77–8.

organization, with one or two notable exceptions that chiefly relate to the positions occupied by the respective leaders.

The leader of the Labour Party is elected by the Parliamentary Labour Party – Labour MPs and peers. While the party is in opposition he is subject to annual re-election, although in most instances this is a formality: in 1960 Harold Wilson offered the first challenge to a Labour leader since 1922 and was soundly beaten by Hugh Gaitskell by 166 votes to 81. The Conservative leader, on the other hand, has, until recently, 'emerged' as a result of private discussion – some would say 'backstairs intrigue' – among various of the leading lights of the party, rather than as the result of openly democratic procedures. Thus, when Anthony Eden resigned in 1957 Winston Churchill and Lord Salisbury were consulted by the Queen, and they, after discussions and a straw poll of Cabinet Ministers, recommended that Harold Macmillan, and not the party's 'number two', R. A. Butler, be sent for. This method of selection did not escape criticism from many within the party, but the outcry was as nothing compared with the feelings that were aroused five years later over the succession to Macmillan. When, in October 1963, Harold Macmillan announced his imminent retirement no one person was firmly established as his successor. Butler was still there, probably the best qualified of the possibles, but he was destined to remain the bridesmaid for, according to Iain Macleod in the *Spectator*,[27] 'from the first day of his premiership to the last, Macmillan was determined that Butler . . . should not succeed him'. Lord Hailsham, eager for the position, announced that he would take advantage of the provisions of the 1963 Peerages Act that permitted him to renounce his title, and thus put himself in the running. He, too, met considerable opposition, and Macmillan advised the Queen, after what Randolph Churchill described as 'full and diligent enquiries',[28] or, according to Macleod, with 'neither the Chancellor of the Exchequer nor the Leader of the House of Commons [having] any inkling of what was happening',[29] to send for Lord Home. Much dissatisfaction and bitterness were engendered by these manoeuvrings and in February 1965 an announcement was made by Sir Alec Douglas-Home that the next Conservative leader would be elected by the Conservative MPs. Five months later

27. Quoted in A. F. Havighurst, *Twentieth Century Britain* (New York, Harper & Row 1962), p. 473.
28. 'The Fight for the Tory Leadership' (1964); quoted ibid. p. 473.
29. ibid. p. 474.

Edward Heath became the first Conservative leader to be selected in this manner.

Conservative practice, then, in the selection of a leader now closely resembles that of the Labour Party, although the Conservative leader does not have to submit himself for annual re-election when the party is in opposition. Furthermore, he is not subject to the constraints that hedge the freedom of action of his Labour Party counterpart. When in opposition the Labour leader does not have the authority to select his own front-bench colleagues, his shadow Cabinet. It is the Parliamentary Labour Party as a whole that elects the frontbench (the Parliamentary Committee), while in the Conservative Party the leader has the same right to choose his frontbench colleagues in opposition as he has to pick his Cabinet when in power. (This right to choose also carries with it the power to dismiss, as Enoch Powell discovered when he was sacked from the Conservative front bench after a controversial speech on immigration in April 1968.) Closely allied to this, the Conservative leader, in or out of power, has the ultimate authority to determine party attitudes, while the Labour leader, in opposition, may well be bound by a majority vote of the Parliamentary Labour Party.

Both parties make use of specialized committees of backbenchers, dealing with such topics as defence, foreign affairs, trade and industry, health, and social security, but, generally speaking, these have more influence on the Conservative than on the Labour side.[30]

The main organization of the Conservative Party in Parliament is the Conservative and Unionist Members' Committee (usually known as the 1922 Committee from the date of the first meeting of the Parliament in which it originated,) a committee of the backbenchers which meets weekly during the parliamentary session and provides a valuable means of keeping the leadership informed of feeling within the party. The executive of this committee in no way resembles the parliamentary committee of the Labour Party, and has no claim to front-bench status.

The counterpart to the Conservatives' 1922 Committee is the Parliamentary Labour Party, which comprises all Labour Members, including the Cabinet or Shadow Cabinet. When the party is in opposition, the leader of the party presides; when it is in power a backbencher is elected as Chairman of the PLP, and of

30. See J. P. Mackintosh 'What's wrong with British Parliamentary Democracy?' in *Westminster Bank Review*, May 1968, p. 27.

course there is no parliamentary committee, as the task of filling the front bench and forming the Cabinet belongs to the Prime Minister, and in the performance of it he is subject to no direction from the PLP. In the absence of a parliamentary committee, the PLP elects a liaison committee to maintain contact between the Government and the backbenchers.

The rank and file members of the parties in the House are expected to toe the line set by their leaders, and failure to do so may lead to withdrawal of the party whip (i.e. suspension of party rights and privileges in the House for a period of time) and/or outright expulsion from the party – which can mean the end of a political career. (We should note here that those who thought Mr Taverne had ended his political career in Parliament when he resigned from the Labour Party and from the House of Commons over the question of British membership of the EEC were confounded when, on 1 March 1973, he succeeded in his bid for re-election as Member for Lincoln, standing on his own Social Democratic Party label. In the general election of February 1974 he was once more returned to Parliament, although with a greatly reduced majority. At the same general election Mr Edward Milne, the outgoing Labour Member for Blyth in Northumberland who had been rejected as a candidate by the local party management committee, successfully defended the seat against an official Labour candidate and candidates of the Liberal and Conservative parties. (In the October 1974 election, however, both men lost their seats to regular candidates of their former parties.) Generally speaking the Labour leaders have shown themselves less tolerant of deviant behaviour in the division lobbies than have the Conservatives. Indeed, in the Conservative Party it seems that the whip has been more a tool in the hands of the back-benchers – to be resigned as an expression of disagreement with the leadership – than a scourge to be used against them.

By and large the organizational differences between the parties now appear to be marginal. The embourgeoisement[31] of the Labour Party and the development of central control have occasioned conflict with the original notions of egalitarianism and direct democracy that motivated the founders of the party, but this conflict has been resolved in favour of the leadership. Labour activists still remain suspicious of party authority, but the

31. W. L. Guttsman's term in *The British Political Elite* (MacGibbon & Kee 1968), p. 226.

'leadership has largely assimilated the attitudes traditionally held by representatives of the older political parties'.[32]

Just as the parties have moved closer together in questions of organization and power distribution, so in questions of policy there is little of major importance to distinguish them. There is general agreement over the constitutional framework itself, although the position and role of the House of Lords and the dispute over the implementation of the recent report of the Boundary Commissioners represent two fairly minor exceptions to the general consensus. Nor can the parties be differentiated according to their attitudes over what many would consider to be the most central questions of recent years – retention of the H-bomb, membership of the Common Market, immigration control, relations with the Commonwealth, the goal of social security, the role of the state in the economy. In most instances the differences within the parties have proven greater than those between them. The movements concerned with the more controversial social issues of the sixties – the law relating to capital punishment, homosexuality, divorce, or abortion – have been largely inspired and directed by private individuals and groups, while the parties, eager to avoid possible vote-losing controversy, have preferred the mugwump attitude of sitting on the fence ('with the mug facing in one direction and the wump in the other').

Nevertheless, having said this, certain differences in attitude are perceptible. We have already noted the different origins of the two major parties – the one hierarchical, the other egalitarian in nature. Angus Maude postulates a simple, though hardly acceptable dichotomy, with the Labour Party chasing equality while the Conservatives concern themselves with quality. Certainly the folklore of the parties, their history, the interests of the various groups that tend to support them, do work to produce distinct images in the minds of the voters. However, while it may be, as Beer has written, that in opposition the Labour Party still has a 'conception of purpose and an order of priorities readily distinguishable from those of the Conservatives',[33] as indeed its 1973 Annual Conference was at pains to display, its record in power seems to justify R. T. McKenzie's remarks that 'two great monolithic structures now face each other and conduct furious

32. ibid. pp. 26–7.
33. Beer, *Modern British Politics*, p. 242.

arguments about the comparatively minor issues that face them'.[34] 'Massive continuity',[35] not vast disagreement, stands out. No longer do general elections consist of 'pitched battles between opposing social philosophies': they represent, rather, 'small raids on interest groups',[36] and politics is now conducted at the margin.

34. McKenzie, *British Political Parties*, p. 586.
35. Beer, *Modern British Politics*, p. 357.
36. ibid. p. 242.

Chapter 4

Parliament

(1) The House of Commons

Parties exist to control the Government, and the path to this goal lies through the House of Commons, for it is the party that secures a majority of seats in the elected branch of the legislature that has the right to have its leaders form the Government. This being so, the primary task of the House is generally seen to be that of maintaining the Government in power. Indeed, as long ago as 1867 Walter Bagehot, in his famous work, *The English Constitution*, suggesting a possible reply that a Minister might give to a question concerning the functions of Parliament, wrote 'Parliament has maintained ME, and that was its greatest duty.'[1] Life in the House then is lived in terms of the party system, which in normal circumstances assures the Government of the majority necessary to ensure its continuance in office. The organization of the House for action is a party function: committee assignments are made along party lines as nearly as possible in proportion to party strength in the House; the timetable of the House is decided by the leaders of the majority party, usually after consultation with leaders of the Opposition; backbench Members are given voting directions by party whips; loyalty to the party is regarded by the party leaders as the most desirable characteristic of a Member of Parliament. The House of Commons is essentially a body in which the backbench Members ratify decisions taken elsewhere. It legitimizes but does not legislate. Legislative initiative, indeed, probably could not rest with the House without the importation of the anarchic practices of the American Congress which seem to validate John Stuart Mill's dictum that 'a numerous assembly is as little fitted for the direct business of legislation as for that of administration'.[2]

Nevertheless, even though Parliament does not have a legislative role in much more than a technical sense, it does have very specific and vital functions to perform. There is, first, the task to which we have already referred, of legitimizing, i.e. of giving authority to, decisions taken by the Cabinet. Bills before Parlia-

1. Walter Bagehot, *The English Constitution* (World's Classics), p. 117.
2. J. S. Mill, *Representative Government* (ed. R. B. McCallum), p. 168.

ment are subject to general debate, which takes place on the second reading and may take place on the third, and to detailed examination, which is conducted during the intervening committee and report stages. (The so-called first reading is no more than the formal introduction of a bill.)

The first major hurdle a bill has to surmount is the second reading, at which the general principles embodied in it are debated. Second readings are usually taken on the 'floor of the House' – but not invariably. Scottish bills, for instance, receive their second readings in Scottish Standing Committee (unless ten members object), and there is a comparatively new procedure, dating from 1965, whereby any Government bill may be sent to standing committee for its second reading, on the proposition of the Minister producing it, if there are fewer than twenty Members who object to this course.

When the House has signified its approval of the general principles of the bill, it is sent to committee for clause-by-clause debate – unless, as happens rather rarely, the House decides that it should first be examined and reported on by a select committee. Nowadays most bills are sent to standing committees, comparatively small bodies of Members which meet 'upstairs', but some are still considered by a 'committee' which consists of the whole House, meeting in the debating chamber and using special rules of procedure. When the committee reports the bill, amended or unamended, to the House, there is a further debate, in which new amendments may be moved. This 'report' stage is of particular importance when a bill has been committed to standing committee and when, therefore, not all Members have had a chance of moving amendments; but it is of limited value when the bill has been examined by a committee of the whole House.

The report stage completed, the bill may, if the House so wishes, be subject to further debate on third reading, which resembles the second reading in that discussion is about the bill as a whole, and amendments to its individual clauses are now out of order. After the third reading, it is sent to the other House, where it goes through a series of similar stages. If both Houses approve, it receives the Royal Assent and becomes an Act – part of the law of the land.[3] If there are disagreements between the two Houses, the lower House can invoke the provisions of the 1949 Parliament Act, whereby, if a bill is re-passed by the Commons in identical

3. The monarch may in fact refuse assent for any bill, but this power of veto has not been used since 1707.

form in two successive sessions, with at least one year separating the second reading in the first session from the third reading in the second session, the Lords' objections are finally overruled. As yet, however, no bill has ever been passed in this manner. By what may be described as custom rather than convention, the Lords gracefully or ungracefully climb down when the Commons have decided, after consideration, to reject certain of the amendments that their Lordships have proposed.

Thus, in theory at least, machinery exists for ample publicity of the terms of proposed legislation and for detailed consideration of all its aspects. In debate are heard the general arguments for and against the principles of a bill; in committee there are opportunities for amendment, improvement or emasculation.

Debates on Government legislation, in the disciplined two-party system that prevails in the House of Commons, are more often than not set-piece exercises, carefully managed by party leaders through the party whips. With votes on such legislation regarded as votes of confidence, backbench revolt of any significance is remote.[4] Debate on the floor of the House publicizes the general principles of a bill, but no longer provides opportunity for their rejection.

The tasks of a committee are to consider a bill in detail, and to offer opportunity for amendment. Amendments offered to bills are essentially of two kinds – those aimed at improvement in the light of the principles approved at the second reading, and those intended to frustrate those principles.[5] Much useful work can be done in committee, but the value of this work is very much dependent upon the attitude of the Government and of the Minister in charge of a bill. Since party discipline reaches from the floor of the House into the committee rooms, few amendments will succeed in a committee of the House of Commons against the wishes of the Minister. Further, the Government may well make use in Committee of the guillotine, by which debate on particular clauses

4. But twice in February 1973 we saw Tory revolts in Committee. On the 13th of that month the Government was defeated over the length of time powers over prices and incomes would continue. Nicholas Ridley and John Biffen both voted against their party. One week later, when the question of disclosure under the terms of the Counter-Inflation Bill was being discussed, two Conservatives, Sir Edward Brown and Dr Anthony Trafford, voted against the Government while three others, N. Ridley, J. Biffen and W Proudfoot abstained.

5. For more detailed analysis see Hanson and Wiseman, *Parliament at Work* (Stevens 1962), pp. 145–6.

is cut off at a pre-determined time. If, by the appointed hour, certain clauses and amendments to those clauses have not been debated they are put to a vote without the benefit of discussion. Such a procedure, while essential if governments are to cope with ever-increasing legislative burdens, does nevertheless arouse hostility from Oppositions and at times from the Government's own backbenchers, who may accuse Ministers of using steam-roller tactics. These accusations are also levelled against that other time-saving device, the kangaroo, which permits selection of the amendments to be discussed. This latter procedure is aimed at preventing an Opposition from being obstructive by putting down numerous amendments of similar nature.

Criticisms concerning the manner in which a Government can curtail the rights of backbenchers to be heard should also be considered in connection with Private Members' bills.[6] About 50 per cent of the time of the House of Commons is taken up with legislation,[7] and the vast bulk of this time is given over to government legislation. From his mid-nineteenth century ascendancy the private member has been relegated in terms of legislative initiative to a very minor place. Since the changes that came into effect in 1967, an average of twenty Fridays and four half-days (Wednesdays) per session have been made available to private Members. Of these, sixteen are set aside for bills and the remainder for motions. Members ballot among themselves for the right to introduce a bill – those successful being assured of a second reading debate for their bills. However, the right to the debate is one thing, securing a second reading quite another. A backbench Member cannot ensure that he will have a quorum for the debate on his bill, and he is in no position to prevent the bill from being 'talked out'. He faces danger from apathy, hostility, or both, and lacks the resources of the Government to overcome them. Thus, even many of those who are successful in the ballot find that their victory is shortlived. Many of the bills that are introduced in this manner are of a fairly non-controversial nature – which is usually important if they are to succeed – but this is by no means always the case. They may at times deal with topics that the major parties

6. These should be clearly distinguished from private bills, which are promoted by bodies of persons outside Parliament (e.g. local authorities and nationalized industries) in order to acquire new powers for themselves, and which are subject to a special parliamentary procedure of a quasi-judicial type. Private legislation, being a highly technical subject, is not dealt with either in this chapter or elsewhere in this book.

7. See Hanson & Wiseman, *Parliament at Work*, p. 121.

regard as too controversial to be adopted officially. In this category, in recent years, we find bills concerned with the death penalty, obscene publications and homosexuality. An MP may also get permission to introduce a bill under the ten-minute rule, but such permission does not carry with it any guarantee that time will be found for a second reading. All that can be said for this procedure is that it does enable the Member to secure publicity for his chosen subject-matter.

In addition to its role as a legitimizer, the House of Commons also acts as a body in which complaints and grievances may be raised and discussed. A Government must be prepared to defend its actions both specifically and generally before the House. This it does in response to Questions raised at Question Time, in debates initiated on the adjournment, or in debates on motions of censure put down by the Opposition.

Question Time has long been regarded as a vital part of the processes whereby the House of Commons attempts to hold a Government accountable for its actions. Questions may be put by any Member on any topic that is within the competence of a Minister. Two questions for oral reply, and any number for written reply, may be put down by a Member for a particular day. The right is undoubtedly 'amongst the most prized of a private Member's privileges',[8] although to describe it as 'perhaps the readiest and most effective method of parliamentary control over the executive', as did the 1945 Procedure Committee,[9] seems an overstatement of its usefulness. Certainly matters of great importance may be raised at Question Time. Questions, and the supplementaries that follow, may oblige a Government to defend and explain its actions, and help to keep the Civil Service on its toes.

There is undoubted value in this procedure, which offers an opportunity to backbench Members to publicize their grievances and to prod governments into action, even though, at times, the occasion is used for political point-scoring rather than for extracting information or explanation, and despite the fact that the time available for oral replies, something under one hour, four days a week, does not permit lengthy answers or detailed cross-examination. Testimony to that value is found perhaps in the threat to Question Time posed by the question-rigging affair of 1971. In that year the *Sunday Times* revealed that four Ministers

8. *Parliamentary Reform* (Cassell for the Hansard Society, 2nd Edn 1967), p. 86.

9. Quoted ibid. p. 88.

in the Department of the Environment were involved in question-planting in the House of Commons. A memorandum of 10 May 1971, circulated by the head of the Directorate of Research and Information in the Ministry of Housing (and reproduced in the *Sunday Times*), began: 'You will remember we were asked a few weeks ago to provide a number of PQs [*Parliamentary Questions*] which could be "planted" so as to forestall the Opposition's onslaught on days when our Ministers are first for questions . . .' and went on: 'Ministers have asked for the exercise to be repeated every time the Department is first for questions – every three weeks'. These revelations occasioned considerable criticism, and as a result a Select Committee on Parliamentary Questions was established. In its report, published in July 1972, the Committee declared that 'it is not the role of the Government machine to seek to redress the party balance of questions on the Order Paper, and Civil Servants should not in future be asked to prepare questions which have this object'. This view was accepted by the Government and hopefully the practice has now ceased.

Question time is supplemented, as it were, by the half-hour debates on the adjournment which close each day's proceedings. The topics for these debates are the choice of the Members, and apart from one day a week when the Speaker decides, from a list of subjects submitted by Members, what shall be discussed, the right to initiate the debate on the adjournment is determined by a fortnightly ballot. These debates are often limited to the introductory speech and the reply by a representative, usually junior, of the Government. The topic for debate must, like Questions, lie within the sphere of a Minister's responsibility and in many respects the adjournment debates represent extended question and answer, providing further opportunities for raising and publicizing grievances and for requiring governmental defence and explanation.

Governments are also obliged to explain and defend their actions in the full-scale debates that take place in the House. They may be initiated by the Government itself, or by the Opposition, using one of its supply days,[10] or moving a motion of censure on the Government. While these debates offer opportunity for rank and file contributions, Privy Councillors tend to pre-empt much

10. Twenty-nine days are given over to 'discussing' the Estimates, but these are in fact used as excuses for much more general debates concerning aspects of departmental administration. The Opposition has the right to choose the topic for debate on such days.

of the time that remains between the lengthy front-bench speeches from both sides of the House that open and close the debate. These set-piece confrontations, followed by usually predictable votes, occasion critical comment from outside the House and their worth is challenged. However, they have value, for the Government is obliged to state a position at some length and the Opposition accorded an opportunity to publicize a coherent alternative. Much of the criticism stems from the voting-predictability which to many observers gives the whole process the character of a charade. This is to ignore the fact that the votes associated with these debates are largely irrelevant in terms of the subject-matter,[11] being regarded by party leaders as necessary expressions of party solidarity.

These debates are however often limited by the fact that the House of Commons in this dialogue with the Government is insufficiently informed. If a Government is to be watched, if its actions are to be questioned, if censure is to be moved in compelling terms, then those watching, questioning, and censuring need to have much greater knowledge of and access to the facts than they currently have. The situation was perhaps unwittingly highlighted by Frank Stacey in his book, *The Government of Modern Britain*, when he wrote, 'Until 1963 . . . an Economic Survey . . . appeared before the Budget and helped to make more fully informed the subsequent discussion of the Budget in the Commons. It was discontinued . . . because the forecasts in some previous years' surveys had proved to be very inaccurate. This was an unfortunate step, as the Economic Survey was a valuable contribution to debate.'[12] It is surely a sad commentary upon the resources available to MPs that even 'very inaccurate' forecasts could be welcomed as valuable contributions.

11. There are of course exceptions to this general statement. Some recent examples are the rebellion by 23 Labour MPs who voted against the penal clauses of the Prices and Incomes Bill on 25 June 1968, and the 45 Tory MPs who defied the Shadow Cabinet and voted against the Race Relations Bill on its Third Reading in July 1968. In 1972 a large revolt by Labour MPs helped provide the crucial majority of more than 100 for joining the European Economic Community. On 22 November of that same year the House of Commons rejected the Conservative Government's Immigration rules by 275 votes to 245 after 45 Tories had abstained and 7 had actually voted against the Government. In June 1973 there was a revolt against the Government's plans for siting the third London airport at Maplin; seven Tories voted with the Opposition.

12. Frank Stacey, *The Government of Modern Britain* (Oxford 1968), pp. 129–30.

If the major task of the House of Commons is to sustain a Government, the price it should be able to exact for performing this task is that of being sufficiently informed to criticize adequately the policies and actions of the Government. Parliamentary control of the executive stands as a fundamental precept of the British system of government and yet more and more often complaints are raised that such control is diminishing while executive power increases. In consequence the demand is often made that this trend be reversed, and that better opportunities should be provided for Parliament to exercise its essential role. Such control, however, should mean, in the words of the Study of Parliament Group,[13] 'influence, not direct power, advice not command, criticism not obstruction, scrutiny not initiative, and publicity not secrecy'.

The House of Commons is not devoid of all means whereby it can exercise a control function. Debates on the floor of the House can, as we have seen, publicize issues and offer opportunity for the raising of grievances, while Question Time and the debates on the adjournment can prove useful for extracting information from Ministers. As already noted, however, both are limited, providing little occasion for scrutiny or informed advice. Nor are the standing committees,[14] that now consider the bulk of legislation after second reading, equipped for an expert consideration of Government proposals. Such committees may not be as non-expert as some critics would claim, for they usually contain members particularly knowledgeable about or interested in the subject matter of a bill. But much of the membership tends to be drawn at random from the ranks of MPs – members unlikely to possess that interest or knowledge. When consideration of the bill is completed the committee is dissolved. There is no attempt to retain for a future date the collective knowledge or wisdom that the committee may have acquired.[15] It should also be emphasized that a standing committee is a 'debating' committee, not one of inquiry.

There are, nevertheless, certain committees of the House of Commons which do engage in detailed scrutiny and investigation of certain aspects of the functioning of the executive.

13. Memorandum by the Study of Parliament Group to the Select Committee on Procedure. See the Fourth Report, 1964–65: HC Paper 393, p. 139

14. Such a misleading name.

15. Exceptions to this general rule concern the Welsh and Scottish Standing Committees to which all Welsh and Scottish bills are sent.

There is, first, the Public Accounts Committee, a body of 15 members reflecting party strength in the House but chaired by a member of the Opposition. Concerned with a study of Government expenditure, the Committee is aided in its work by the Comptroller and Auditor-General, whose staff audit the accounts of the Government departments. It is these audits, and the Comptroller's subsequent report to the House of Commons, that provide the basic material for the enquiries made by the PAC. In large part the Committee is examining the expenditure of money voted by Parliament at least two years ago, and at times it looks rather like a watchdog barking outside an empty stable. However, the committee has an important check on potential bureaucratic mismanagement. Again, while the horse may have been stolen, the committee has an important role to play. Its very existence is an important check on potential bureaucratic mismanagement. Again, while the horse may have been stolen, the Committee's revelations may lead to the return of the beast, or at least a substantial part of it. Thus in 1964 the PAC revealed that Ferranti had made what it considered excessive profits on a Government contract, and this eventually resulted in a considerable sum being returned to the Treasury.

The Committee's work can also lead to an improvement in Government procedures. For instance, in the summer of 1967 the Committee roundly condemned Bristol Siddeley Engines for making 'exorbitant' profits on engine overhauls between 1959 and 1963,[16] and the Ministry of Aviation for permitting such profits to be made. As a result of the PAC report and of the recommendations it contained, a new approach to the question of development contracting for the Government was announced in February 1968. A formula agreed to by the Treasury and the Confederation of British Industries included nearly all the safeguards recommended against the hidden escalation of costs and profits.

The second committee which, in the past, enabled the House of Commons to maintain a watchful eye upon Government expenditure and administration was the Estimates Committee. The Committee, replaced in 1971 by the Select Committee on Expenditure, did its work through a series of sub-committees which, from December 1965 until the start of the 1967/68 session, were specialized in nature: in addition to the steering sub-committee these sub-committees dealt with defence and overseas affairs,

16. In February 1967, after long negotiations, BSEL agreed to refund £3.96 million in respect of excessive profits.

economic affairs, social affairs, technological and scientific affairs, building and natural resources, and the supplementary estimates. While the Committee had the twin ideas of economy and efficiency before it when commencing its work, it spread itself over a wider field than was usually comprehended by 'financial', and was also 'an instrument of general administrative review and scrutiny, and a major source of information about how the Departments operate'.[17] Much of its time was spent, as Nevil Johnson has written, in 'finding out whether the procedures they use seem to be intelligent and comprehensible, and whether the distribution of functions and the overall administrative organization are effective for carrying out Government policies'.[18] That the work of the Committee was wide-ranging is evidenced by the reports it produced,[19] but a survey of such reports also reveals a lack of systematic investigation and oversight of particular areas. Thus, while the Departments of State paid not inconsiderable attention to the reports that concerned them, the effect of such reports was weakened by the fact that the Committee did not follow up its work to discover what actions, if any, had been taken as a result of its recommendations.

In 1971, as we mentioned earlier, the Estimates Committee was replaced by a Select Committee on Expenditure with power to examine projections on public expenditure and to consider the policies behind those projections. This change came as a response to recommendations made in 1968 by the Select Committee on Procedure, and to growing criticism that Parliament was failing to match the expertise to be found in Whitehall. In its work, which has been aimed at revitalizing Parliament in the complex area of Government expenditure, the Committee has done much solid work producing reports which have covered the whole range of the public sector's main activities. The work of the Committee has been remarkably free from party political controversy as the then chairman, Edward Du Cann, pointed out in September 1972 when he reported that there had been only one division on party lines in agreeing fourteen reports. And yet the Committee has not been afraid to plunge into politically controversial areas. In

17. Nevil Johnson, *Parliament and Administration* (Allen & Unwin 1966) p. 128.

18. ibid. p. 129.

19. A complete list of reports and special reports of the Estimates Committee for the years 1945–65 can be found in Appendix 1 of Johnson, *Parliament and Administration*, pp. 173–81.

February 1973 it published *Public Expenditure to 1976–77* (Cmnd 5178) in which it strongly criticized the Government's spending plans. The report was prepared by a general sub-committee of nine chaired by Robert Sheldon, the Labour Party spokesman on Treasury Affairs, and adopted unanimously by the full committee of 49 with its Conservative majority. However, although the Committee has much solid work to its credit it has failed, like the Estimates Committee before it, to make much impact on public awareness or on debate in the House of Commons. Nevertheless, many have argued, and still argue, that other specialist committees are essential if the House of Commons is to offer adequate oversight of Executive activity.

One of the most telling cases advanced in favour of more specialist committees in Parliament was that presented by the Study of Parliament Group to the Select Committee on Procedure 1964–5. The main burden of their argument was that 'the main weakness in Parliament's present methods of scrutinizing administration, and indeed of debating policy matters, is the limited ability to obtain the background facts and understanding essential for any detailed criticism of administration or any informed discussion of policy'.[20] To strengthen Parliament's hand the Group recommended, first, that the sub-committees of the Estimate Committee should be organized along specialist lines. (as we have already seen, this recommendation was adopted for a two-year period.) In addition, it argued that specialist committees were needed 'to scrutinize the actions of Government in their own fields, to collect, discuss, and report evidence relevant to proceedings in Parliament whether legislative or other'.[21] It considered that such committees of advice and scrutiny might initially be concerned with scientific development, the prevention and punishment of crime, the machinery of national, regional and local government and administration, housing, building and land use, and the social services.[22] As they developed, they could then take over the relevant functions of the Estimates Committee.

There was already in existence, at the time the Study of Parliament Group presented its evidence to the Procedure Committee, a committee that was operating more or less along the lines that the Group envisaged. This was the Select Committee on Nationalized Industries. Established in 1956, with wider terms of reference than

20. HC Paper 303, 1964–65, p. 137.
21. ibid. p. 137.
22. ibid. p. 138.

its predecessor of 1955, the Committee was instructed to examine the reports and accounts of the nationalized industries. A series of reports on the different industries has been published, dealing with matters of both policy and administration. In addition, in 1962, the committee produced a follow-up report to discover to what extent its recommendations had been followed. Evidence has been taken not only from the various public corporations but also from representatives of related Ministries and even from academics. Indeed, such have been the relations of the Committee with certain Government departments that one commentator was led to suggest that 'in many respects it has behaved sometimes like a specialist committee attached to the Ministries of Power, Transport and Aviation'.[23]

The success of the Committee on Nationalized Industries must in large part be attributable to the non-partisan way in which it has approached its work. Few votes have been taken during the course of its proceedings, and even fewer have been along party lines: that this should be so in such a politically-contentious field is remarkable, and a hopeful sign for future developments in other areas. The lesson that may be drawn from this experience, and one well taken by some, but not all, of the members of the Study of Parliament Group, concerns the necessary distinction that must be drawn if specialized committees are to have any real value. Such committees must attempt to make not artificial distinctions between policy and administration, but real distinctions between party and non-party issues. If useful work is to be done by members of these committees they need to be free of the heavy hand of party whips. Such freedom is usually only given to MPs when non-party-political questions are under discussion or when questions of confidence in the Government are unlikely to arise. Only in these circumstances can one expect sufficient objectivity from the committee members. The suggestion that such committees should also be concerned with work on bills and resolutions is one that would involve them in partisan matters. The Government's need to safeguard its policies would involve the use of the whip when divisions were taken, and the committees would therefore divide along party lines. Such a division would probably carry over to consideration of other less controversial matters and the sense of unity of purpose would be lost.

This is not, however, to argue that there is no room for more

23. David Coombes, *The Member of Parliament and the Administration* (Allen & Unwin 1966).

specialized knowledge to be brought to bear by standing committees when considering legislation. Rather it is to suggest that the work of specialized investigatory committees should not be confused with that of any specialized legislative committees which might be established. The demands of the former are not the demands of the latter, and attempts to combine the different functions can only be to the detriment of the investigatory function.

An outcome of the clamour for the introduction of specialist committees into the House of Commons was the announcement in December 1966 by Richard Crossman, Leader of the House, that two such committees, on agriculture and on science and technology, would be established. To these was later added a third, on education and science. This and the Agriculture Committee were, so to speak, attached to specific Government departments, whereas the Committee on Science and Technology was concerned with a subject that overlapped departmental responsibilities. The first two began their work early in 1967. They were empowered to send for persons and papers and to sit in public during their examination of witnesses. The Committee on Agriculture produced a report during 1967 that criticized certain aspects of the preparations made by the Ministry of Agriculture for possible British entry into the Common Market, while the Committee on Science and Technology went to work on two separate enquiries – the nuclear reactor programme, and the question of oil pollution around the country's shores.

Important evidence of much wider relevance than the committee's terms of reference might lead one to expect emerged in June 1968, when minutes of evidence to a sub-committee of the Select Committee on Science and Technology were published. Ostensibly concerned with coastal pollution, the evidence contained a vigorous attack on the Treasury and on succeeding Chancellors of the Exchequer by Sir Barnett Cocks, Clerk to the House of Commons. The gravamen of his charges was that the Treasury was depriving the House of Commons of the staff it needed to do its job properly. Sir Barnett testified that he had under his control only thirty-eight clerks to look after all the House of Commons' select committees, its standing committees, all the committee work arising out of private Members' bills, and all the business involved in parliamentary Questions. The very sub-committee before which this criticism was made had to share a clerk with the Select Committee on Agriculture, and the same clerk also carried out part-time work for the Council of Europe. Dr David Owen remarked in committee: 'It is an intolerable situation whereby we can have a Government department in effect limiting the scope and power and effectiveness of any select committee that might be established.' Sir Barnett agreed with Dr Owen and went on: 'The travel of select committees overseas has been fixed at £7,000 for this year. In this year of great economy, I notice there is a grant in the Estimates to encourage sport and recreation among servants of the Crown. The grant last year was £120,000. In this year of great economy the grant has mounted to £170,000 . . . and the select committees can have only £7,000 for investigation overseas.'[24]

This complaint voiced to the sub-committee by Sir Barnett forms part of a general series of complaints concerning the lack of facilities available to MPs for carrying out their tasks of scrutiny and criticism in an effective manner. British MPs, when they arrive at the House of Commons, find facilities available to them which seem designed to ensure that they encounter the greatest possible difficulty in performing their duties: a locker too small to contain an average-sized briefcase; perhaps a shared room for a few lucky ones; no telephone, apart from a public kiosk; no secretarial or research assistance unless paid for out of personal resources.[25] The Library of the House of Commons, within the limits set by its budget, does provide excellent service to Members in digging out information for them. But when one realizes that, for this task of meeting the needs of the bulk of MPs, who have no research assistance of their own, the Library employs a mere twelve researchers to handle some 2,000 requests a year that come from Members, one can appreciate that the budget for this work is sadly lacking.

This situation contrasts sharply with that to be found in the

24. For a report of Sir Barnett's accusations see *The Times*, 26 and 27 June 1968.

25. The Select Committee on House of Commons Services recommended in its Sixth Report of the 1968–69 session that 'provision should be made at public expense for secretarial assistance of an allowance to meet the cost of up to a maximum of one full-time secretary per member'; that 'MPs should be allowed free trunk calls, and that they should be allowed to send all letters on official business free from October 1st.' (Sixth Report from the Select Committee on House of Commons (Services), 1968–69: services and facilities for members. [HC Paper 374].) On 11 December 1969, Mr Peart, Lord President of the Council, announced in the House of Commons that MPs would be able to claim an allowance for secretarial assistance of up to £500 a year.

United States Congress. In Washington each Representative and Senator, in addition to a salary, liberal by British standards, is given a sizeable allowance for the employment of personal staff: a member of the House of Representatives is thus able to employ four or five assistants while the Senator's allowance permits him a staff of a dozen or so. Further, the work of these Congressmen is not conducted on benches in the corridors of the Capitol, or in shared rooms, but in the well-equipped suite of offices allocated to each of them. When, in addition to the services of their own employees, these American Representatives and Senators need further research assistance they do not compete for the services of a handful of clerks in a useful but modest library. They turn instead to the largest library in the United States, the Library of Congress, which employs more than 200 staff, many of them specialists, in its legislative reference service, and which is capable of dealing with 100,000 Congressional requests a year.

The contrast is stark and yet some commentators suggest that the comparison drawn between Congress and the House of Commons is not a viable comparison, as members of the two legislatures are engaged in different activities, and that facilities which would be indefensible in the American context, where Congressmen are actively engaged in the legislative process, may well be acceptable in a system like the British, where legislation is not the function of rank and file MPs. Thus we find Professor Birch, in a recent book,[26] displaying what almost amounts to complacency about the situation in the House of Commons. The duties of a backbencher are, according to Birch, to take care of the interests of his constituents, to vote as his party leaders direct, and to attend parliamentary party meetings. He may also, if he is so inclined, specialize in a certain field of activity, or take an interest in the work of one of the select Committees of the House. His 'role is more like that of a chorus boy than that of a leading actor'.[27] This might well be described as a 'lobby-fodder' analysis of the role of the House of Commons, ascribing to MPs a passive role in which the dictates of party leaders are expected to be followed in the battle between Government and Opposition.

If this analysis is accepted then one can also accept the lack of facilities provided for British MPs. But this is in fact only half the picture, the half easily recognized by the general public. By concentrating in large part on the Government/Opposition con-

26. A. H. Birch, *The British System of Government* (Allen & Unwin 1967)
27. ibid. p. 150.

flict it ignores, in substantial measure, that other vital interaction which should continually take place between the legislature and the executive. 'The redress of grievance before the granting of supply' has long been considered a vital role of the House of Commons, but in these days of strict party discipline this form of words is archaic: back bench revolts that bring down Governments – which would be the outcome of a refusal to vote Supply – are no longer expected. Nevertheless, the right to scrutinize and investigate adequately the policy and administration of the Government, even though reports and recommendations that may emerge from such investigation may be rejected, is still considered a highly important part of the work of the House of Commons. This right can be exercised effectively only if 'adequate research and information facilities' are provided 'for both committees and individual members'.[28] Such facilities are, as we have seen, not available, and one cannot defend their absence and the obstacles this places in the way of the House's performance of its watchdog functions.

The development of the new system of specialized committees (if 'system' is not too strong a word here) has not followed the lines originally envisaged. The promise of 1966 that two departmental select committees would be set up each year until 'all domestic policy was subject to scrutiny'[29] has not been fulfilled. The committees that are now in being as a result of the innovations of the 1960s are those on Science and Technology, Race Relations and Immigration, and Scottish Affairs. (There is, in addition, a Select Committee on the Parliamentary Commissioner established in conjunction with the introduction of the 'Ombudsman' into the British system of Government.) Matters that might have been deemed suitable for scrutiny by a departmental select committee are now in the competence of the committee on expenditure. Nevertheless, the period since 1966 has undoubtedly seen a radical increase in Parliamentary scrutiny of the executive branch of government. Ministers, Civil Servants, Local Government officials have all been subjected to investigation, and backbenchers have managed in part to unshackle themselves from the Palace of Westminster by securing Treasury backing for overseas visits considered necessary for their committee work.

The improvement in the ability of the Commons to criticize has not met with universal approval. As one might expect, many

28. Memorandum by Study of Parliament Group, p. 139.
29. See J. P. Mackintosh in *The Times*, 13 March 1969.

Ministers, Civil Servants and local officials have resented this oversight, but opposition to the growth of these investigatory bodies has also come from Parliamentarians concerned with the status of the House itself. Mr Michael Foot has described the Committees as 'a "pretentious" distraction from the main problem of restoring to the central chamber the role of chief forum for political debate in Britain,'[30] while Mr John Mendelson is afraid that 'fringe committees' could be the death of the Chamber. Certainly the fears of both men would appear to find some justification in the proliferation of committee sittings in the last six years of the 1960s. In 1964 there were 240 such sittings, in 1969 629, and Government business managers often found business hampered by the difficulty of finding men to carry the work on bills. However, these arguments disregard the fact that it was precisely because the Chamber of the Commons was unable to act as an effective, informed forum for debate that specialized committees were proposed. The reports of such bodies, it was hoped, would then provide the essential ingredients for revitalized confrontation in the Chamber. That, all too often, the reports have gone undiscussed, the information produced unused, is an unfortunate reflection on the way in which business in the whole House is conducted. It is not an argument against the continued use of such committees for, unless the legislature is to remain a 'dignified' part of the constitution, performing little more than the ceremonial functions of legitimization, it must have the information that will permit it to hold the Executive accountable for its actions. If such information is not readily available, and if the House of Commons is denied the opportunity to fulfil the wider role, MPs will be forced to continue to exercise what influence they can through party as opposed to Parliamentary channels and the decline of the House will continue, perhaps to the point that it will come to warrant that description unjustly applied by Congressman Short to the American Congress: 'a supine, subservient, soporific, supercilious, pusillanimous body of nitwits'. Government in Britain will have degenerated still further towards rule by bureaucrats under the general guidance of alternating sets of oligarchs.

In addition to the old bogey of 'ministerial responsibility', much of the opposition to increasing and strengthening the role of the House of Commons finds its origin in fear that party control of the House will thus be weakened. Many who seek change would

30. Ronald Butt in *The Times*, 22 October 1970.

of course argue for just that, seeing in party control the source of all that has gone wrong with the British parliamentary system. However, one does not need to become involved in the controversy concerning the desirability of a strong party system to argue for change. Improvement need not be concerned with sharpening the watchdog's blunted teeth but rather with improving the functioning of its senses. Thus what is sought is a body capable of uncovering and publicizing facts concerning administrative practices, and also capable of making informed suggestions for improvement. What is not generally sought is a body that would obstruct or hinder the necessary work of administration, or seek to wrest responsibility for the running of the country from the Government. It is the task of the Government to govern, the function of the electorate to deliver a verdict on the performance of the Government, and the duty of the House to ensure that the governing is subject to as much scrutiny as possible, and that the verdict is passed in the light of as much information as can be reasonably expected.

The paradox of the House of Commons is that, organized as it is in party terms, MPs perform some of their most valuable work in the House when they put party behind them, as for instance in the select committees where deliberation and reports cut across party lines. This is not to argue that backbenchers do not have an important role within the party and cannot influence the decisions of their leaders. Rather it is to suggest that that role, apart from providing the necessary support in the division lobbies, is largely exercised outside the chamber of the House, in party offices and committee rooms. It is in the meeting of the specialist committees that exist within the major parties, in the contacts between leaders and supporters, that the backbencher may well hope to have some influence upon his party's policy. The presentation of a programme in the House is the end product of party discussions and bargaining in which backbenchers will have an opportunity to present their views. A backbencher who openly disagrees in the House with certain aspects of his party's policy may embarrass the leadership a little; he will rarely occasion a change of that policy.

The development of powerful party political machines has been described as the 'most serious political menace' to the system of parliamentary government,[31] and yet it is through these machines that British political life is organized for coherence. The tightly-

31. L. S. Amery, *Thoughts on the Constitution* (Oxford, 1947), p. 42.

whipped votes on the floor of the House of Commons, reflecting decisions that have so obviously been taken elsewhere, occasional cynicism about the parliamentary process. Yet only by taking the decision-making process out of the 'numerous assembly' that Mill considered ill-fitted for legislation, only through the presentation to the electorate, via the House of Commons, of comprehensive, alternative programmes can responsible government be achieved. It may be argued that the activities of the whips extend further than is necessary for the maintenance of party images and that more issues could be made subject to free vote and thus removed from the realm of party politics. But this is not to argue for any fundamental change in the present party situation in the House. Burke's address to the electors of Bristol has little relevance today. MPs owe to the electorate not so much their judgment as their loyalty to the party label that took them to Westminster. Only through the parties can one attempt a crude approximation of the 'wishes of the electorate' and at the same time hold responsible those to whom the power to govern is accorded. A significant reduction in party discipline might well produce the series of shifting coalitions that are a feature of the American Congress: the task of the electorate would be made more difficult, the fixing of responsibility well-nigh impossible.

It is, then, through the medium of the House of Commons that opposing parties put their programmes before the nation: the Government explains its policies and defends its actions; the official Opposition advances its considered alternatives. The system is geared to the encouragement of a sense of responsibility on both sides of the political fence. The Government is expected to give adequate time for the Opposition to make its case, while the Opposition for its part is obliged to present reasoned argument, to criticize but not to obstruct.

(2) The House of Lords

The House of Lords stands as a paradox in the British parliamentary system, the antithesis of representative and responsible government. Members of the House are not responsible to any electorate and the bulk of their number sit by virtue of birth and not of merit. Breaches have been made in the hereditary principle, as is evidenced by the presence of the law lords,[32] and of the life

32. First introduced under the terms of the Act of 1875 to provide for sufficient judicially-experienced peers to cope with the judicial work of the H ouse.

peers introduced under the terms of the 1958 Life Peerages Act. But even so, these, in addition to the twenty-six senior bishops of the Church of England, still represent fewer than 250 out of a total potential membership of more than a thousand.[33]

That such a chamber should have survived for so long in a democratic society is indeed strange, but mere survival should not be taken to imply total lack of change. Bagehot's fears of a century ago that the House might never be reformed have proven ill-founded, for changes have taken place in both the powers and the composition of the Lords. Nevertheless, until the introduction of the Parliament (No. 2) Bill, following the 1968 White Paper, there was no systematic attempt at reform. Rather, there was a series of piecemeal acts which amounted to something considerably less than the thoroughgoing reform of both powers and composition needed to make the House relevant to mid-twentieth century political life.

The only major change in the powers of the House of Lords came with the passing of the 1911 Parliament Act. A reaction against the way the Upper House had rejected the Liberal Government's Finance Bill of 1909, the Act legalized the convention that the Lords did not reject money bills, but it also went further. The absolute veto that the Lords had possessed over legislation sent up from the Commons was abolished and replaced by the power merely to impose a two-year delay: in 1949 this period was reduced to one year.

The 1911 Act, in addition to curbing the powers of the Lords, made promise of a reconstitution of the chamber, declaring that a House constituted on a popular rather than an hereditary basis would be set up. This followed the lines of a resolution passed by the House of Lords itself the previous year in which, *inter alia*, it was stated that the possession of a peerage should no longer, of itself, give the right to sit and vote in the House. In 1918, the report of the Bryce Conference, set up by Lloyd George to consider the possible composition and powers of a reformed Upper House, declared that such a chamber should, in the main, be elected by members of the House of Commons, and that any marked permanent one-sided political bias should be avoided.

Suggestions for reforming the composition of the House and for modifying, if not totally abolishing, the hereditary element have,

33. On 1 August 1968 the House of Lords consisted of: 736 hereditary peers by succession; 122 hereditary peers of first creation; 155 life peers; 23 serving or retired law lords; 26 bishops – a total of 1,062.

then, a long history, and yet only comparatively recently have efforts been made to implement such proposals. The Labour Party came out for the abolition of the House of Lords in its manifesto of 1935, but was slow to do anything about this chamber, whose composition must clash with its notions of equality. Certainly the Party pledged itself to overcome any resistance it might encounter from the Lords, but when it came to office in 1945 it met in general with co-operation rather than obstruction. Indeed, the Upper House received much praise during the earlier part of this period for the constructive manner in which it dealt with the task of improving the legislation that came up to it from a relatively inexperienced Government. Nevertheless, the Labour Government did feel that as its term of office drew to a close it might encounter opposition from the Lords over its plans to nationalize the steel industry. Consequently it proceeded to enact the Parliament Bill of 1949, which reduced the delaying period of the upper chamber to one year. During discussions on this bill, there were attempts by party leaders to secure a thorough-going reform of the House. Agreement among the parties was far-reaching. It was thought that the second chamber should be complementary to, and not a rival of, the House of Commons; that reform should be based on a modification of its existing constitution rather than on its substitution by a totally new type of chamber based on election. Further, such a House would not be so constituted as to give a permanent majority to any political party. Possession of a peerage would not, in itself, give voting or attendance rights; appointment would be on the grounds of personal merit alone, and the doors would, for the first time, be open to women. Payment would be made to members, who would also be subject to removal for neglect of duties. Members of the peerage not eligible for the new chamber would be entitled to stand for the House of Commons.

The talks produced a remarkable degree of agreement, but they were brought to nought by the failure to reach accord as to the powers that such a reformed body would possess. Ostensibly, the breakdown was caused by an inability to agree over the period of delay that the House would be able to interpose. But, bearing in mind that eventually only three months separated the two sides, it seems that a more fundamental question was involved – should a second chamber be merely a 'useful' chamber, revising bills, debating issues of national interest, or should it be more? Should it be a body with enough power and authority to act, if the need arose, as a balancing factor in the constitution? Generally, the left tended towards the former view, the right towards the latter.

Following the 1948 talks and the 1949 Parliament Act, nothing further was done about the power of the Lords for another twenty years. Action was confined to its composition.

In 1957, the payment of expenses to peers attending the House was introduced at the far-from-princely rate of three guineas a day.[34] The following year a step was taken to encourage the 'backwoodsmen' formally to absent themselves from the House, either for a session or for a whole Parliament. Rather surprisingly, some 200 peers have taken advantage of this opportunity for self-denial. The Life Peerages Act, also of 1958, represented the first opportunity for a wide-scale breach of the hereditary principle and for the abolition of the sex-discrimination that had hitherto kept women out of the House. The introduction of life-peerages did not, however, imply that no more hereditary peerages would be created: indeed, during the Conservative administrations that followed the 1958 Act the creation of hereditary peerages far outstripped the appointment of life peers. But the picture changed when the Labour Government came into power in 1964; for since then no more hereditary peerages have been created. Finally, in 1963, there was the passage of the Peerage Act which permitted peers to renounce their titles and privileges and thus become eligible to sit in the Commons.[35] This Act represented a victory, after a long struggle, for Anthony Wedgwood Benn, briefly the second Viscount Stansgate, who had no wish to have his political ambitions ruined by translation to the Lords. There has not been a rush by peers to disencumber themselves of their titles, but two notable members of the Upper House who, with Benn, were quick off the mark to render themselves eligible for membership of the Commons were two leading contenders for the Conservative Party leadership, the Earl of Home, now Sir Alec Douglas-Home, and Lord Hailsham, who reverted to his previous style of Quintin Hogg, but who is now once more back in the Upper Chamber as Lord Hailsham.

While the Life Peerages Act proved a useful means of increasing Labour Party representation in the House of Lords, without

34. Increased to 4½ gns. in 1965, £6 10s. in 1969 and £8.50 from 1 January 1972.

35. This Act also gave seats in the Lords to peeresses in their own right, and to all the Scottish peers, instead of their 16 elected representatives.

giving succour to the hereditary principle, there still remained a considerable party imbalance in the upper chamber. Thus, in 1968, of those peers who took a party whip, 351 were Conservative, 116 Labour, and 41 Liberal.[36] While, if one looks at the regular attenders, the picture is by no means as stark as the global figures would indicate – Labour 95, Conservative 125, Liberal 19, Crossbench 52 – the existence of this Conservative 'reserve', to be trotted out as the occasion demands, for instance on such issues as the Transport Bill or the Rhodesia sanctions,[37] has to be reckoned with by any non-Conservative Government.

However, the seriousness or otherwise of this imbalance is in larger part dependent upon the functions it is thought a second chamber should perform. At the moment, in addition to its power to delay legislation, the House of Lords has three tasks.

First, the House provides a useful and convenient place for the introduction of non-controversial bills which, receiving detailed examination by the Lords, are thus prepared for quick and easy passage through the Commons. Secondly, the House has a role as a forum in which issues of national moment may be debated, free from the strict reins of party discipline. Finally, the House acts, as we have seen, as a reviser of bills, having the time, that may not be available in the Commons, for closer examination of the details of proposed legislation.

Generally, the fact that the House of Lords has a political imbalance would appear to be of little consequence for the adequate performance of the first two of these tasks. One, by definition, is outside the scope of political controversy, while the other provides ample opportunity for the expression of all shades of opinion. The third function, however, can and does involve the Lords in matters which are directly political and which can lead to votes taken along party lines. In such instances the question of relative party strengths can become important. The point should not be overemphasized. After the hectic years of the post-war Labour Government, the number of Lords' amendments dropped considerably, which was understandable in the light of the Conservative Governments that held office until 1964; but Humphrey Berkeley was able to write of the 1964–65 session, when Labour was back in power, that 'the number of amendments . . . had dwindled to about 130, many of them being of a purely formal or

36. White Paper on House of Lords Reform. Cmnd 3799, Nov. 1968.
37. See below pp. 89–90.

drafting character'.[38] Nevertheless, the importance of this Conservative majority became once more evident when in 1968 twelve amendments – two of major importance – were made to the Labour Government's Transport Bill. As most of the amendments concerned matters to which the House of Commons had given full attention, the Lords could not claim to be providing an adequate examination that had been denied elsewhere. It was apparent, therefore, that the Lords' objections were primarily 'ideological'. When this was coupled with the rejection on June 18 of the Government's Order in Council extending the sanctions against Rhodesia[39] many Labour voices were raised in favour of the complete abolition of the chamber.

An analysis of the unusually large vote on the issue of sanctions against Rhodesia certainly provided heavy ammunition for those who sought, at the least, the abolition of the hereditary principle in the legislative context. Thus, of the 193 votes cast against the Government's Order in Council, '142 came from hereditary peers (119 Tories and 23 crossbenchers) and 51 from life peers. Of the 184 votes cast for the Government, 129 were from nominated peers and 55 from peers by succession.'[40] The hereditary peers had offered a direct challenge to the Labour Government and in so doing they revived the whole question of the reform of the House of Lords, a question which, despite the Labour Government's pledge in the Queen's speech, and the inter-party talks that had been in progress since the previous November, had long been semi-dormant. Indeed, immediately following the rejection of the Sanctions Order, the Government suspended the inter-party talks and proceeded itself to produce a comprehensive scheme of reform. A White Paper duly appeared in November 1968 and most of the proposals contained therein were incorporated in the subsequent bill.

The reform proposed in the Parliament (No. 2) Bill was concerned with the more anachronistic features of the old House. The role of the hereditary peers was to be radically transformed through the introduction of a two-tier structure and the abolition of the right to a seat in the House that succession to a peerage has

38. Humphrey Berkeley, *The Power of the Prime Minister* (Allen & Unwin 1968), p. 112.

39. This was a gesture of defiance by the Conservative peers which embarrassed the Government, but which could not prevent sanctions being continued. Indeed, when the Order was reintroduced in identical form it was approved without a division.

40. Article by David Wood in *The Times*, 20 June 1968.

hitherto carried. Existing peers by succession were to be allowed to retain their places in the Lords and their right to speak in debates and serve on committees, but the right to vote was to be exclusively limited to 'created peers' i.e. peers of first creation or life peers.[41] Existing peers by succession who renounced their membership of the reformed House and any future peers by succession were to be eligible for election to the Commons, while all peers were at last to leave the company of felons and lunatics and become qualified to vote in parliamentary elections. This reformed 'voting House' was initially to consist of about 230 peers, distributed among the parties in such a way as to ensure that the Government had a small majority over the combined opposition parties but stilll remained as a minority of the total membership of the House. To use the example given in the White Paper, in a voting House of 230, the appropriate figures might be: government 105, main opposition party 80, other opposition parties 15, and cross-benchers 30. (These figures exclude the law lords and the bishops.) The size of the House would, of course, vary over time as adjustments were made to reflect changes in governments, but the fixing of a retirement age (of 72) was calculated to avert an 'unreasonable increase in its size'. It was expected that voting peers would play a full part in the work of the House, a part reflected by the requirement that they attend at least one-third of the sittings. However, the suggestion in the White Paper that they should receive remuneration for their work which adequately reflected their responsibilities and duties was not incorporated into the subsequent bill.

The powers of the second chamber were also to be amended. The period of delay that the Lords could interpose was to be reduced to six months from the date of disagreement 'provided that a resolution directing that it should be presented [for Royal Assent] had been passed in the House of Commons'. Outside the field of taxation and other financial matters, the Lords, hitherto, have had co-equal powers with the Commons over subordinate legislation. A reformed House would lose its power of final rejection, and would be able merely to require that the Commons reconsider an affirmative order or consider a negative order to which the Lords had objected.

The most telling argument of those who have favoured reform rather than abolition of the House of Lords was that, if there was

41. Peers by succession were to be eligible for appointment as life peers and therefore for membership of the voting section of the House.

no second chamber then the functions it at present performs would have to be transferred to an already over-burdened House of Commons or go undone. The initiation of non-controversial legislation and the technical revision of bills undoubtedly help ease the timetable of the lower House, and abolition of the Lords would probably 'subject the House of Commons to severe strain and paradoxically would result in less procedural flexibility and speed because of the need to guard against the overhasty passage of legislation'.[42] Many would also argue for the role of the House as a debating chamber – as an institutionalized Speakers' Corner, where men of experience can debate issues in a less politically-charged atmosphere than that which prevails in the Commons. Free of the whips, free of immediate concern for the outcome of the debate, speakers in the Lords can be more objective in their approach than their closely-whipped colleagues of the other House. However, this is essentially peripheral to the main argument. Little would be lost if this function were to go. The publicity accorded debates in the Lords is not great, and most people of experience who have something of value to say can usually find outlets in the mass media – press, radio, or TV – or can join Lord Soper in Hyde Park or on Tower Hill.

The role of the second chamber is that of useful adjunct to the House of Commons. For the adequate performance of this task, it is important that the permanent political one-sidedness be removed and the Government assured of the major voice in both Houses of the legislature. This does not render the Upper House superfluous, as the Abbé Sieyès' famous dichotomy would have us believe; for a reformed House should be seen to be a creature of the Commons, providing the time so lacking in the lower House for initiation, revision, and perhaps investigation. Further, a guarantee to Governments of the largest bloc of votes in a reformed House should not be taken to involve a threat to British constitutional safeguards. Bi-cameralism in the British context does not involve a concept of checks and balances between two rival branches of the legislature. The idea of the House of Lords as a 'guardian of the Constitution', a sort of Supreme Court to the House of Commons' Congress, has never been very viable, having relevance only when non-Conservative Governments were in office, and then relating to a body that had no logical excuse for its existence in a democratic society.

Herbert Morrison once expressed fear that 'rational reform or

42. Cmnd 3799, p. 10.

democratization of the second chamber' would strengthen 'its position against that of the House of Commons'. Indeed, he considered 'the very irrationality of the composition of the House of Lords and its quaintness . . . safeguards for . . . modern British democracy'.[45] It is unlikely that he would have been alarmed by the recent proposals for reform, for there still remained an element of the irrationality he found so reassuring. Fears that reform would result in a more powerful House were misplaced. By (rightly) denying the Lords a power base in the country, and by (more controversially) making membership, in effect, a matter of prime ministerial appointment (after consultation with the leaders of the opposition parties), the strictly subordinate role of the House was emphasized, and possible claims for greater authority averted. But having introduced the phasing out of the hereditary element, the reformers then fell into an uncomfortable and untenable position between two stools. For instance, having decided that the Government of the day should have a majority in the Upper House, they proceeded to deny it an *absolute* majority, preferring to leave the balance of power in the hands of those Michael Foot has described as 'political neuters'. Again, having decided to produce a 'working House', the Government also decided not to pay those who were to do the work. The delaying power was to be reduced but not abolished – which smacked of recognition of its role as guardian against 'rash, hasty and undigested legislation' from the Commons – while in the field of subordinate legislation, the significance of which has increased greatly in recent years, the role of the Lords was to be reduced.

However, in the event, reform – rational or irrational – was not to be. On Thursday, 17 April, the Prime Minister announced in the House of Commons that the Government had decided not to proceed further with the Parliament (No. 2) Bill 'in order to ensure that the necessary parliamentary time' was available for its Industrial Relations Bill and the Merchant Shipping Bill. This bland announcement represented in fact a considerable triumph for the Labour left-wingers and the Conservative right-wingers who had combined to use every procedural device available to delay passage of the Bill and had thus occasioned such pressure on the time-table of the House that the Government was forced to retreat.

Norman Shrapnel, in *The Guardian*, once wrote of the House of

43. Herbert Morrison, *Government & Parliament* (3rd Edn, Oxford 1964) p. 205.

Lords as fulfilling 'a deep instinctive need for tough fantasy and topsyturvydom. Ideally. W. S. Gilbert should be the permanent Lord Chancellor, with Edward Lear as Black Rod, and Lewis Carroll somewhere on the bishops' benches.' Fantasy and topsyturvydom may be acceptable in a wonderland of Savoy Operas, where the House of Lords 'did nothing in particular, and did it very well', but they would seem to have little relevance to the political needs of the twentieth century. Britain cannot afford the luxury of a 'dignified' chamber, and while the recent proposals for reform recognized this it is unlikely that the Parliament (No. 2) Bill would have created a straightforwardly 'efficient' one. Some would argue that a root-and-branch approach is needed that proceeds from acceptance of the British system as essentially uni-cameral, with a House of Commons assisted in its work by another body known as the House of Lords. If such argument is valid, all reform should be directed towards enabling that assistance to be given more effectively. To this end, a body would be needed which reflected party strengths in the Commons and which was adequately rewarded for the tasks it performed – the tasks of initiation, revision and investigation. Fears that reform of a thoroughgoing nature would bring with it increased party domination would appear to be misplaced. The initiation of non-controversial bills is by definition, as mentioned before, outside the scope of such domination, while one would expect work of a select committee nature to be as free from party interference as it is in the Commons. The one area in which the hands of the party whips might be more in evidence is that of amendments to Government bills, and here it is not unreasonable to expect that those who bear the electoral responsibility should want the final choice in determining the shape of legislation.

Ultimate responsibility for the nature and direction of British government must lie with those answerable to the electorate. Any future reform of the House of Lords, then, should recognize this fact and be concerned with securing the more efficient functioning of the part of the system which is representative and which hence bears the responsibility.

Chapter 5

The Cabinet

Slow to develop, barely known to the constitution save through convention,[1] the Cabinet represents the major instrument of government in Britain. While the House of Commons is the body which legitimizes and the forum in which the major parties present and defend their policies, it is not the main fount of legislative proposals. Most legislative as well as administrative initiative comes from the Cabinet, which derives its authority from the electoral decision that has given its supporters a majority in the House of Commons. It is therefore rooted in the party system. Elections are fought in party terms; the House of Commons is organized for action along party lines, and the Cabinet depends on party support in the legislature for its continued existence.

The monarch, in whose hands rests the constitutional task of appointing the Prime Minister, is now normally limited by convention to inviting the leader of the majority party in the House of Commons to form a Government. In the past this has permitted, as we have seen, the exercise of some discretion where the Conservative Party was concerned, but since 1965, when that party decided that its leader should be elected rather than be allowed to 'emerge', the role of the monarch has been reduced, conditions of coalition aside, to a formality in which the supremacy of party wishes is acknowledged. The monarch's power of veto over any of the Prime Minister's nominees for Cabinet posts is now also a legal fiction, since the right of the Prime Minister to select his own governmental colleagues is never again likely to encounter monarchical challenge. Such is the party base of a Prime Minister's authority that any sustained opposition to his wishes by a monarch would necessarily result in a constitutional crisis in which the monarchy would be endangered. As the only logical arguments for the retention of the monarchy are founded upon the non-involvement of that institution in the political processes, it is the task of the monarch, as Jennings has written, 'only to secure a government, not to try and form a government of which he approves'.

1. The first mention of the Cabinet in an Act of Parliament came in the Ministers of the Crown Act, 1937.

Party considerations, however, definitely impose certain restrictions upon the Prime Minister's freedom to choose his colleagues. As a party leader he will almost certainly be limited to selecting members of his own party. In England there is none of the bi-partisan or a-political approach to Cabinet-building that one finds in the United States. Usually the selection will be made from members of the legislature, although MPs defeated at a recent general election or, on rare occasions, persons without previous parliamentary experience may be invited to join. It is expected, however, that any appointee who is not a Member of Parliament should be made answerable to the legislature by seeking election, or re-election, at the earliest possible opportunity, or by being given a peerage. The Cabinet-making of Harold Wilson in 1964 provides two examples of these exceptions to the general rule. In the first Patrick Gordon Walker was appointed Secretary of State for Foreign Affairs, even though he had lost his parliamentary seat at the general election. Through the elevation of the sitting member to the Lords, the constituency of Leyton was made vacant for Gordon Walker, but he lost the subsequent by-election and had to resign his Cabinet post: The other example was that of Frank Cousins, Secretary General of the Transport and General Workers' Union, who, although never having been a member of either House, accepted the office of Minister of Technology. The Nuneaton constituency was made vacant for him, again by elevating the sitting member to the Lords, and at the by-election Cousins, more successful than Gordon Walker, was elected to the Commons and thereby enabled to retain his place in the Cabinet.[2]

The limits on a Prime Minister go even further than this. In all normal circumstances the party will contain several potential leaders whose personal ability and authority is such that their presence in the Cabinet can hardly be avoided: indeed, their membership may be essential if party unity is to be maintained.

This fundamental need to build a Cabinet acceptable to the parliamentary party as a whole is matched by the concern a Prime Minister must have to create a corporate entity, the members of which will be prepared to be responsible for each other's actions and, in public, to speak with one voice. Unity of action and utter-

2. War has provided the only exceptions to the general practice. Neville Chamberlain and Jan Smuts were both members of Lloyd George's War Cabinet, and Robert (later Lord) Casey was a member of Churchill's War Cabinet from March 1942 to December 1943. None of these three was a member of either House of Parliament while in the War Cabinets.

ance – the doctrine of collective responsibility – is a fundamental principle of the British Cabinet system. It originated in the eighteenth century from the determination of politicians to present the monarch with a united front, developed as a means of confronting the legislature and the electorate with a similar unity, and received its classical exposition in 1878, when Lord Salisbury proclaimed that 'for all that passes in Cabinet, each member of it who does not resign is absolutely and irretrievably responsible, and has no right afterwards to say that he agreed in one case to a compromise, while in another he was persuaded by his colleagues'. The 1932 Coalition Government's 'agreement to differ' on the tariff question, which provided the exceptional spectacle of Cabinet Ministers airing their differences in public, constituted a breach in the doctrine, but the 'deviation' was short-lived. As Jennings has suggested, it can hardly be regarded as precedent.

The doctrine does, in fact, extend further than Lord Salisbury's statement would suggest, for it reaches out beyond the Cabinet to include all members of the Government. The effect of this is that decisions which emerge from a Cabinet of twenty or so Ministers, after varying degrees of debate and consideration, must be accepted by the much larger government establishment which now extends to the unpaid parliamentary private secretaries. As something like a third of a Government's parliamentary supporters hold some kind of office, the convention facilitates the task of the leadership in securing party support for its policies. Decision-taking cannot be diffused over so large a body, and the 'collective responsibility' of all members of the Government has, therefore, become more of a myth than a convention of the constitution. What was once seen as a valuable device for harmonizing the individual views of Government leaders is now much more a method of reinforcing party discipline. Having said this, however, one must note that if an office-holder cannot square his individual conscience with the collective decision he can always resign. Failure to take advantage of this opportunity implies public acceptance of the decision. If the member chooses to retain his office he must be prepared to vote for the decision in the House, and must refrain from criticizing it, except in private.

One exception to this general rule was provided by Mr Frank Cousins who, while Minister of Technology in the Wilson Government, publicly expressed his approval of resolutions passed by the union of which he had been General Secretary (the Transport and General Workers' Union) which condemned the

Government's policies on prices and incomes and on the war in Vietnam. This breach of the doctrine, however, was short-lived, for in July 1966 Mr Cousins, having come to the conclusion that he could no longer remain a member of a government that implemented a prices and incomes policy, decided to resign. In the Spring of 1969 the Home Secretary, Mr James Callaghan joined with a majority of the National Executive Committee of the Labour Party in repudiating the Government's proposals for trade union reform. He continued in his Cabinet post and indeed it was the Government, facing strong pressures from the party membership both within and without Parliament, which eventually backed down. Most recently, in 1974, three Ministers, Mr Benn, Mrs Hart and Miss Joan Lester, were reprimanded by Mr Wilson for supporting a national executive resolution critical of the Government for permitting joint naval manoeuvres with the South African Navy. They were not, however, dismissed or required to resign.

An example of just how far flung are the tentacles of collective responsibility was seen in 1967. On 10 May seven Parliamentary Private Secretaries failed to support the Government on a motion seeking authorization for a British application to join the Common Market, and their abstention led to their prompt dismissal. This was undoubtedly harsh treatment for men who occupy 'a no-man's land between Government and backbenches', receive no extra pay for their services, and are appointed not by the Prime Minister but by their 'own' Ministers; but it was probably felt, as Mackintosh has suggested, that such 'dissent by a PPS [could] be taken to indicate that his master has disagreed in Cabinet but been overruled'.[3] If the image of Cabinet unanimity was to be maintained, the Parliamentary Private Secretaries had to go. The differences of opinion that had obviously occurred in Cabinet, and which Mr Douglas Jay's subsequent departure from it confirmed, could not be permitted even indirect expression.

The principle of the collective responsibility of Governments has evoked a corresponding response from Oppositions, which are anxious to appear united in support of a coherent alternative. Hence there is now a very real sense in which the collective responsibility of the Cabinet is matched by the collective responsibility of its Shadow counterpart. While, understandably, greater latitude is permitted to a party in opposition than to one in power,

3. J. P. Mackintosh, *The British Cabinet* (2nd Edn, Stevens and Methuen 1968), p. 521.

there have been sufficient examples in recent years to illustrate the doctrine at work. In 1960, for instance, Hugh Gaitskell, then leader of the Labour Party, told R. H. S. Crossman, Labour frontbench spokesman on social security matters, that persistent, public opposition to official party policy would be incompatible with his continuing to be a recognized party spokesman.[4] In 1966, Angus Maude, a frontbench spokesman for the Conservative Party, 'resigned after writing articles which were taken to be critical of the party leadership'.[5] Enoch Powell, after several years of expressing views at variance with official party policy on a variety of subjects, was expelled from the Shadow Cabinet in 1968 because of his controversial speech on immigration. He eventually left the Party and now sits as an Ulster Unionist from South Down. More recently, in 1972, Roy Jenkins resigned as Deputy Leader of the Labour Party and from the Shadow Cabinet because of disagreement with the majority of his colleagues over the Labour Party's attitude towards membership of the EEC, but in 1974 returned to the Labour front-benches as Home Secretary.

In addition to the responsibility he accepts as a member of a collectivity when he joins a Government (or an Opposition front bench), a man who becomes head of one of the Departments of State also accepts responsibility for the affairs of that department. This doctrine of individual ministerial responsibility means, first, that for each department of State there will be a parliamentary spokesman to whom questions may be directed and of whom criticism may be made. The existence of such a person is of great importance in enabling the House of Commons to subject the work of any department to close scrutiny, while at the same time preserving the anonymity of the civil servants involved. It is fundamental to the British system of government that those who administer should be answerable, through their respective Ministers, to those who, technically at least, legislate. It has also been suggested that the doctrine involves resignation (the modern version of eighteenth-century impeachment) following disclosures of misconduct, mismanagement, or misconceived policies associated with a particular Minister. But here the doctrine is vague, defying generalization or the formulation of prescriptive rules.

Personal misconduct by a Minister calls forth the clearest application of the rule. If misconduct is proved, resignation is expected.

4. Referred to in Alderman and Cross, *The Tactics of Resignation* (Routledge 1967), p. 71.
5. ibid. p. 70.

Thus in 1936 J. H. Thomas resigned from the Cabinet after a tribunal of enquiry upheld the allegation that he had leaked Budget details to friends. In 1947 an indiscreet remark by Chancellor of the Exchequer Hugh Dalton to a lobby correspondent, just before making his Budget speech, resulting in premature disclosure of one small item of the Budget, was the occasion of his resignation. In 1963 came the resignation of the Secretary of State for War, Mr John Profumo. In March of that year, he had told the House of Commons that there had been no impropriety in his relationship with Miss Christine Keeler, intimate friend of a Russian diplomat, but later confessed to having lied. His resignation was then inevitable. Ten years later, newspaper revelations about Lord Lambton's associations with call-girls led to his resignation from the Government.

Mere mismanagement of a department, however, by no means involves automatic resignation. Whether the Minister goes or stays is largely a party matter. Thus, when Sir Thomas Dugdale resigned as Minister of Agriculture in 1954, after criticisms of his department's actions in the Crichel Down affair, it was mainly as a result of his failure to retain the confidence of Conservative backbenchers. Had the case not involved compulsory land purchase powers, anathema to many Conservatives, Sir Thomas, who had assumed an active role in the affair only at a comparatively late stage, might well have survived. By way of contrast there was the retention of office by Mr Lennox-Boyd, Secretary of State for the Colonies, after the revelations of brutality at the Hola camp for Mau Mau detainees in Kenya, where in 1959 several inmates had been beaten to death. Lennox-Boyd, unlike Dugdale, had the support of his backbenchers, who rallied behind him against the attacks of the Labour Party opposition.

Finally, calls for resignation may arise when policies with which a Minister has been personally associated come under attack. Here again generalization is difficult, for it is the Cabinet that decides whether to throw around the Minister the cloak of collective responsibility, as with John Strachey and the groundnuts fiasco of the late 1940s, or to sacrifice him to political expediency, as with Sir Samuel Hoare and the Ethiopian 'sell-out' of the 1930s.

In general, the doctrine of ministerial responsibility cloaks civil servants with anonymity, gives MPs opportunities for the exacting of information about the working of the administration, and provides oppositions with targets against which they can vent their spleen. It does not, however, give the House the power to determine whether or not a Minister shall remain in office. Party is now the determinant of ministerial tenure, and a minister's relations with his Cabinet colleagues, plus the support he is accorded by the backbench members of his party, are the major factors that decide his future. Nevertheless, while it is to the party that he is now accountable, the judgment that his party colleagues pass on him will be coloured by his actions both in his department and in the House; for a party is loth to carry in positions of authority those who bring it into disrepute or open it to attack.

The size of the Cabinet is itself a matter of Prime Ministerial discretion, and he it is who decides which departmental heads shall form part of this supreme directorate. Here again, however, the Prime Minister's freedom of manoeuvre may well be hedged about by party expectations that certain members shall be included, and by the necessity of ensuring that certain departments shall be represented. This means that not all Heads of Departments are members of the Cabinet, but those excluded do attend meetings of that body when topics with which they are concerned are under discussion.

Although recent Cabinets have varied little in size, each having about 20 members, there has been much argument, spread over a considerable number of years, between those who favour a small and those who favour a large Cabinet.

Arguments for a small Cabinet have reflected a belief that the increase in the departmental duties with which most Ministers have to cope distracts their attention from the planning and execution of long-term policies. Departmental 'interests', and the rivalries that go with them, inhibit the adoption of a truly 'overall' view. The only solution is to separate the policy-making from the administrative functions. What is needed is a body of six to eight Ministers, largely free of departmental worries, who, through policy committees, could simultaneously take the 'big' policy decisions and exercise a general supervision of their implementation.

The first practical application of the 'small Cabinet' plan came during the First World War. In February 1916, L. S. Amery and Sir Mark Sykes suggested to Prime Minister Asquith that 'the only Government that could carry on the war was a Cabinet of four or five men entirely free from all departmental responsibilities and in a position to give their whole time to the thinking out, shaping and execution of policy'.[6] Asquith rejected the idea, but it was taken up by Lloyd George when he became Prime Minister at the

6. L. S. Amery, *Thoughts on the Constitution* (Oxford 1947), pp. 78, 79.

end of 1916. The 'War Cabinet' initially comprised only four members in addition to Lloyd George himself – Lord Curzon, Bonar Law, Arthur Henderson, and Lord Milner – but it was only a matter of days before Neville Chamberlain joined the group. During the next two years the size of the Cabinet fluctuated a little, reaching a peak of nine in July 1917,[7] but the emphasis remained on keeping the membership free of departmental duties. Not even the Foreign Secretary, Lord Balfour, was an official member, although he did attend all meetings. In fact, during this period, only two members had departmental responsibilities. One was Neville Chamberlain, Director-General of National Service, who resigned in August 1917 and who, incidentally, was not a Member of the House of Commons during his tenure of office. The other was Bonar Law, Chancellor of the Exchequer and, perhaps more importantly as far as membership of the Cabinet was concerned, leader of the Conservative Party and deputy leader of the House of Commons. In the absence of departmental routine, the Cabinet was able to meet together almost daily for the planning of policy as a whole, while its members also provided the chairmen for nearly all of the most important ministerial committees. The separation of policy from administration was, however, by no means absolute, for the appropriate Ministers would attend meetings of the Cabinet when the affairs of their departments were under discussion.

Successful though the War Cabinet system was, it did not long survive the end of the war. As Amery has written, 'the force of tradition and the claims of individuals proved too strong, and by November 1919 Mr Lloyd George reverted to a typical pre-war Cabinet of twenty'.[8]

Argument as to the ideal size of Cabinets continued between the wars. L. S. Amery, elaborating his previous thesis, wrote in *The Forward View* that 'the "normal" Cabinet is really little more than a standing conference of departmental chiefs where departmental matters take up most of the time. . . . It is quite incompatible with any coherent planning of policy as a whole, or with the effective execution of such a policy.' Others, most notably Harold Laski and Herbert Morrison, have suggested that the arguments of those who advocate the adoption of the small Cabinet are based upon a misguided belief in the possibility of

7. Lloyd George, Lord Curzon, Bonar Law, A. Henderson, Lord Milner, Sir E. Carson, G. Barnes, J. Smuts and Neville Chamberlain.

8. Amery, *Thoughts on the Constitution*, p. 81.

drawing viable distinctions between policy and administration. The two are so closely intertwined, principles being so dependent upon detail, that it is unrealistic to consider the exclusion of departmental ministers from the policy-making process. Further, the creation of a 'super-group' might well promote jealousy and rivalry between the 'Ins' and the 'Outs', and in any conflict between the two, the 'subordinate' Ministers, backed by the resources of their departments, might well frustrate the intentions of the 'policy-makers'. A suspension of the 'normal' processes might be accepted in conditions of national emergency, but in the absence of such conditions (e.g. war), demands for a 'return to normalcy' are likely to prevail. It was also argued that a 'two-tier' system would involve a threat to the doctrine of ministerial responsibility, since confusion would arise as to who was the most appropriate person to whom to direct questions and criticisms. Finally, the Cabinet could not provide party and national leadership from the Olympian heights to which Mr Amery's proposals would elevate it.

In 1939, war, which had made possible the first experiments with the small Cabinet, once more provided the occasion for a drastic reduction in the number of Cabinet Ministers. Following the declaration of war against Germany, all members of the Cabinet formally resigned, and the same evening Neville Chamberlain, the Prime Minister, announced the formation of a War Cabinet of nine members, six of whom headed Departments of State. When Winston Churchill became Prime Minister in May 1940, his first Cabinet bore close resemblance to that of Lloyd George, containing only five members in all. Churchill himself had taken over the Defence Ministry, but of the remainder only the Foreign Secretary had departmental responsibilities. By October 1940, however, three more departmental Ministers had joined the Cabinet – Sir Kingsley Wood, Chancellor of the Exchequer; Mr Ernest Bevin, Minister of Labour and National Service and Lord Beaverbrook, Minister for Aircraft Production. The Amery concept of a small band of 'supervising Ministers' was thus abandoned and replaced by a compromise scheme which, while making use of Ministers without portfolio as co-ordinators and chairmen of committees, incorporated into the Cabinet those Ministers whose departments were most closely associated with the war effort.

When Clement Attlee became Prime Minister after the General Election of 1945, he formed a Cabinet of traditional size, but the debate has continued. Most recently, Lord Gladwyn in *The Times*,[9] arguing for drastic changes in the whole governmental structure, suggested that the Prime Minister should choose five of his parliamentary colleagues as the 'Great Officers of State'. Each of these 'big five' would be responsible, in a general way, for a major policy area. Gladwyn suggested groupings of: Foreign Affairs, Defence, and Overseas Development; Finance, Trade, Technology, and Economic Affairs; Home Affairs, Social Affairs and Labour; Education and 'Culture'; Agriculture, Transport, Civil Aviation, 'and everything else'. The day to day running of the individual departments would be left to junior Ministers, but the 'real government of the country' would be in the hands of this Cabinet of six whose members would 'preside over the highest level inter-ministerial committees within their spheres'.

While it does appear, however, that the arguments of those who consider the small Cabinet suitable only as a temporary expedient for emergency conditions have prevailed, there have been attempts to render the large Cabinet more capable of meeting the criticisms levelled against it, and of coping with the ever-increasing demands made upon it. The creation and expansion of the Cabinet Secretariat, Winston Churchill's experiment with co-ordinating Ministers or 'Overlords', the amalgamation of departments, and greater use of committees have all aimed at securing better direction and co-ordination in government.

The Cabinet Secretariat, one of the least publicized parts of the Whitehall machine, was introduced by Lloyd George during the First World War. It was intended to bring order to the proceedings of the Cabinet, and to end the situation whereby, in the absence of an agenda, Ministers could attend Cabinet meetings insufficiently prepared for the business of the day, or, in the absence of minutes, be left with conflicting notions of decisions reached or of actions authorized. Lord Curzon pointed to the weaknesses of the pre-secretariat system when speaking in a debate in the House of Lords (19 June 1918): 'The Cabinet often had the very haziest notion as to what its decisions were. . . . Cases frequently arose when the matter was left so much in doubt that a Minister went away and acted upon what he thought was a decision which subsequently turned out to be no decision at all, or was repudiated by his colleagues.'[10] Amery quotes the Duke of Devonshire as a characteristic example of the dangers of the

9. *The Times*, 23 May 1968.
10. Quoted Amery, *Thoughts on the Constitution*, p. 77.

situation: 'As you know, I am rather deaf, and, I am afraid, sometimes inattentive. I certainly altogether failed to understand that . . . a decision was even provisionally taken of such importance as that to which you refer, and it must have been taken after very little discussion.'[11] A secretariat was the logical solution to these problems, and, following its war-time introduction by Lloyd George, the Haldane Committee on the Machinery of Government recommended in 1918 that it should be retained as a permanent part of the government machine 'for the purpose of collecting and putting into shape the agenda, of providing the information and material necessary for [the Cabinet's] deliberations, and of drawing up the results for communication to the departments concerned'.[12] While support for the new institution was by no means unanimous, it did become so indispensable that Bonar Law's 1922 campaign pledge to abolish it proved impossible to fulfil.[13] Today, it is some one hundred strong, with a Cabinet secretary, three deputy secretaries, five under-secretaries and seven assistant secretaries. There is a functional division of labour among the deputy secretaries, the work being grouped under the general headings of economic affairs, social policy and overseas policy.

After he became Prime Minister in 1964, Harold Wilson did much to strengthen and expand the scope of the Secretariat. Sir Solly Zuckerman and Dr Balogh were recruited to advise, respectively, on scientific and economic policy. After the appointment of Professor Moser as its director, there was a reorganization of the Central Statistical Office which greatly improved the services it provided.[14] Mr Wilson was also responsible for extending the sphere of influence of the Secretariat into Whitehall itself. Before he became Prime Minister, the 'high-level inter-departmental conclaves of senior officials', the committees by which Whitehall lives, by tradition 'met always under the chairmanship of an official from the Treasury or perhaps the Foreign Office'.[15] By giving the Cabinet Office the responsibility for providing most of the chairmen, the Prime Minister gave it more control over the work of these committees and, in a sense demoted the Treasury

11. Both Amery (ibid. pp. 75–6), and Mackintosh (*British Cabinet*, pp. 288–90) have further examples of the confusion that could arise.
12. Quoted H. Berkeley, *The Power of the Prime Minister* (Allen & Unwin, 1968), pp. 47, 48.
13. ibid. p. 48.
14. See Ian Trethowan in *The Times*, 6 June 1968.
15. Mark Arnold Foster in *The Guardian*, 8 Nov. 1967.

from a position of impartial splendour to that of another department with an axe to grind'.[16]

The growth of the Office continued under Prime Minister Heath when, in 1970, he announced the establishment of a Central Policy Review Staff based on the Cabinet Office. This body was designed to act for the Cabinet as a whole, providing the material and producing the analyses that enable Ministers to make informed policy decisions. Many, however, have attacked this innovation as one leading to greater bureaucratization and, because the chairman Lord Rothschild had direct access to Mr Heath, as one which would inevitably strengthen the position of the Prime Minister in his dealings with his colleagues.

The Cabinet Office is, then, a high-powered body that does much more than act merely as a secretariat for the Cabinet and its committees. It now provides an important means whereby Downing Street can keep a closer eye on Whitehall. Furthermore, the Cabinet Secretary has a vital role to play, for, in addition to attending Cabinet and preparing minutes – 'in itself a critical function when a Cabinet discussion has been blurred' – he also acts as chief official adviser to the Prime Minister, and might be regarded as 'roughly the equivalent to a Departmental Minister's Permanent Under-Secretary'.

When Winston Churchill became Prime Minister for the second time, in October 1951, he took tentative steps back along the path towards the 'small Cabinet' principle. Cabinet membership was initially restricted to 16, but by September 1953 it had risen to 19. More significant, however, was the introduction of co-ordinating Ministers or 'Overlords'. Lord Woolton, Lord President of the Council, was appointed co-ordinator of the Ministries of Food and Agriculture; Lord Leathers was made Secretary of State for the co-ordination of Transport, Fuel and Power, and Lord Cherwell, the Paymaster-General, was given oversight of scientific research and development.

The announcement of these appointments brought immediate criticism from the Opposition, largely on the grounds that the arrangement constituted a threat to the doctrine of ministerial responsibility. It was argued that the existence of such co-ordinators would leave the House of Commons confused as to where ultimate responsibility rested, while the fact that all three were members of the House of Lords, and therefore not directly accountable to the House of Commons, only served to increase

16. ibid.

the suspicions of those who saw these appointments as yet further attempts to limit Parliament's control over the executive.

Lord Salisbury attempted clarification on behalf of the Government when he argued that this co-ordination was merely 'an allocation of duties by the Prime Minister for purposes of administrative convenience. It does not affect the direct responsibility to Parliament of Departmental Ministers, which, as before, remains with the Ministers once the Government have taken their decisions.'[17] He did not, however, allay the suspicions, and on 6 May 1962 Churchill himself addressed the House on the arrangement:

The coordinating ministers have no statutory powers. They have in particular, no power to give orders or directions to a Departmental Minister. A Departmental Minister who is invited by a coordinating Minister to adjust a Departmental policy to accord with the wider interests of the government as a whole always has access to the Cabinet; and if he then finds that he cannot win the support of his Ministerial colleagues he should accept their decision. No Departmental Minister can, of course, be expected to remain in a Government and carry out policies with which he disagrees. *Thus the existence and activities of these coordinating Ministers do not impair or diminish the responsibility to Parliament of the Departmental Ministers whose policies they coordinate.*[18]

Opposition to the 'Overlord' experiment does appear to have been more emotional than rational. While Churchill's decision to have his co-ordinators sit in the Lords rather than the Commons may have been an error of judgment guaranteed to stir the passions of a Labour Opposition, this certainly did not constitute a serious threat to the rights of the popularly-elected chamber. After all, if the House of Commons was concerned with matters of administration within a department then there was the Minister to whom questions could be directed: if about matters of policy then, as always, there was the Cabinet as a whole to be castigated. Reaction to the whole idea was, nevertheless, so hostile that the experiment was ended in 1953. Lord Leathers resigned from his post, and Lord Woolton, Chancellor of the Duchy of Lancaster since November 1952, ceased to co-ordinate the Ministries of Food and Agriculture, and was appointed Minister of Materials.

Some of the rationalization that was sought through the use of the 'Overlords' has been achieved in recent years through the

17. Quoted in Morrison of Lambeth, *Government & Parliament* (3rd Edn, Oxford 1964), p. 63.

18. Quoted ibid. p. 64. Authors' italics.

amalgamation of Ministries. For instance, between 1947 and 1964, the work of the Admiralty, the War Office and the Air Ministry was co-ordinated under the Minister of Defence who, unlike Churchill's co-ordinators, did have statutory powers 'which gave him a special position *vis-à-vis* the service ministries'.[19] In 1964 co-ordination became integration. The existing Departments were swept away and a new Ministry of Defence was established. Responsibility was now concentrated in the hands of one Minister. In other fields, the Ministry of Pensions merged with the Ministry of National Insurance in 1953, became the Ministry of Social Security in 1966, taking over the National Assistance Board, and in 1968 emerged as the Department of Health and Social Security. (See below, Chapter 6, pp. 120–3.) In like manner, the Commonwealth Relations Office, having taken over the Colonial Office, was, in 1968, itself merged with the Foreign Office – now the Foreign and Commonwealth Office. In the Government re-organization of October 1969, which reduced the Cabinet in size from 23 to 21, the Ministry of Technology took over the Ministry of Power and the industrial responsibilities of the Board of Trade, while a new Department of Local Government and Regional Planning assumed responsibility for housing, local government, transport and regional planning. At the same time, the short-lived Department of Economic Affairs was broken up and its responsibilities allocated among the Ministry of Technology, the Treasury, the Ministry of Local Government and Regional Planning and the Cabinet Office.[20] This process of amalgamation was continued by Prime Minister Edward Heath, most notably in his creation of two super-ministries – for Trade and Industry and for the Environment. The former brought together the Ministry of Technology, the Board of Trade and the Ministry of Aviation and Supply; the latter encompassed the work of the Ministries of Housing and Local Government, Transport and Public Buildings and Works.

The most important development in post-war governmental operations has probably been the increased use of committees of the Cabinet. While they have long formed a significant, if unpublicized, part of Cabinet organization, the role of these com-

19. ibid. pp. 55–6.

20. The creation of the Department of Economic Affairs in 1964 had appeared to run directly counter to the trends apparent in the other spheres of government, involving the Treasury, as it did, in the loss of much of its responsibility for economic planning.

mittees has increased considerably in recent years along with the increasing work which the Cabinet has had to deal. Only through their use could a 'group of over-worked departmental chiefs' be enabled to give adequate consideration to the problems that faced them. Indeed, the extended recourse to committee has permitted much of the co-ordination that was sought with the introduction of the Overlords, without the attendant accusations that departmental Ministers were being relegated to a secondary role, and that the doctrine of ministerial responsibility was being breached.

The committees are of two kinds – the numbered, ad hoc, usually short-lived committees generally established to deal with particular inter-departmental problems, and the named, standing committees set up in the major areas of government activity. Examples of the latter are: defence and overseas policy, home and social, economic strategy, parliamentary, legislative, future legislation, economic policy, emergency, regional and environment, industrial relations, counter-inflation, European, agriculture, broadcasting, the third London airport and immigration and community relations.

In the past, committee chairmen have often been Ministers without Portfolio – that is, Ministers without departmental burdens or commitments – who have thus been in a position to mediate between the claims of interested parties. Douglas-Home's appointment of Selwyn Lloyd, Lord Privy Seal, as chairman of the Standing Committee on Agricultural Policy, a post previously held by the Chancellor of the Exchequer, was a good example of this. As an impartial chairman, Lloyd's task was to mediate in disputes between the Treasury and the Ministry of Agriculture over the annual price review.[21] The idea of senior non-departmental Ministers presiding over Cabinet committees was carried over into the first few years of Harold Wilson's Prime Ministership. For example, Douglas Houghton, Minister without Portfolio, chaired the committees on social services and home affairs. The use of non-departmental Ministers as chairmen was not, however, made into a firm principle, and Mrs Barbara Castle, Secretary of State for Employment and Productivity, became chairman of the Economic Committee dealing with Prices and Incomes, while Mr Jenkins, Chancellor of the Exchequer took over the Public Expenditure Scrutiny Committee, and Mr Callaghan, the Home Secretary, the Home Affairs Committee.

21. See Mackintosh, *British Cabinet*, p. 503.

During Mr Heath's premiership Mr Carr, Home Secretary, Mr Barber, Chancellor of the Exchequer and Mr Prior, Lord President of the Council, along with Mr Heath himself, most often chaired the leading committees.[22]

These trends of recent years have led to many issues being settled in committee without reaching the full Cabinet, although it was possible for a matter to be brought up if a Minister dissented or 'reserved his position'.[23] In June 1968, however, John Mackintosh wrote that 'the old system whereby any Minister who disliked a committee decision could "reserve his position" and thus take the matter to the full Cabinet has ended. Mr Wilson has given instructions that when the general opinion of the committee is clear and the chairman is satisfied that is the end of the matter'.[24] The powers of the major standing committees and of their chairmen would, then, appear to have been much enhanced (a situation which does not appear to have changed during the Heath Prime Ministership), and in the light of this development it is not unreasonable to expect that Cabinet meetings will be 'chiefly occasions for co-ordination and for keeping busy departmental Ministers in touch'.[25] Nevertheless, to accept this is not necessarily to subscribe to some of the more extreme interpretations of the British Cabinet system that are current.

In recent years there has been much heated discussion about the manner in which Cabinet government in Britain is developing, with such terms as 'Prime Ministerial dictatorship' or 'autocracy tempered by public opinion polls' being put about as suggested descriptions of the new order. The role and power of the Prime Minister are emphasized by some commentators to the extent that the Cabinet itself is relegated to the rank of the 'other dignified elements in the Constitution'.[26] This line of argument has its origins in the rigidly-disciplined two-party system that, it is claimed, renders each general election an occasion for choice between two potential Prime Ministers. The parties are now personified in their leaders, and the personalities of the leaders become, in the eyes of the electorate, the personalities of the

22. An interesting discussion of the work of Cabinet committees is to be found in a leading article – Whitehall's Needless Secrecy – in *The Times* of 3 May 1973.

23. ibid. p. 518.

24. *The Times*, 2 June 1968.

25. ibid.

26. R. H. S. Crossman, Introduction to Bagehot, *The English Constitution* (Fontana 1963).

parties. Such pre-eminence enables a Prime Minister to maintain a tight rein over members of his party in the House of Commons, for if they prove recalcitrant he can threaten to dissolve Parliament and appeal to the country through a general election – a prospect which few MPs would welcome because of the cost and effort involved in electioneering, and which rebels might fear as an occasion for their rejection by an electorate demanding unswerving obedience to the party leader.

These arguments are not, however, substantiated by the evidence available from election studies and public opinion polls. The major influence upon voters is not the personality of the leader but the image of the party – its record when in office, complemented by its proposals for the future and the personnel likely to be charged with the implementation of such proposals. The fate of Governments is essentially dependent upon achievement and overall record rather than upon the ability or charisma of an individual.

It would also appear that the power to dissolve Parliament is a two-edged sword which might well prove more damaging to a Prime Minister than to those he is trying to coerce. Some two-thirds of the seats in the House of Commons can be regarded, in normal circumstances, as 'safe', and a general election is therefore of no overwhelming concern to their holders: the same cannot be said for the Government which is always put in jeopardy at such a time. Thus, while most MPs can face an election with a fair degree of equanimity, with little arduous canvassing required of them, and with their expenses met by the party, a Prime Minister is concerned not only to retain his own seat but also to retain a majority for his party in the House of Commons. His campaign cannot, then, be limited to his own constituency: his appeal must be to the country at large. By dissolving Parliament, a Prime Minister puts at stake his position and power as leader of the country, an exercise which, more often than not, he is likely to avoid if his party is split. The right to dissolve Parliament, therefore, while important as a weapon of electoral strategy,[27] cannot be regarded, in any real sense, as a power to keep his parliamentary party in line.

27. Subject only to the approval of the monarch (which has not been withheld for more than a century) the Prime Minister can dissolve Parliament at which he considers to be the most electorally-propitious time. Indeed, to some extent the power permits him to plan measures so as to produce a favourable electoral climate.

Arguments concerning the growing 'dictatorial' power of the Prime Minister are not based solely on his relations with the electorate: they rest also on interpretations of power relationships within the parliamentary party. It is suggested, for instance, that from the Prime Minister's power to appoint and dismiss Cabinet colleagues flows the power to control the party: that the party, by elevating a man to the leadership and thus to the Prime Ministership, inevitably subordinates itself to that man and to his policies. The Cabinet chosen, the Prime Minister is said to have the final word in deciding how it shall operate, what shall appear on the agenda, what subjects shall be discussed, and, ultimately, what course shall be followed.

Much has also been made of the increased use of committees of the Cabinet which is seen by some as a method of by-passing the full Cabinet, and hence as another technique by means of which the Prime Minister is enabled to impose his will upon the Government. The two most-quoted examples of the increased Prime Ministerial power supposedly inherent in this development relate to the decisions to manufacture atomic weapons and to engage in the Suez 'adventure'. In the first instance, it is alleged that, by confining discussion of the project to the Defence Committee of the Cabinet, the Prime Minister was able to act without the prior knowledge of several Cabinet Ministers,[28] while in the second, it has been suggested that Anthony Eden revealed his plans for the invasion of Egypt only when it was too late to reverse them. Charles (now Lord) Hill, Chancellor of the Duchy of Lancaster in the Macmillan Government, has added some weight to the argument. In a passage which expresses general approval of the way Macmillan ran things, he does criticize the fact that at times 'the Cabinet was consulted at too late a stage in the evolution of some important line of policy: he [Macmillan] seemed to forget that many of us had not been present at the Cabinet committee concerned with the topic'.[29]

According to this intrepretation, then, policy-making is seen as the prerogative of the Prime Minister, aided and abetted by a 'handful of trusted friends',[30] with the doctrine of collective responsibility invoked to ensure collective obedience.

28. See Crossman, Introduction to *The English Constitution* and Mackintosh, *British Cabinet*.

29. In *Both Sides of the Hill*. Quoted Mackintosh, *British Cabinet*, p. 502.

30. Crossman, Introduction to *The English Constitution*.

This description of the power of the Prime Minister depends, in the first instance, upon acceptance of the two parties as monoliths, united in aims and solid in their support of the only possible leader. Such a picture does not accord with the facts. The major British political parties are not united over their respective aims, or over the means of achieving the ends upon which they are agreed. Factions exist within both, with disagreements between them as to the long and the short term objectives to be pursued. Again, it is rare for a major party to have but one potential Prime Minister. A leader usually has to face the fact that some of his colleagues are also his rivals, eager at almost any time to step into his office. To check any hopes they may have to replace him, he must retain the support of the bulk of his parliamentary party. To ride roughshod over the opinions and desires of senior colleagues, or to alienate any sizeable group within the party, would be to create a situation in which a challenge to the leadership might be made.

The Prime Minister's power to fill the one hundred or so posts in the Government of non-Cabinet rank is undoubtedly important in attaching to his apron-strings a considerable number of the lesser lights in the party. On the other hand, his freedom of action in making appointments to the major offices of State is, as we have already noted, severely limited by party expectations and political necessity. A Prime Minister, in forming his Cabinet, must be aware that apart from rewarding some of his supporters he is also providing a power-base for those who are his potential successors. Conversely, the expectations that require that certain men be appointed to the Cabinet require also that their membership continue. While he may have some latitude as to who shall occupy which posts, a Prime Minister does not, normally, have a free hand as to the dismissal of the more influential members of the Cabinet.

Harold Laski pointed to these restrictions when he wrote that a Prime Minister could not long survive the dismissal of any important member of his Cabinet. It has been suggested that Harold Macmillan's 1962 'massacre of the Ministers', when he dismissed, at one fell swoop, the Chancellor of the Exchequer (Selwyn Lloyd), the Lord Chancellor (Viscount Kilmuir), and five other members of the Cabinet, is a rebuttal of the Laski maxim and indicative of the supreme power of the Prime Minister *vis-à-vis* the Cabinet. In fact, the interesting thing to note about the 1962 dismissals is that not one of those dismissed could be regarded as a serious contender for the leadership. Even so, this attempt to give the Government a new look by changing the supporting cast while retaining the leading players, occasioned much hostility within the Conservative Party and the Prime Minister acquired a reputation in some quarters as being a man 'prepared to lay down his friends for his life'. Confidence in Macmillan was badly shaken, and little more than a year later he resigned on the grounds of ill-health.

The suggestion that the Prime Minister, through control of the Cabinet agenda, and through the use of committees, can determine which topics shall receive Cabinet consideration and which shall be subject to his own personal discretion, is a misleading oversimplification. A Prime Minister could not long prevent the discussion of topics unless he had the support of several of the more influential members of the Cabinet. Control of the agenda does not, in itself, permit of any large-scale or continuing restriction of debate. As for the assignment of topics to committees of the Cabinet for consideration, this, far from representing a device for by-passing the Cabinet, must surely be seen as a means of permitting that body to perform its functions more efficiently and effectively than would be possible if all topics were considered, ab initio, at full Cabinet meetings. The increased use of committees is but a logical outcome of the increased tasks that face British government. Furthermore, it should not be overlooked that these committees are composed of Cabinet members, and that all decisions taken in committee are placed before the Cabinet. Thus with the two examples we have cited – the decision to manufacture atomic bombs, and the Suez policy – lengthy committee study had preceded their eventual circulation in the Cabinet agenda. One cannot argue from this procedure that these were essentially Prime Ministerial policies foisted upon an unwilling and unwitting Cabinet. Had, for instance, the Defence Committee split sharply on the question of atomic bomb manufacture then undoubtedly full discussion in the Cabinet as a whole would have followed. Such a policy could only be implemented in the manner it was implemented because the Prime Minister had important Ministerial support.

Finally, to suggest that Government policy is essentially Prime Ministerial policy is to ignore the multiple sources of policy initiatives that exist. Declared party policy, civil service recommendations, administrative necessities, the personal policies of departmental Ministers, group representations, the pressure of events, all go to make up the composite that is a party's programme. The Prime Minister will make his own contribution – a contribution which may be especially valuable in the light of his special position – but he is in no position to *impose* his will. For example, when Harold Macmillan decided to promote British entry into the Common Market he could not force the policy upon the Cabinet. It took several months of persuasion before the climate of opinion was such that attempts to implement the policy could be made. Lord Hill has outlined the relationship between one Prime Minister and his Cabinet in a work already quoted. He wrote that if Harold Macmillan dominated the Cabinet, 'he did not do it by ex cathedra pronouncements or by laying down the law or by expressing his views too early in a discussion. . . . It was done by sheer superiority of mind and of judgment. He encouraged genuine discussion provided it kept to the point. *If he found himself in a minority he accepted the fact* with grace and humour.'[31] The Prime Minister's task is one of persuasion and negotiation. He is undoubtedly the most important member of the Cabinet, and this does increase the persuasiveness of his arguments, but this is a long way from the 'Prime Ministerial system' that would have him the fount of policy and the master of his colleagues. He is Prime Minister because his fellow party members are prepared to accept him as such. He remains in office for just so long as that acceptance continues. What he makes of the power of the office is dependent upon many factors – variables such as his own ability and personality; the ability and status of the principal members of the Cabinet; the state of the nation; the ends he is seeking to promote. What is certain is that, unless his fellow Cabinet members are prepared to abdicate, in the sense that they are ready to accept without question his policies and his leads, the Prime Minister is very much a member of a team and must act accordingly. Indeed, the establishment by Mr Wilson, in 1968, of the Parliamentary Committee would appear to be open acknowledgement of the manner in which the Prime Minister must work with the other leading members of his party. This body, which in 1968 comprised, in addition to the Prime Minister himself, the nine senior members of the Cabinet, and which early in 1969 was reduced to seven, represented in effect an inner Cabinet which met twice weekly to discuss the important political issues. The reports of the

31. Hill, quoted Mackintosh, *British Cabinet*, p. 502. Authors' italics.

Committee were open to discussion by the full Cabinet, but the extent to which such discussions could achieve anything was necessarily a function of the degree of unanimity within the Committee, or of the strength of feeling within the Cabinet as a whole.[32] Similarly, the Prime Minister's freedom of action depended to a great extent upon the support afforded him by the Committee.

Power, then, lies, in Mr Wilson's words, not with the Prime Minister but with the Prime Minister in Cabinet, 'to the extent that the Cabinet keeps the confidence of the House'.[33] As a statement of constitutional legalism it is difficult to quarrel with this assertion. A Government is dependent for its continuance in office upon the support of a majority in the House of Commons. Withdrawal of that support, the defeat of the Government on a vote of confidence,[34] involves either the resignation of the Government or the dissolution of Parliament and an appeal to the electorate. As, however, in normal circumstances, the Government is in power because members of its own party have a majority in the House of Commons, defeat can only be accomplished through the defection of Government backbenchers. This being so, it is clear that, conditions of coalition apart, power in fact rests with the Prime Minister in Cabinet, to the extent that the Cabinet retains the confidence of its parliamentary party. The vital dialogue that takes place between the Government and members of the legislature is, essentially, the dialogue between the Government and its own backbenchers. It is in private party meetings that controversial issues are discussed and attempts made to set the lines for the confrontation with the Opposition. Party loyalty, backed up by party discipline, minimizes the occasions upon which private discord bursts into the public eye. It does not, of course, eliminate them altogether, as has been evidenced in recent years by discord concerning the Government's policies on Rhodesia, Vietnam, prices and incomes, trade union reform, Nigeria and the Common Market. However, it would appear that those who lead such

32. A recent example of the leadership group failing to get its way was seen on 15 May 1969 when the full Cabinet rejected the Parliamentary Committee's proposal to bring forward the Pensions Bill for higher weekly contributions. (See the report by James Margach in the *Sunday Times*, 18 May 1969.)

33. In an interview with Ian Trethowan published in *The Listener*, 9 Feb. 1967, p. 185.

34. Nowadays most votes are regarded as votes of confidence.

revolts against the Government are careful to ensure that while they embarrass they do not destroy.[35]

The power to effect changes in Government policy is, then, a power which, in the main, rests not with the Opposition, or with the House of Commons as a whole, but with the supporters of the majority party. Checks on mal-administration may come from the House acting in non-party-political fashion, although here, as we have seen, the machinery for scrutiny is still inadequate. Checks on policy come largely from intra-party consultation and in the final analysis, of course, from anticipation of electoral reaction. Robert McKenzie opened his study of British political parties with Lord Holland's remark of 1830 that 'party seems to be no more',[36] and yet it is now apparent, as McKenzie went on to write, that since then party has emerged 'as the dominant factor in British politics'.[37] British government is now comprehended within a party political framework which determines the interaction of electorate, legislature, and executive, and which provides the organizational structure necessary to the coherent functioning of these three branches. The vote is cast in party terms, the House of Commons is organized along party lines, and Cabinet government can be seen to be party government.

35. Mackintosh, *British Cabinet*, p. 585.
36. McKenzie, *British Political Parties*, p. 1.
37. ibid. p. 5.

Chapter 6

Central Administration

1. The Apparatus

Under this heading we propose to deal only with that part of the central machinery of government which is organized as 'regular' departments, each responsible to Parliament through its ministerial chief. Although nowadays far from covering the whole of central administration, this still constitutes the greater and more important part of it; moreover the other parts of the central administrative apparatus, since they are related to it in various ways, cannot be properly understood until it has been described and analysed. The regional agencies upon which considerable emphasis is now being placed are 'derivative' in a similar sense. Although in many cases part of the central administration (i.e. 'out-stations' of the central departments) and always in some way connected with it, they are reserved for treatment in a separate chapter (see below Chapter 10) because they present a number of distinct problems.

A list of the departments that exist today provides evidence of the extensive changes in the structure of British Administration that have taken place in the twentieth century and particularly since the Second World War. Of ministries that can trace an uninterrupted development from the nineteenth century and beyond there are eight – the Foreign and Commonwealth Affairs Office, the Exchequer, the Lord Chancellor's Office, the Home Office, the Scottish Office, the Department of Education and Science, the Ministry of Agriculture, Fisheries and Food and the Ministry of Posts and Telecommunications. (Some of these Ministries have, of course, undergone changes of name to indicate their duties more precisely when they have acquired new responsibilities – for example, the addition of Commonwealth Affairs to the Foreign Office, of Science to Education, of Food to Agriculture and Fisheries.)

Of the newer ministries, two, Transport (now part of Environment) and Health (now part of Social Services) date from the period of the First World War and another, Defence, from that of the Second. More recent creations are Employment (Employment and Productivity in the Wilson Government), to which the responsibilities of the former Ministry of Labour were transferred; Housing and Local Government, itself now swallowed up by the Department of the Environment, which was a product of the splitting up of the Ministry of Health; Technology, which took over many of the functions of the Board of Trade and absorbed the Ministry of Power, and which is now part of the super-ministry of Trade and Industry; Wales, a ministry created in response to the nationalistic demands of the Welsh; Overseas Development, the recipient of 'aid' functions formerly dispersed among other ministries, including the Foreign Office, and which is now amalgamated into the Foreign and Commonwealth Affairs Office; and of course the two conglomerate ministries already mentioned – Trade and Industry and Environment.

To account for the contours of this departmental structure and to explain the reasons why each department has acquired a particular bundle of powers would involve writing a comprehensive administrative history of Britain. There has been a continuous process of creation, fission, fusion and transfer, rapid at some times, slower at others. The resultant changes are to be largely explained by the expansion of the functions of government, by the development of new areas of policy (e.g. social security and economic planning) and the disappearance of old ones (e.g. India), and by the fluctuations in the degree of emphasis accorded from time to time to different fields of administration. Political factors internal to the party currently in office have also been of major importance; for it often happens that a ministry is created for a particular politician rather than a politician being found for a particular ministry.

Except for periods of wartime 'emergency', it would be difficult to find an example of the creation of a new ministry in direct response to the discovery of a new need. Needs become gradually, rather than suddenly, evident, and when first 'adopted' politicially are provided for through an existing ministry or other Governmental agency, as far as possible on the principle of associating like with like.

The process of ministerial creation may be illustrated with reference to the growth of the social service and regulatory functions of government during the nineteenth century. In those days there were few ministries to which such functions could conveniently be attached – although the Home Office and the Board of Trade, which were the more obvious ones, steadily acquired fresh duties of a highly miscellaneous kind. Hence the

'Privy Council' came to play the role of the hold-all, acquiring committees for the performance of a variety of administrative duties such as those relating to education and agriculture. This was a reasonable and convenient way of doing things, so long as the main jobs were the doling out of subsidies to private organizations (with the normal concomitant of inspection) and the application, also to private organizations, of comparatively simple regulations. When the administrative duties of these 'committees' however, became both more complicated and more direct, the demand that they should be confided to separate departmental organizations under responsible Ministers increased in strength and eventually became irresistible. Thus the relevant committee of the Privy Council developed into what was called, or rather mis-called, a 'board' under a 'president' of Ministerial status (e.g. education, agriculture) and eventually into a fully-fledged Ministry, as when the Ministry of Health was created to take over, among other responsibilities, those previously exercised by the Local Government Board. The principle would seem to be that, given favourable political conditions, a new ministry is created at a point where a function or a series of related functions become sufficiently important and sufficiently complex to require separate departmental organization with separate Ministerial responsibility to Parliament.

Fusion and fission may perhaps best be illustrated by following the changes in the distribution of those functions formerly lumped together under the heading of 'Health'. On its creation in 1918 the Ministry of Health gathered together by inheritance from other authorities functions which appeared to be closely associated, in so far as they were all concerned with the relief of poverty and the amelioration of the conditions of life. As we have already seen, it took over the powers of the Local Government Board. It also replaced the English and Welsh Insurance Commissioners (dating from 1911), acquired the Privy Council's powers over the midwifery service and those of the Home Office over infant life protection, the practice of anatomy and the treatment of lunacy and mental deficiency. A variety of other functions were transferred to it from the Board of Trade, the Ministry of Agriculture and Fisheries, and the Board of Education. Among its most important responsibilities in the 1920s was the implementation of Lloyd George's 'homes fit for heroes' promise, and the operation of the as yet very rudimentary town and country planning legislation. At the time, such a gathering together of services in one Ministry seemed good policy on the principle of ensuring the coherent development and adequate co-ordination of 'all those activities of the central government which are directed to maintaining or improving the physical well-being of the population at large or of any particular section of the community[1] But with the considerable development of all these functions both between the wars and more particularly after the Second World War, the diseconomies of concentrating them under one roof came to exceed the economies. Not only did the Ministry of Health become unwieldy; there was also a danger that certain of its responsibilities might through sheer administrative inertia, take arbitrary preference over others – a danger of which illustration had been actually provided in former days by the Local Government Board, which had tended to apply cheeseparing and restrictive 'Poor Law' standards towards the other local government services it was supposed to be assisting. For these and other reasons the process of fission was set in train, with the result that the responsibilities of the former Ministry of Health became divided between three ministries, viz. Health, Housing and Local Government, and Social Security. At the time of writing, the fusion process has once more taken charge, with the result that Housing, Local Government and Planning are now part of the Department of the Environment, while Health and Social Security are to be found in the Department of Social Services.

Another example of the fusion–fission process is provided by the evolution of the former Ministry of Fuel and Power. A wartime innovation, the new ministry acquired the old Mines Department and the new Petroleum Department of the Board of Trade and also the Board's regulatory powers over the generation and distribution of electrical energy. Its most important tasks, however, were the rationing of fuel and the reorganization of the production of coal – both of them wartime necessities. Generally regarded at the time as a temporary expedient, this Ministry (later rechristened the Ministry of Power) seemed during the post-war period to have become a permanent part of the administrative landscape, as a result of its being given supervisory responsibilities for the newly-nationalised fuel industries (i.e. coal, gas and electricity). However, as a part of Mr Wilson's ministerial reorganization of 1969, it was merged with the more recently-established Ministry of Technology to become the Ministry of

1. Report of the Machinery of Government Committee, 1918. Cd 9230, p. 58.

Technology and Power, during which transformatory process it also acquired some of the industrial responsibilities formerly exercised by the Board of Trade. (In 1970, as mentioned earlier, it became part of the new Department of Trade and Industry. But in response to the energy crisis of 1973 Mr Heath created a new Department of Energy with Lord Carrington as its Secretary of State.)

Fission and fusion inevitably involve transfer, but the converse does not necessarily apply. Over the years one can observe an almost continuous process of administrative 'rationalization' by transfer of functions from one existing Ministry to another. This has now been facilitated by legislation that enables the process to be effected comparatively swiftly, and usually with a minimum of parliamentary discussion, by statutory instrument (see below, Chapter 11, pp. 242–51). In so far as purely political factors are not involved in transfers (and it should be remarked that they usually are) the aim is to produce Ministries which have what the late Paul Appleby described as 'coherent missions'. To have functions consistently transferred away from it has been the fate of the Home Office. Traditionally, this department has been the repository of 'miscellaneous duties in the domestic sphere for which no other department has a strong or clear claim'. When, however, a department (usually a new one) can and does present such a claim, the case for the transfer of the particular function to it is overwhelming and the transfer normally effected. In 1920 the Home Office surrendered its powers over the mining and quarrying industries to the newly-created Mines Department of the Board of Trade; between 1919 and 1921 it lost its 'infant life protection' functions to the Ministry of Health; in 1940 it surrendered the factory inspectorate to the Ministry of Labour and National Service; in 1945 it lost workmen's compensation to the Ministry of National Insurance; in 1947 the control of advertisements to the Ministry of Town and Country Planning and in 1953 and 1954 its regulatory powers over slaughterhouses and markets to the Ministry of Housing and Local Government.

The transfer of one of these responsibilities, that for factory inspection, illustrates the inter-penetration of political and administrative factors which so often accompanies the transfer process. The case for transferring the factory inspectorate from the Home Office to the Ministry of Labour was first made in 1916 but the actual transfer was not effected until 1940, and then only at the insistence of the very powerful wartime Minister of Labour and National Service, Ernest Bevin. During the intervening period 'departmental policy' in the Home Office, reinforced by the prestige enjoyed by the Home Secretary as a leading member of the Cabinet, inhibited this rather obvious piece of administrative rationalization. Even when made, it was regarded as only temporary and did not become permanent until 1946. From this example it is clear that a 'transfer' decision cannot always be made when administrative convenience would appear to require it. The political status of the department concerned and the Minister at the head of the department have also to be taken into consideration, and if there is strong opposition from a powerful department and powerful Minister to the loss of a function which has been long-performed and regarded as of value, the change-over may well be delayed until sufficiently strong countervailing forces have been built up. In the case just quoted a prestigious civil servant, consistently supported by his Minister, seems to have been the villain of the piece. During the period immediately following the First World War 'the Home Office had a redoubtable champion in the person of Sir Malcolm Delevingne, the head of its Industrial Division', who, it was said, 'was prepared to die on the steps of the Home Office rather than yield one iota of its prerogative to any upstart department', and 'defended the fort with such fiery pertinacity and such unexhaustible ingenuity that he held it triumphantly'.[2]

One may reasonably ask whether there is any discernible principle governing the distribution of functions between Government departments. It is certainly very difficult to discover such a principle. The only serious attempt to define one was made in 1918 by the 'Haldane' Committee, which, after stating that there was a choice to be made between 'distribution according to the persons or classes to be dealt with and distribution according to services to be performed', came down very firmly in favour of the latter.[3] This principle, although sensible to the point of sheer obviousness, is too general to be of much practical use and consequently of little interest to us today. Departmental reorganizations have not followed and are not likely to follow any consistent pattern. They are the product of specific attempts to remedy recognized imbalances and incoherences, to place functions

2. F. M. G. Willson (ed.), *The Organisation of British Central Government 1914–1956* (Allen & Unwin 1957), p. 82.

3. Report of the Machinery of Government Committee, 1918. Cd 9230, p. 7, para. 18.

where they may be most effectively performed, to emphasize certain responsibilities of Government at the expense of others and to give satisfaction to political demands whether emanating from party, politicians or public.

The division of responsibilities interested the Haldane Committee largely because it was seeking for a rational principle which might be applied to the job of cleaning up the very considerable administrative mess left by the vigorous instututional improvisation of the First World War period. One must also remember that in 1918 it was still possible to think in terms of clearly separated departmental functions (with the inevitable proviso, stated by the Committee itself, that what was a 'major' function of one department would be a 'minor' function of another). Today, while still confronted with a plethora of reform proposals which attempt to justify themselves in terms of convenience and rationality, if not in terms of principle, we know that it is impossible to divide Governmental functions into a series of neatly defined blocks, each to be occupied by one Government department or a small number of closely-related departments. We can see that we are faced with a continuous process of creation, fusion, fission and transfer and are aware, to a degree which was impossible for the Haldane Committee in 1918, that any important decision taken in one department will immediately affect the work of almost every other. Consequently our interest is much more strongly focused on the problems of co-ordination and overall planning than on those of demarcation. In respect of the latter the motto is 'solvitur ambulando'. It might even be 'sauve qui peut'.

How, then, is co-ordination effected in the British system of administration? Clearly the ultimate responsibility lies with the Cabinet and the Prime Minister. The Cabinet secretariat has a key role to play, and so does the system of committees which a modern Cabinet invariably maintains as a means of organizing its work.[4] At the official (i.e. civil service) level, there is a

4. During Mr Churchill's post-war ministry, an abortive experiment was made with the establishment of co-ordinating *Ministers*, generally described as 'overlords' (see above, pp. 106–8). This was revived, in a different and much stronger form, by Mr Harold Wilson, who in his 1969 reorganization of ministries created 'empires' for Mr Richard Crossman (social services), Mr Anthony Crosland (housing, local government, regional planning and transport) and Mr Anthony Wedgwood Benn (technology and power). Mr Heath pursued a similar line when he became Prime Minister in 1970, creating the Departments of the Environment and of Trade and Industry.

complicated network of inter-departmental committees, both permanent and ad hoc: but the institution which, at least in the past, has been the co-ordinator par excellence is undoubtedly the Treasury, the so-called 'department of departments'.

Its position is unique and without parallel in any other country. In Britain the Treasury is not merely a ministry of finance, but the fact that it *is* the Ministry of Finance has given it a strategic position highly advantageous for the development of its co-ordinating role.

The foundations of Treasury control over the national finances were laid in the eighteenth and nineteenth centuries. Two dates mark important stages in the process. The first was 1787, when the Consolidated Fund was brought into existence – 'a fund into which shall flow every stream of revenue and whence shall issue the supply for every public service'. As the administrator of the Consolidated Fund the Treasury found itself placed in a position of power from which it has never subsequently been dislodged. The second date is 1861, when the Treasury acquired the right to vet and approve the annual estimates of *all* Government departments before presentation to Parliament. (Before that date only *some* of the estimates passed through its hands.)

In earlier days the Treasury used its powers to vet departmental estimates and authorize departmental spending in the interests of a cheese-paring 'economy' described by Mr Gladstone, who was largely responsible for promoting it, as 'saving candle ends'. In the twentieth century it has abandoned its purely restrictive attitude and become primarily concerned with securing 'value for money'. In collaboration with the departments themselves and under the ultimate authority of the Cabinet, it adjudicates between competing demands for resources, and attempts to organize the 'forward planning' of national expenditure. The annual review of Estimates, of course, continues. It will remain necessary so long as parliamentary authorization of expenditure remains on an annual basis; but the expenditure control that the Treasury exerts is essentially a *continuous* process, operating throughout the year and using criteria which go far beyond the comparatively narrow considerations which apply to the annual budget. Whenever a department proposes to engage in activities involving new expenditure or new distribution of existing expenditure the consent of the Treasury becomes necessary – a consent which rests not upon any rule of law, but on a constitutional convention now so well established as to be automatically accepted. The requirement of prior approval, it has been said, is 'the principal foundation of the Treasury's power to co-ordinate financial policy'. Although the giving or withholding of such approval is contingent upon ultimate statutory authorization, there is great freedom to incur financial liabilities in advance of parliamentary sanction and before the necessary appropriations have been made.[5]

This fact, together with the virtual automatic approval by Parliament of the annual estimates, provides the basis for the *forward planning* to which we have referred above. Such planning, as applied to the totality of national expenditure on both current and capital account, is a very recent development. The so-called 'forward look', whereby expenditure was surveyed 'over a period of years in relation to prospective resources'[6] was first undertaken for defence expenditure and, more generally, for public investment. In 1958, however, the Select Committee on Estimates, while recognizing the value of this technique, criticized the Treasury for still concentrating 'too much attention on the policy of expenditure proposals for the coming financial year with too little regard to commitments and consequences for future years'.[7] This criticism was repeated by the Plowden Committee (appointed in 1959 to examine the Treasury's methods for controlling public expenditure) which strongly advocated 'the development and use by Government of long term surveys of expenditure and resources' and proposed an internal reorganization of the Treasury to facilitate the making of such surveys and their translation into terms of practical policy. As we shall see, the kind of reorganization proposed by the Plowden Committee was effected and new techniques of expenditure control were brought into operation.

It is clear that financial control involves the maintenance of continuous relations with the spending departments. This, together with the fact that the Treasury is the department not only of the Chancellor of the Exchequer but also of the Prime Minister (as First Lord of the Treasury), has caused it to be regarded as the most suitable location for the central control

5. See S. H. Beer, *Treasury Control* (Oxford 1957), pp. 45–6.j
6. Lord Bridges, *The Treasury* (Allen & Unwin 1964), p. 138.
7. Sixth Report from the Select Committee on Estimates, Session 1957–58, Treasury Control of Expenditure. HC Paper 254/1, para. 23.

of the machinery of administration as well as for that of finance. From the mid-nineteenth century onwards it became a Ministry for the civil service, acquiring responsibility for the numbers, pay and distribution of civil servants, together with the general principles governing their grading, promotion, discipline and organization. The methods it has employed are predominantly informal, and, particularly after the First World War, have involved continuous and mainly co-operative relations with the spending departments – although the antagonism characteristic of the relationship between controller and controlled has by no means been absent. 'The postwar theory of the control of the civil service organization,' wrote the Committee on Public Expenditure in 1931, 'rests on active co-operation and goodwill between the Treasury on the one hand and the Department on the other. They are jointly trustees for the efficient and economical administration of the Service.' But within the velvet glove of informal co-operation there is the rarely-displayed mailed fist of legal power. An Order in Council of 1920, expressing in general terms an authority which the Treasury already exercised, vested in it the right to 'make regulations for controlling the conduct of His Majesty's Civil Establishments and providing for the classifications, remuneration and other conditions of service of all persons employed therein, whether permanently or temporarily'. Moreover, when a new department has been set up by statute, a provision has always been included whereby Treasury authorization is required for the numbers and grades of civil servants appointed to run it.

From 1919 onwards the Treasury acquired a separate Division for such 'establishments' functions, working in close relationship with an Establishments Officer in each department, appointed with Treasury approval. The same date saw the beginning of Treasury interest in wider 'machinery of government' questions, through the appointment of a small Section of Investigating Officers. These, admittedly, were more concerned with office machinery than what is now termed 'organization and methods' but their appointment proved the modest beginning of a long process, considerably speeded up by the Second World War, whereby the Treasury's responsibiity for all matters concerning the structure and *modus operandi* of departmental administration underwent a significant extension.

From the above it will be clear that the Treasury, in addition to its strictly financial functions as defined by the Haldane

Committee[8] has acquired extensive powers of what the Committee termed 'control and supervision'[9] – powers which are now far more extensive than could have been envisaged in 1918. To responsibility for the civil service there has been added, during the inter-war and post-war periods, responsibility for the proper functioning of the machinery of government and for such economic planning as the Government of the day has seen fit to engage in.

Inevitably there have been critics, particularly vociferous of recent years, who hold that such an enormous concentration of power and authority in the hands of a single ministry is objectionable in principle and clumsy in practice. Criticism has been directed particularly at the conferment of responsibilities for the machinery of government, for the civil service, and for economic planning on a Ministry primarily concerned with the nation's finances – a Ministry, moreover, which is alleged to be firmly attached to rather obsolete 'departmental policies' and rarely to have shown conspicuous inventiveness and initiative. Criticism of this kind was considerably stepped up in the later 1950s, when many writers partly attributed Britain's relative economic stagnation to the Treasury's attachment to orthodox financial policies and lack of enthusiasm about radical reforms in the field of public administration. The demand widely advanced was that the newer functions should be removed from its control and given to separate Ministries free from the 'dead hand' of Treasury tradition.

The initial reaction to these mounting criticisms was internal reorganization. Up to 1962 the Treasury was organized in five 'sides' – Economic Affairs, Supply, Home Finance, Overseas

8. '(a) Subject to Parliament it is responsible for the imposition and regulation of taxation and collection of the revenue for which purpose it has the assistance of the Revenue Departments.

'(b) It controls public expenditure in various degrees and various ways, chiefly through the preparation or supervision of the estimates for Parliament.

'(c) It arranges for the provision of the funds required from day to day to meet the necessities of the public service for which purpose it is entrusted with extensive borrowing powers.

'(d) It initiates and carries out measures affecting the public debt currency and banking.

'(e) It prescribes the manner in which the public accounts should be kept.' (Report of the Machinery of Government Committee, 1918: Cd. 9230, p. 17, para. 2.)

9. ibid. p. 18, para. 4.

Finance and Establishments. Originally all had reported to one Permanent Secretary, but a minor reorganization in 1956 bifurcated top-level control through the appointment of two Permanent Secretaries, one made head of the Civil Service and given responsibility for Establishments, the other being placed in charge of Finance, Supply and Economic Affairs. The major reorganization of 1962 preserved this bifurcation but radically changed the Treasury's internal structure in such a way as to make a clear distinction between the financial aspects of its business and those concerned with the machinery of government. This change was in accordance with the recommendations made by the Plowden Committee, as was also the greater emphasis now placed on 'management' functions through the creation of a 'management group' separate from the group responsible for pay and conditions of service, which continued to discharge the old Establishment functions.

Prominent among changes on the Financial and Economic Sides was the loss to Supply, now renamed Public Expenditure and Resources, of its establishment responsibilities, which were now transferred to what was termed the 'management' (i.e. machinery of government) side. (This meant the end of the former mixed Supply and Establishment Divisions.) Even more important in the light of the Plowden recommendations was the creation of a National Economy Group with special responsibility for economic planning, on which the Government was now placing new emphasis with the creation of the National Economic Development Council in 1960. The Group was organized in two divisions, one responsible for economic forecasting and co-ordination and the development of general policies for economic growth, the other having responsibility 'for advising Ministers on certain themes of Government economic policy which are concerned with stimulating economic growth', such as 'incomes policy, restrictive practices, prices, national manpower problems and the stimulation of productivity on a national basis'.[10]

The new stress, therefore, was on the positive responsibility of the Treasury for 'management' in two senses, i.e. (1) the management of the administrative apparatus and (2) the management of the economy as a whole. This went a long way towards meeting the criticism of existing organization and practice implicit in Beer's characterization of the Treasury's former role, viz:

10. Lord Bridges, *The Treasury*, p. 100.

> Treasury control old and new is not positive direct action; that is to say the Treasury does not itself commonly take the initiative, dictating to departments what they shall undertake in order to fulfil government policy or plans. Rather it shapes the initiative already taken by departments by a criticism which is mainly negative, bringing that initiative into accord with policy.[11]

Henceforward, it was hoped, negative criticism would be much more strongly supplemented by positive planning. This inevitably meant a change, the implications of which would have to be worked out, in the traditional relationship between the Treasury

The Treasury, however, was not to be left in peace to see how this reorganization would work in practice. In the 1960s the running was made by those reformers in favour of splitting up the Treasury's functions. First, in 1964, came the creation of the Department of Economic Affairs, to take over the major part of the Treasury's responsibility for economic planning and co-ordination (see below, p. 201). The second blow came in 1968 with the Government's acceptance of one of the major recommendations of the Committee on the Civil Service, chaired by Lord Fulton, viz. that establishment and machinery of government work should be transferred to a separate department on the grounds that 'the central management of the Service is not, under modern conditions, an appropriate function for the central finance department'. For this change three reasons were given: first, that with the expansion, both actual and envisaged, of the central management of the Service, 'there would be reason to fear too great a concentration of power in one department'; second that the management of the Service required 'an expertise separate and different' from that required by the management of Government finance and control of expenditure; third, that central management of the former kind, if it was to be concerned 'positively and creatively . . . with the maintaining and improving of the standards of the Civil Service' required 'a separate institution with a single-minded devotion to its own professional purposes'.[12]

Thus the fusion–fission process noted above was extended to the department of departments itself, the Treasury. This does not mean, however, that the Treasury will cease to be a co-ordinating department. It will obviously continue to be concerned with

11. S. H. Beer, *Treasury Control*, p. 77.

12. *The Civil Service*, Vol. 1: Report of the Committee, 1966–68. Cmnd 3638, Vol. 1, pp. 81–2.

financial co-ordination; moreoever, with the demise of the Department of Economic Affairs in 1969 it had its economic planning functions restored to it. But although the latter event, which cast long shadows before it, appeared to contradict the tendency towards the splitting up of the Treasury, there is still a clear movement in the direction of locating the responsibility for *over-all* co-ordination elsewhere. This location cannot, of course, be the new Civil Service Department, which is solely concerned with questions of machinery of government and personnel, and remains experimental. It can only rest with the Prime Minister. This would imply – and has already begun to imply – the 'building up of Number 10 (Downing Street) under the Cabinet Office to give stronger central direction to the whole government machine'.[13] The Central Policy Review Staff, to which we have already referred, would seem a significant step in that direction.

2. The Personnel

The late but unlamented Joseph Stalin once said that 'cadres decide everything', by which he presumably meant that any apparatus of government is as good as the personnel that man it. Indeed it is a mere truism that no amount of reorganization of the kind that we have been discussing will be effective if the quality of the people staffing the Government department is insufficient and their morale low. Collectively, those who are responsible to Ministerial chiefs for running the administrative machine are known as the 'civil' service. The use of the term 'civil' implies a distinction not with the military service but with the 'political' service, consisting of Ministers responsible to Parliament. Constitutionally, the word 'service' in both contexts implies obedience and subordination to the 'Crown'. In this rather formal sense the Civil Service is a traditional part of the constitution. In so far as both Ministers and civil servants are appointed, dismissed and subjected to specific conditions of service 'at Her Majesty's pleasure', there is no distinction between the political heads of the Government departments and the bureaucrats who staff them. Indeed the dependence of the latter on the 'prerogative' power is seen in the fact that the major reorganizations of the Civil Service during the course of the last century or so have been effected by Orders in Council, such as those of 1855, 1870 and 1920, and not

13. See interview between Norman Hunt and Harold Wilson, *The Listener*, 6 April 1967.

by legislation. In reality, of course, the distinction between the 'civil' service and the 'political' service is of the highest constitutional and practical importance.

Moreover the Civil Service as we know it is a comparatively recent innovation, having been made in the nineteenth century. The need for this new beginning, as we have already noted (see above, Chapter 1, p. 22) was due to the virtual destruction of the Tudor and Stuart royal bureaucracy as a result of the parliamentary victory in the Civil War and the 'revolution' of 1688. The development of modern bureaucracy in Britain may be dated from 1780, and the fundamental principles of its organization were originally laid down by Lord Macaulay in 1833 and Sir Charles Trevelyan and Sir Stafford Northcote in 1853. The principles followed by these pioneers were inspired by the philosophy of Utilitarianism, most clearly expounded in Jeremy Bentham's famous pamphlet with the highly specific title of 'Official Aptitude Maximized, Expense Minimized'. Reflecting the interest of early nineteenth-century reformers in the achievement of governmental honesty and efficiency in the performance of regulatory work still limited in scope and complexity by the predominant laissez-faire outlook, the fundamentals then laid down have remained virtually unchallenged until very recent times, and must therefore be briefly stated.

Macaulay was primarily concerned with Indian administration when he expressed his views on the qualifications required in the upper ranks of the public service and on the methods necessary for recruiting people who possessed them; but his words came to be regarded as having general applicability. Advocating competitive examination based upon performance in academic subjects normally taught in the universities, he told the House of Commons:

> We conceive that under this system the persons sent out (i.e. to India) will be young men above par – young men superior either in talents or in diligence to the mass. . . . Whatever be the languages, whatever be the sciences, which it is in any age or country's fashion to teach, those who become the greatest proficients in those languages and those sciences will generally be the flower of the youth – the most acute, the most industrious, the most ambitious of honourable distinctions.

Accepting this philosophy, Sir Charles Trevelyan and Sir Stafford Northcote, in their Report on Organization of the Permanent Civil Service, laid down four major principles. In answer to the question 'What is the best method of providing (the Civil Service) with a supply of good men and of making the most of them after they have been admitted?' they replied:

(1) recruitment by examination of a 'competing literary' type, standardized throughout the service and conducted by a 'central board';

(2) the making of a clear distinction between those destined for 'superior situations' and those who were to occupy 'the lower class of appointments'. (The former were to be 'the most promising young men of the day', recruited by 'an examination on a level with the highest description of education in this country'; the latter were to be obtained by a competitive examination suitable for candidates of lower educational attainments, and also lower average age. Briefly there was to be a separation between the 'intellectuals' and 'mechanicals');

(3) the unification of the service through the imposition of uniform salary grades and the establishment of the principle whereby a civil servant could be transferred freely from one department to another;

(4) promotion by merit rather than by seniority, with 'every possible security against its abuse'.

At a time when patronage was the normal method of appointment, when admission to the Civil Service was sought after mainly by 'the unambitious, the indolent and incapable', and when success depended on 'simply avoiding any flagrant misconduct and attending with moderate regularity to the routine duties', these principles were revolutionary; and because they were revolutionary they received no immediate implementation. Although the Civil Service Commissioners were created in 1855 to conduct the recommended examinations, it was not until 1870 that an Order in Council prescribed open competitive examination as the normal mode of entry and that a clear distinction was made between the 'intellectuals' and 'mechanicals' (Class 1 and Class 2), by the prescription of separate competitive entrance examinations for each. Not until then, moreoever, was the unification of the Service, advocated by Trevelyan and Northcote, seriously advanced by giving authority to the Treasury to approve the examination regulations of the Civil Service Commissioners, to prescribe the number of vacancies to be competed for and to arrange them in 'groups'. The significance of the Order in Council of 1870 was therefore very great indeed. As Emmeline Cohen has said, 'It was of paramount importance in the reform of the Civil Service not only because it reduced political patronage but because by doing so it paved the way for those other reforms which as previous enquiries had made it clear, would not take place until the methods of appointment had been changed'[14].

The expansion of the Civil Service and the growing complexity and technicality of the work with which it had to cope brought further reorganization, but always within the limits of the broad principles that had already been laid down. New problems of recruitment were created by the employment of an increasing number of specialists (such as doctors, lawyers, educationists, scientists, engineers, accountants, statisticians, social workers and, more recently, economists), some of them common to several departments, others (such as tax inspectors, factory inspectors, inspectors of schools, customs officers etc.) confined by the nature of their work to a particular department. The general principle was that those with professional qualifications should be exempted from special examination and appointed on a basis of competitive interview. This was reasonable enough; but the question of promoting 'professionals' and departmental specialists out of their 'classes' and into the general administrative hierarchy was answered in a manner which gave less satisfaction. Only in exceptional cases was such promotion permitted. Hence the Civil Service tended to develop a marked rigidity of 'class' structure. Professionals, because of the 'narrowness' of their training and the specialization of their work, became generally regarded as 'servants' of the general administrators and unfitted for the discharge of higher administrative responsibilities, which remained the preserve of those with a 'broad' and 'humane' education. Moreover, within the structure of the administrative hierarchy the original distinction between 'mechanicals' and 'intellectuals' was more or less rigidly maintained, although the simple dichotomy between class 1 and class 2 became replaced (after 1920) with a four-class division: Administrative, Executive, Clerical and Clerical Assistant. The principle was maintained that each class should be recruited by competitive examination at distinct educational levels, and class to class promotion, although by no means unknown, was comparatively rare.

These rigidities, however, were considerably shaken by twentieth-century developments and particularly by the impact of two world wars. It was the Second World War that was responsible for the more important developments. During it and after it age limits were relaxed; separate examinations at the lower levels were largely eliminated in favour of accepting evi-

14. *The Growth of the British Civil Service 1780–1939* (Cass 1965), p. 122.

dence of ability provided by public examinations; new forms of examination intended to measure personal qualities rather than academic attainments were introduced for recruitment to the highest class; special methods of entry suitable for those experienced in other fields were introduced; movement from the specialist to the generalist classes was facilitated; and class to class promotion was developed to such an extent that today more members of the Administrative Class are recruited by promotion (or limited competition) from the lower classes than by open competitive examination for university graduates.

These modifications in what had become the traditional civil service pattern inevitably led to a more active and persistent questioning of 'Trevelyan–Northcote' principles than had been heard since the days when these principles were originally enunciated. Criticism of the Civil Service was not of course new. The Service has never had a good 'press', and has been made the subject of a series of caricatures ranging from Dickens' Sir Tite Barnacle to Tommy Handley's Sir Short Supply (of Second World War fame); but most of the earlier criticisms had concentrated on the alleged excessive size, devious ways and arbitrary behaviour of the Service, as expressed in books such as Lord Hewart's *New Despotism*, and in the abuse showered on officials of the Ministry of Agriculture at the time of the Crichel Down affair of 1953–54. In the 1950s, however, the main target became its alleged inefficiency, due to its unpreparedness to adapt itself to the rapidly changing needs of the twentieth century. Specifically, criticisms were directed at (a) its alleged caste-like character, regarded as a source of complacency and of suspiciousness towards new ideas coming from outside; (b) its 'amateurism', particularly at top levels; (c) its lack of adequate training, particularly in the techniques of management; and (d) its domination by persons educated mainly in 'arts' subjects at two ancient universities. Of great significance was the fact that, almost for the first time, critics of the 'best civil service in the world' began to compare it, unfavourably with, the public services of other countries, and particularly with that of France.[15] While neither confirming nor denying the justice of these complaints, one may see in

15. See, for instance, Brian Chapman, *British Government Observed* (Allen & Unwin 1964). The most recent of the 'radical' critics is Max Nicholson, whose book, *The System*, owed much of its impact to the fact that its author had occupied the post of Secretary to the Lord President's Office.

them a reflection of the mood of national self-criticism emanating from Britain's relative economic stagnation and her decline from the status of a world power. From this kind of self-criticism no national institution is at present exempt.

The major target of the critics was the Administrative Class – because it was the highest class in the Service, occupied with policy-making tasks, and allegedly able to tell Governments what they could and could not do, under the guise of giving 'advice'. This most prestigious of civil service classes, formerly the object of so much admiration, was now placed in a defensive position. Its role, therefore, must be briefly examined.

Up to the Second World War, it was overwhelmingly recruited from upper middle-class young men (and, to a very limited extent, women fortunate enough to secure an education at Oxford) or Cambridge and possessing sufficient academic ability to achieve success in the formidable – and predominantly written – competitive examination set by the Civil Service Commissioners. During the war, it was considerably diluted by 'temporaries', and after the war the area of its recruitment was widened by the introduction of a new type of competitive examination ('Method II'), by the extension of the practice of promotion from the Executive to the Administrative Class, by the introduction of 'direct entry' at the Principal grade (i.e. the grade above the lowest one, to which entrants by open competition are recruited), and as a result of the limited but significant democratization of university education, which meant that Oxford and Cambridge (still the main source of 'open competition' recruits) became repositories of high potential talent from a variety of sources rather than an extension of the public schools.

The duties of this class were those of 'intellectuals' in the Trevelyan–Northcote sense. They were first clearly defined by the Report of the Civil Service Reorganization Commission of 1921, which listed them as

> those concerned with the formation of policy, with the coordination and improvement of Government machinery, and with the general administration and control of Departments of the Public Service.

This formulation implied a combination of 'top level management' with policy-making responsibilities; but it was the latter that were most consistently emphasized and most highly prized. Advising ministers about policies to be pursued; working out the implications of policies adopted; preparing Ministerial briefs for parliamentary interventions; conducting negotiations with representatives of interest groups; drafting statutory instruments (see below, Chapter 11; helping to pilot legislation through the House of Commons; and generally facilitating and co-ordinating duties which were generally, and rightly, regarded as typical of the work of the Administrative Class. Management as such was relegated in the main to the upper strata of the much more extensive Executive Class, whose duties were defined by the Reorganization Committee as 'concerned with matters of internal organization and control, with the settlement of broad questions arising out of business in hand or in contemplation, and with the responsible conduct of broad operations'.

Those recruited to the Administrative Class, either by open competition or by promotion, entered at the lowest grade, Assistant Principal, where they received a training which before the war was somewhat perfunctory, being based almost entirely on the 'apprenticeship' principle, but after the war became extended – although somewhat slowly and reluctantly – to include formal 'courses'. Promotion was from Assistant Principal to Principal, and then (at ages varying from the middle thirties to the middle fifties)[16] to Assistant Secretary, the grade at which a civil servant first became faced with major decision-taking responsibilities. Above that level the ladder became narrower and steeper, via Under-Secretary, and Deputy Secretary to Permanent Secretary, the last being Head of Department and chief adviser to the Minister. Total numbers in all grades of the Administrative Class, at the beginning of 1968, were 2,784. The Administrative Class thus constituted a small and powerful bureaucratic 'aristocracy', hierarchically organized and tightly-knit. The aristocrats among these aristocrats were to be found in the Treasury, which, as the central co-ordinating department, succeeded in enlisting to its service a high proportion of the 'cream' of the Administrative Class.

The strength of this system, whereby a small number of highly-educated and very intelligent 'generalists', advised by a larger group of technical specialists, direct the activities of a great administrative machine operated by NCOs of the Executive Class and staffed mainly by persons engaged in comparatively routine operations, is historically attested. It gave Great Britain an administration which was the envy of the world for its combination of intelligence at the top and competence below, and

16. *The Civil Service*, Vol. IV, p. 562.

which is still universally admired for its honesty and virtual incorruptibility. Even the extent of its adaptability should not be underestimated. Indeed, these and other virtues drew forth expressions of admiration from its most severe critics, including the Fulton Committee, which wrote:

There are exceptionally able men and women at all levels. There is a strong sense of public service. Its integrity and impartiality are unquestioned. We believe that the country does not recognise enough how impressively conscientious many civil servants are in the personal service they give the public. It is of high importance that these and other qualities should be preserved.[17]

Nonetheless, it was the weaknesses rather than the strengths of this system that received emphasis. Summarizing the general tenor of post-war criticisms, the Fulton Committee said that in general 'the structures and practices of the Service have not kept up with the changing tasks'.[18] Specifically, the Committee alleged that it was 'inadequate in six main respects for the most efficient discharge of the present and prospective responsibilities of government', viz.

(a) It is still too much based on the philosophy of the amateur (or 'generalist' or "all-rounder'). This is evident in the Administrative Class, which holds the dominant position in the Service.

(b) The present system of classes in the Service (there are over 1,400, each for the most part with its own separate pay and career structure) seriously impedes its work.

(c) Scientists, engineers and members of the specialist classes are frequently given neither the full responsibilities and opportunities nor the corresponding authority they ought to have.

(d) Too few civil servants are skilled managers.

(e) There is not enough contact between the Service and the community it is there to serve.

(f) Personnel management and career planning are inadequate.[19]

To remedy these defects, the Committee proposed, *inter alia*:

(1) the creation of a new Civil Service Department, under the control of the Prime Minister, 'with wider functions than those now performed by the "Pay and Management" group of the Treasury, which it should take over'.[20]

17. ibid. Vol. 1, p. 13, para. 22.
18. ibid. p. 11, para. 14.
19. ibid. p. 104. Summary of Main Findings, para. 1.
20. ibid. p. 104, para. 3.

Non-industrial staff of the home Civil Service

Staff Group	*Perma-nent*	*Tem-porary*†	*Total*	*Per cent of whole*
Administrative	2,624	160	2,784‡	0.4
Executive (general and departmental)	87,907	3,159	91,066	12.0
Clerical officer (general and departmental)	117,308	22,869	140,177	18.5
Clerical assistants	35,419	53,849	89,268	11.7
Typing	11,079	18,880	29,959	3.9
Inspectorate	2,785	93	2,878	0.4
Messengerial	19,039	16,361	35,400	4.7
Post Office minor and manipulative	182,961	42,090	225,051	29.7
Professional, scientific and technical I	20,518	6,000	26,518	3.5
Scientific and technical II	42,343	16,803	59,146	7.8
Ancillary, technical and miscellaneous supervisory grades, etc.	38,085	17,877	55,962	7.4
Total	560,068	198,141	758,209	100.0

* Central Staff Record figures.

† From departmental returns.

‡ Nearly 300 more than the total in paragraph 97, largely due to the inclusion of civil servants who, although not members of the administrative class, are more appropriate to the administrative staff group than to any other.

Notes: Diplomatic Service staff at home and abroad (5,223 permanent and 1,396 temporary) and Post Office engineering etc. staff formerly classified as industrial (92,415 permanent and 21,382 temporary) are excluded from the above figures. Home Departments' staff serving abroad are included, but not locally engaged staff. Part-timers totalling 44,774 have been counted as half. The total for the Non-industrial Home Civil Service excluding the Post Office was 465,000 on 1 January 1968.

Source: *The Civil Service,* Vol. 4: Evidence submitted to the Committee under the Chairmanship of Lord Fulton 1966–68, London 1968.

(2) The development of 'greater professionalism both among specialists (e.g. scientists and engineers) and administrators'. (For specialists this would mean 'more training in management, and opportunities for greater responsibilities and wider careers'; for administrators, greater specialization, i.e. orientation towards 'particular areas of government' such as economic and financial administration on the one hand and social administration on the other.[21])

(3) More specialization in the recruitment of administrators, particularly by taking more fully into account the relevance of their university courses to the job they are being recruited to do.[22]

(4) More attention to training, and in particular the establishment of a Civil Service College to provide 'major training courses in administration and management and a wide range of short courses' and to engage in 'important research functions'.[23]

(5) More attention to career management, so as to enable all civil servants to 'have the opportunity to progress as far and as fast as their talents and appropriate training can take them'.[24]

(6) Greater mobility between the Civil Service and other forms of employment, through such devices as 'expanded late entry, temporary appointments for fixed periods, short-term interchanges of staff, and freer movement out of the Service'.[25]

The most important proposal of all, which struck at the very root of the Trevelyan–Northcote 'philosophy', was for the abolition of the Service's class structure. 'All classes,' said the Committee 'should be abolished and replaced by a single, unified grading structure covering all civil servants from top to bottom in the non-industrial part of the Service'. In the new structure, to be devised by the new Civil Service Department in collaboration with the other departments of government, 'the correct grading of each post should be determined by job evaluation'.[26]

'Fulton' was obviously controversial and it provoked plenty of controversy. There were some who regarded its proposals as the most radically constructive to appear since the publication of the Trevelyan–Northcote Report, well over one hundred years

21. ibid. p. 105, para. 7.
22. ibid. para. 8.
23. ibid. para. 9.
24. ibid. para. 10.
25. ibid. para. 11.
26. ibid. p. 104, para. 6.

ago. According to this view, their implementation meant a root-and-branch adaptation of the structure and spirit of the Service to late-twentieth-century needs. Others were more sceptical. Critics of 'Fulton' may be divided into two groups: those who feared that the Committee's proposals could not be implemented without sacrificing the essential characteristics of the British Civil Service that had made it a uniquely valuable instrument of policy implementation, closely adapted to the peculiar requirements of British parliamentary democracy; and those who considered that, in view of the reforms already made or under way, little real change would be effected. The former group, the 'traditionalists', did not produce any great vocal effort; the latter, the 'unbelievers', expressed themselves more forcefully. Among them was Professor J. A. G. Griffith, here selected as an example because of the massive knowledge of British administration he accumulated during the production of a major research study of 'Central Departments and Local Authorities'.[27]

The abolition of classes he welcomed 'if only for the shake up that may follow'. As, however, each recruit would presumably enter the unified class structure at a different point and with unequal chances of promotion, he did not consider that the abolition would make much difference to the present dispensation. 'It may be,' he said, 'that more scientists and lawyers and economists will be admitted to the Senior Policy and Management Group'; but 'what is unknown is whether they will, because of their professional expertise, make better Under, Deputy and Permanent Secretaries than those who, under the present system, are recruited to those jobs'. While also welcoming the new Civil Service Department, he wondered whether it would be really capable of developing the degree of dynamism that 'Fulton' clearly hoped that it would acquire. Although its creation would offer a challenging assignment, the danger was that, once established, it would settle down to a life as unadventurous as that of the old Treasury 'Pay and Management' side. As for the Civil Service College, this would be only a 'laudable' extension of what was already going on, in the already-established Centre of Administrative Studies.

Professor Griffith, in fact, tended to dismiss the 'Fulton' proposals as irrelevant rather than as harmful. In his view, they concentrated on 'sub-machinery, while the superstructure of

27. London, Allen & Unwin, for Royal Institute of Public Administration, 1966.

policy decisions, Departmental "views", strong and weak civil servants, annual changes of Departments for Ministers, and all the other major determinants of power', remained unchanged. 'We may not get the Civil Service we deserve,' he concluded, but 'we do get the Civil Service which is determined by our educational, social and economic structure'.[28]

This less than enthusiastic view of the 'Fulton' proposals derived from a radicalism more fundamental than that of the committee members themselves, resting as it did on the opinion that a mere revamping of Civil Service organization was no substitute for the basic changes in social system that Britain allegedly required. Less radical, although partaking of the same attitude, was the criticism that, in promoting the reorganization of the Civil Service without first having considered what changes were needed in the machinery of administration, the Government was guilty of putting the cart before the horse. According to this view, which has been forcibly expressed by Professor Max Beloff,[29] the task given to the Fulton Committee – 'to examine the structure, recruitment and management, including training, of the Home Civil Service, and to make recommendations' – could not be effectively accomplished until there was a clearer idea of what a reformed Civil Service was required to *do*.

This point may well have some validity. Nevertheless, the Fulton Committee, despite its apparently restrictive terms of reference, could hardly avoid dealing with certain 'machinery of government' matters which touched closely on the role and *ethos* of the Civil Service. Among these were the well-established traditions of anonymity and secrecy and of political neutrality, to which we will now turn.

Both doctrines may be derived from the fundamental principle of *obedience*, any denial of which would challenge the convention of Ministerial responsibility itself. As the latter, although not without elements of fiction, is basic to the whole system of British parliamentary government, it is not surprising that Mr Harold Wilson in announcing the terms of reference of the 'Fulton' Committee, disclaimed, on behalf of the Government, 'any intention . . . to alter the basic relationship between Ministers and Civil Servants'. Civil servants, he added, 'however eminent, remain confidential advisers of Ministers, who alone are answerable to Parliament for policy; and we do not envisage any change

28. 'The Civil Service We Deserve' in *Socialist Commentary*, August 1968.
29. *The Times*, 19 June 1968.

in this fundamental feature of our parliamentary system of democracy'.[30]

How far this 'basic relationship' requires for its maintenance the strict application of the anonymity–secrecy doctrine is much open to discussion. So is the question of how far anonymity and secrecy are necessary for the effective performance of the civil servant's duties. The joint doctrine, of course, has never been literally applied. Names of leading civil servants, although not exactly household words, are well known to people interested in politics and administration, and all senior departmental office holders are listed (together with their salaries) in the standard works of reference, such as *Whitaker's Almanack*. Regularly they give evidence to parliamentary committees, speaking 'on behalf of' their Ministers but sometimes expressing distinctly individual views, which are published in Minutes of Evidence. Some write articles in journals, learned and otherwise, and in the 'quality' press, and a few have even appeared on television. It is well known, moreover, that Government departments have distinctive outlooks and well-established policies, which are not invariably those favoured by the current Ministerial incumbents. The public, therefore, is by no means entirely ignorant of who, at the official level, is advising the Minister, and of what kind of advice he is likely to be giving. Although, in the British system, there is far less openness than in the American, Swedish or even French systems, neither anonymity nor secrecy is absolute, and the present tendency would seem to be towards the erosion of both.

Those such as Professor Brian Chapman, who criticize the lack of openness in British processes of government, would carry this erosion further. For him, it is partly a matter of legal re form by way of modifying the doctrine of Crown privilege and liberalizing the Official Secrets Act. These, together with the rules of contempt of court and the libel laws, are said to 'constitute a mas-

30. *HC Debates*, Vol. 724, cols 209–10. Whereas there is no doubt that civil servants are responsible to Ministers, there is rather less certainty about the responsibility of Ministers (apart from the formal constitutional one) *for* the actions performed by civil servants in their name, particularly when the civil servants concerned are acting in contradiction to or outside the scope of clearly-defined ministerial policy. This question was fully ventilated during the course of the discussion of the 'Crichel Down' Case, 1953–54. Sir David Maxwell-Fyfe, Attorney-General, then produced the nearest thing we yet have to a definition of the conventions or customs prevailing in this twilit area of the constitution. (See D. N. Chester, 'The Crichel Down Case' in *Public Administration*, Vol. XXXII, Winter 1954, particularly p. 399.)

sive hindrance to the proper understanding, discussion and control of the Executive's activities'. Chapman even suggests that 'some of these powers have been cynically misused to protect the reputations of ministers and civil servants'.[31] He also holds that, quite apart from its legal foundations, secrecy is an habitual vice, firmly built into the 'system'. Although constitutionally supported by the doctrine of Ministerial responsibility, it 'clearly has much profounder psychological and sociological origins. Secrecy in public life panders to a craving for a sentiment of self-importance of belonging to an inner circle.' Its 'total effect . . . has been fundamentally to weaken Britain's capacity to cope with the economic, social and foreign problems of the contemporary world'.[32]

This general line of argument would appear to have been accepted by the 'Fulton' Committee. Predicting that erosion of anonymity would continue, it 'saw no reason to seek to reverse it'. The convention it said, 'has depended in part on the assumption that the doctrine of Ministerial responsibility means that a Minister has full detailed knowledge and control of all the activities of his department' – an assumption that is 'no longer tenable'. Hence, 'the convention of anonymity should be modified and civil servants as professional administrators should be able to go further than now in explaining what their departments are doing'.[33]

On secrecy, it held that 'civil servants and perhaps also Ministers are apt to give great if sometimes excessive weight to the difficulties and problems which would undoubtedly arise from

31. *British Government Observed*, pp. 46–7.

32. ibid. pp. 61–2. Max Nicholson, another radical critic, is of the view that 'civil servants and others in similar positions should not be permitted to continue to hide beneath the woolly folds of the Prerogative', from which he proposes to extract them by passing 'a clear and comprehensive Statute of Administration' in which 'all administrative law and major practice which has the force of law should be reviewed, modernised, and codified in clear and understandable forms, eliminating all quasi-judicial, quasi-gibberish and other forms of Whitehall double talk' (*The System* (London 1967), p. 432). Lord Salter, a former civil servant of vast experience, considers that anonymity has actually increased during the last fifty years. 'To the shelter of Ministerial responsibility has now been added the further shelter of greater anonymity,' he writes, adding that he regards this as 'highly regrettable'. The Service, in his view, 'should in this respect go back to where it was at the beginning of this century' (*Slave of the Lamp*, London 1967 p. 286). It seems probable that Lord Salter's capacious but necessarily selective memory has exaggerated the extent of 'openness' in the civil service at the time when he was in the early stages of his career.

33. *The Civil Service*, Vol. 1, p. 93, para. 283.

more open processes of administration and policy-making'; it called in the Swedish example to show that 'open government is possible'; and it put forward the suggestion that 'the Government should set up an enquiry to make recommendations for getting rid of unnecessary secrecy in this country'.[34]

There is indeed a general opinion among students of British public administration that greater openness and less anonymity have become desirable, and that both are compatible with the maintenance of the principle of obedience which is the foundation of the convention of Ministerial responsibility. The danger is that reforms designed to give effect to these desiderata will invade a principle of equal if not greater importance, that of political neutrality. If this materialized, a crisis of confidence in the Civil Service might well develop; for, in a parliamentary democracy, such confidence depends upon the maintenance of belief on the part of the public that the Civil Service will serve governments of any likely political complexion with equal loyalty. To ensure that civil servants, particularly those in policy-making positions and those who have frequent contact with the public, should not be open to accusations, however unjustified, of political bias, elaborate rules have been devised.

Civil servants from this point of view have been divided into three groups, viz. (1) the 'politically free', consisting mainly of those in the industrial and minor and manipulative grades; (2) the 'intermediate' group, who could engage in most political activities but only with the permission of their departments and subject to certain conditions. (This includes the sub-clerical, clerical and corresponding grades, together with certain specialists, such as leading draughtsmen and experimental officers, equivalent in status to Executive Officers); (3) the 'politically restricted', a category embracing all the rest, including the Administrative Class. A 'politically-restricted' civil servant is debarred from engaging in 'national' political activities, but is free to seek his department's permission to engage in 'local' activities. It should be added that both the 'intermediate' and 'restricted' groups are bound by what is called a 'code of discretion' aimed at avoiding 'embarrassment to Ministers or their Department'.[35]

This is a complicated scheme. Its main aim has been to avoid the political 'neutralization' of a considerable body of British

34. Ibid. Vol. 1, p. 92, para. 280.
35. See *The Civil Service*. Vol. 4: 'The Political Activities of Civil Servants', pp. 401–5.

citizens on the specious grounds that they belonged to the public service, yet simultaneously to ensure that the civil servant's reputation for political impartiality was preserved. Some seem to have argued that nothing has been achieved by all this, and that the sensible thing would be to trust the civil servant, at whatever level, not to make a political ass of himself. This argument is reinforced by the political freedom granted, without dire consequences, to civil servants in certain other countries such as Sweden. However, it would be false to argue that what is politically acceptable in one country would be equally acceptable in another, with different forms of government and different traditions; and there is a danger that if greater political freedom were to be combined with greater openness and less anonymity, 'grave disquiet' would be the reaction in those influential quarters where such disquiet is the normal reaction to any proposal to tamper with what are regarded as fundamental constitutional conventions. This is a field, therefore, in which progress, if such it may be called, is likely to be slow, and in which would-be reformers might well be advised to proceed cautiously. It is perhaps significant that the Fulton Report avoided the subject,[36] except by way of referring to 'the over-riding importance of good relations between the Service and the public', and underlining the duty incumbent upon 'the Head of the Civil Service and the Prime Minister ... to safeguard the political neutrality of the Higher Civil Service'.[37]

3. Conclusion

This chapter has illustrated two allied problems of adaptation, typical of twentieth-century Britain and felt with particular acuteness in the field of public service.

The first is the adaptation of existing administration institutions, whether old or comparatively new, to rapidly changing needs. We have seen, for instance, that the central machinery of government is faced with new tasks of control, co-ordination and planning imposed on it by a situation in which the Government virtually runs the economy, and has assumed direct responsibility for welfare in the widest possible sense. The Civil Service, too, has to face demands for greater technical expertise, greater managerial competence and a career more genuinely open to tal-

36. Despite its receipt of a paper from the Treasury on 'Political Activities of Civil Servants', ibid. Vol. 4, pp. 401–5.

37. Ibid. Vol. 1, p. 96, para. 289; p. 95, para. 286.

ents, all of which have been stimulated by the development of wider, deeper and more varied governmental responsibilities. Adaptation has certainly been more rapid and more successful than the severer critics of British administration would suggest; but there is a notable time-lag, made particularly evident by Britain's crises of the 1950s and 1960s; and it was this that stimulated the spate of books, articles and pamphlets 'knocking' Britain for its administrative failures. This, too, was responsible for the recent implementation of reforms along the lines suggested by Fulton – the abolition of classes (the merging of the Administrative, Executive and Clerical classes into one Administration Group), the setting up of a Civil Service College and the creation of a Civil Service Department. It remains to be seen how serious and adequate the recent changes will prove, bearing in mind the capacity of the Establishment (defined as those who run the System) and of the System (defined as what is run by the Establishment) to dilute the reforming impetus and to absorb its product with the minimum of real impact.

The second problem of adaptation is that of modifying constitutional concepts and practices to bring them into a more coherent relationship with changes in politico-administrative reality. We have already emphasized on several occasions the ambiguity of the doctrine of Ministerial responsibility in the face of the increasing complexity and ubiquity of administration. Yet an unduly rigid attachment to the venerable doctrine has tended to inhibit the development of new techniques designed to achieve its ostensible object, viz. 'popular control' of administration. Here again there has been considerable exaggeration on the part of some of the critics, particularly those who talk in terms of the replacement of Ministerial responsibility by Civil Service dictatorship. Such dictatorship is a figment of the imagination; reality is to be found in the concoction of policy in semi-secret by a triad of Ministers, civil servants and pressure group representatives, with Parliament hovering critically and vocally in the background, sometimes able to influence policy even in a radical way, at others being forced to accept a series of *faits accomplis*. More serious critics demand not that the triad should be broken up (which would be undesirable as well as impossible) but that its operation should be brought more out into the open and exposed more thoroughly to the light of public and parliamentary criticism. This demand, once condemned as extreme, seems well on the way to becoming current doctrine. If taken seriously it will mean important changes in methods of administration and a corresponding modification of constitutional doctrines and practices.

Administration cannot be treated as a separate entity – as a neutral machine designed to carry out the 'will of the people', democratically expressed through parliamentary institutions. In all countries, but particularly in those where politics and administration are deliberately joined through making Ministers individually and collectively responsible to a parliament of which they are members, the administrative 'machine' is an integral part of the political system. It therefore cannot be changed or fundamentally modified without affecting the way in which politics is conducted and – ultimately – the way in which constitutional doctrine is conceived.

Chapter 7

Group Activity

We referred in the preceding chapter to pressure groups which form part of that triad principally responsible for policy formulation, and we turn now to a consideration of that 'anonymous empire' which has such a vital role to play in the political process.

The electoral system in itself is of only limited value as a means of influencing policy. Electoral strategy demands that the parties, in their search for votes, blur the differences that exist between them in order that their appeal to the all-important 'centre' may be that much greater. Specifics are exchanged for generalities, and general elections become occasions for handing down general verdicts. But behind the generalities lies a host of specific interests which derives from the citizens' various roles in society or from the particular causes they embrace. While most voters do not translate interest into action – for example, many workers do not belong to a trade union; many motorists do not belong to one of the motoring associations – associations do exist in great number to serve almost every conceivable interest or cause. Such organizations may range in size and influence from the Trades Union Congress and the Confederation of British Industries down to the Proportional Representation Society, the oddly-named Society of Individualists and the host of small groups that spring up to promote some local cause or to combat some local nuisance. The life of the groups may be long or short, according to their aims and their success in achieving them.

These organizations offer important channels through which the views of sections of the electorate may be communicated to Governments or administrators. Indeed, in Robert McKenzie's view, they are far more important than the parties 'for the transmission of political ideas from the mass of the citizenry to their rulers'.[1] Through this communication, groups seek to influence Government, either in the defence of common interests or in the promotion of common causes. Thus the motoring associations may seek to prevent the enactment of legislation they consider inimical to the best interests of their members, while the Anti-

1. R. T. McKenzie, 'Parties, Pressure Groups, and the British Political Process' in *Political Quarterly*, Vol. XXIX, No. 1, 1958.

Vivisection society is eager to secure the abolition of experiments on animals.

While influence is the common aim of all groups in their dealings with Government, a useful, though by no means absolute, distinction may be drawn between those groups which seek to protect the interests of their members and those which seek to advance a cause in which their members are interested. For instance, where a trade union may be concerned to negotiate with a Government about legislation which directly affects its members, a group such as the Royal Society for the Prevention of Cruelty to Animals is occupied with problems that have little bearing on the self-interest of those who support it.

Potential membership of the former, the 'defensive' groups, is usually easily definable, while that of the latter, the 'promotional' groups, is more open-ended. Membership of BLESMA for instance, is directly related to the number of limbless ex-service men in the country, and membership of the AUT to the number of university teachers, while that of, say, the League Against Cruel Sports is limited only by the size of the population and by the League's degree of success in persuading others of the merits of its cause. But by and large, although the potential membership is greater for the promotional groups, it is the defensive groups, in which employer and employee associations figure so largely, that have the greater actual membership. That this should be so is understandable, for certain situations encourage, even if they do not actually require, group membership. In many jobs, membership of a trade union is obligatory, or at the least regarded as socially desirable. A host of associations exists to serve the interests of producers of all kinds. To many people, buying a car involves joining one of the motoring associations. Promotional groups, on the other hand, do not have a ready-made clientèle; their membership is not drawn from occupational or ownership groups that have a built-in tendency towards corporate activity. They depend for their support on the strength and appeal of their arguments. Furthermore, while defensive groups may be found across the whole social spectrum, from trade unions to the Country Landowners' Association, promotional groups tend to draw their greatest support from the more publicly-active sections of society, namely the middle and upper classes.

Another distinction might also be drawn here. Many of those groups that have been termed 'defensive' might also well be labelled 'service', for much of their time is taken up with the provision to their members of services which have nothing to do with the political system. For instance, trade unions are primarily concerned with the wage rates and working conditions of their members, and most of their efforts to these ends are directed towards the employers and the corresponding employers' organizations. (Recent prices and incomes legislation has, however, now brought the Government much more closely into this relationship.) Employers' associations are much occupied with presenting a united front to the unions and with the dissemination of information among their members. The motoring associations, from service to stranded motorists to the provision of legal aid, do much for the car-owner that is remote from the realm of political activity. In only part of their work, then, do these groups qualify for study here, and this bifurcation has led Maurice Duverger to describe them in *The Idea of Politics*[2] as 'partial'. The activities of the 'promotional' groups on the other hand are much more concerned with the political system – with influencing Governments to achieve their ends, whether they be the restoration of capital punishment, the legalization of abortion, reform of the penal system, or the preservation of rural England. There is little or no 'service' element involved here, but rather a singularity of purpose that Duverger has termed 'exclusive'.[3]

While the distinction between defensive and promotional, or between partial and exclusive groups is necessarily crude and, as already indicated, by no means absolute, it does permit of more detailed analysis of group roles than would otherwise be possible. The nature of a group – its membership, its objectives, at times the services it is able to render the Government – is an important determinant of which channels of influence will be most readily available to it, the degree to which it is accorded formal acceptance, the extent to which it must battle for recognition.

On the other side of the coin, the constitutional relationship between the legislative and the executive branches of Government, and the nature of the party system at work within a State, help to determine which avenues will provide the most fruitful opportunities for group action. For instance, in the United States, where the Constitution separates the executive from the legislature, and where neither the President nor the political parties

2. M. Duverger, *The Idea of Politics* (Methuen 1966) pp. 116–20.
3. ibid. pp. 116–20.

provide tight, overall policy direction and control, groups find their most potent pressure point in individual Congressmen. In Britain, on the other hand, subordination of the legislature to the executive, through the medium of party, focuses much group attention on the executive and the political parties to the neglect of the legislature.

With the notable exception of the trade unions and the co-operative movement, group influence on the political parties has not been accomplished through formal affiliation. Indeed, in the Conservative Party, there is no provision for corporate membership. Most groups choose to remain uncommitted, overtly at least, to any political cause, preferring to be free to negotiate across the political spectrum. Nevertheless, political partisanship does exist and many organizations can be seen to be 'politically orientated'. For instance, the Economic League, British United Industries, Aims of Industry and Common Cause are all committed to causes usually associated with the Conservative Party, and they receive financial support from large firms which also donate generously to that party.[4] Further, when one considers the Conservative orientation of businessmen, and their heavy representation among Conservative MPs and Peers, it is apparent that many trade associations and business organizations do feel themselves aligned with the Conservative rather than with the Labour Party.

By and large, however, the bulk of group activity is directed not at the political parties but at the administration, and there is considerable institutionalization of groups within the British governmental framework. In particular, the defensive or partial groups find ready access to the major channels of influence in the administrative corridors of Whitehall. As Government activity has extended into all sectors of society so there has developed a realization that, for effective administration, those directly affected should be consulted and, if possible, their consent and co-operation obtained. There is now a general acceptance of group representation in the administrative processes, which finds formal expression in the plethora of advisory committees that exist to provide vital links between the Government on the one hand and the various producers' groups – comprehending employers', employees', and professional associations – on the other. There are something like 500 effective central and national advisory committees on which producers' groups have representation.

4. See *The Times*, 9 Dec. 1968.

Many of these are of a very specialized or technical nature – Guttsman quotes the Committee on the Preservation of Wooden Vessels, and the Committee which advised on the licensing of Bulls and Boars[5] – but many have a much wider scope, being concerned with the general condition of industry, or with the problems of particular industries. For instance, the Economic Planning Board existed to advise the Government on the best use of the country's economic resources. While it did not in any sense direct or supervise the 'planning' of the economy. the Board was a major consultative committee through which senior officials were able to test outside reaction to possible policies at an early stage in their formation'.[6] A committee of narrower scope is the National Advisory Council for the Motor Manufacturing Industry, which is made up of three Governments representatives, seven representatives of the employers, appointed on the recommendation of the Society of Motor Manufacturers and Traders, two officials of the SMMT (ex officio), four trade union representatives nominated by and coming from the Amalgamated Engineering Union, the National Union of Vehicle Builders, and the Confederation of Shipbuilding and Engineering Unions, and one 'independent' member.[7] The terms of reference of the Council are 'to provide a means of regular consultation between the Government and the motor manufacturers on such matters as the location of industry, exports, imports, research, design and progress of the industry'.[8]

That these contacts are regarded as a necessary part of the political process is indicated by the formal provision made for them in certain statutes, as for instance in the 1947 Agriculture Act which obliges the Ministers to 'consult with such bodies of persons as appear to them to represent the interests of producers in the Agricultural Industry'.[9] Indeed, in the list of Advisory Committees in 1958 in the PEP study, more than a hundred had been set up under statutory authority. This concern for consultation was also highlighted by answers to a questionnaire circulated by the Select Committee on Delegated Legislation, 1952–53, which emphasized the extent to which various Ministries re-

5. W. L. Guttsman, *The British Political Elite* (MacGibbon & Kee 1963) p. 339.
6. PEP, *Advisory Committees in British Government* (Allen & Unwin 1960), p. 134.
7. S. H. Beer, *Modern British Politics* (Faber 1965) pp. 337–8.
8. Quoted ibid. pp. 338–9.
9. Quoted J. D. Stewart, *British Pressure Groups* (Oxford 1958), p. 7.

garded contacts with representative organizations as a normal part of their regulation-making process.[10] Attention was also drawn to this obligation to consult by Prime Minister Harold Wilson when he declared in a speech in the House of Commons in October 1966 that 'it is *our duty* to consult with the CBI, the TUC and others ...'.

The formal contacts are also supplemented by continuous interchanges of a more informal but still highly important nature. Thus phone calls, face to face encounters between public and private bureaucrats, lunches at the Athenaeum, where Beer reports that 'you can hardly hear yourself for the grinding of axes'.[11] all provide occasion for the exchange of information and for all efforts in persuasion.

There is involved here much more than the mere 'duty' of which Mr Wilson spoke. Necessity also enters into the picture. Governments are often in need of information from those they administer. Thus, as the Committee on Intermediaries stated in its report in 1950: 'collectively, one of these organizations knows far more of Government policy over a wide field than any individual can hope to attain to';[12] and as Blondel has pointed out, 'if firms and other interests were to starve the Civil Service of information the administration of the country would come to a halt'.[13] Again, many Government policies would fail, or prove at the least difficult to implement, without the active co-operation of certain groups. Doctors, by withdrawing from the National Health Service, could create chaos. The Government's agricultural policies need the assistance of the National Farmers' Union for their implementation. The motoring associations have for many years provided sign-posting and traffic-directing services that have greatly eased the burden on official agencies.

There is, then, a two-way traffic, with groups seeking consultation and access to the decision-taking and decision-executing processes, and with Governments seeking consultation and information for effective planning and administration. This is a mutual dependence recognized by Pendleton Herring as long ago as 1936, when he wrote that 'the greater the degree of detailed and technical control the Government seeks to exert over indus-

10. ibid. pp. 15–16.
11. Quoting an official of one of Britain's largest corporations, ibid. p. 339.
12. Quoted S. E. Finer, *Anonymous Empire* (Pall Mall 1958), p. 37.
13. J. Blondel, *Voters, Parties, and Leaders* (Pelican 1963), p. 225.

trial and commercial interests, the greater must be their degree of consent and active participation'.[14] Contacts between groups and Government are now so close that one writer has been led to comment that 'the intermixing between outsiders and the civil servants has now reached a point where the distinction between "administrative decisions" and "decisions taken by private individuals" is more and more difficult and more useless to make'.[15]

The fact that consultation takes place on a fairly regular basis does not imply that harmony will at all times prevail. Occasions are bound to arise when a group fails to achieve its objectives through the 'normal' channels, and it has to decide whether to accept the position or to press its case further through other available avenues, such as the legislature and the electorate. For instance, questions may be put in the House of Commons by Members associated with a group, or by others who welcome an opportunity to embarrass the Government. Public campaigns may be initiated with the aim of forcing the Government to reconsider its decision, under the threat of possible loss of electoral support. Strikes or boycotts may be threatened and implemented. All of these are accepted means whereby a group may hope to influence Government action, but all have limited value for the 'partial' groups in the British political context.

The various group interests have links, at times close, with Members of Parliament, as the volumes of *The Times* 'House of Commons' reveal. Such links may arise in two principal ways. First, a group may have one or more of its members or officers elected, through the medium of one of the major parties, as an MP. (The most obvious example of this is to be found in the numerous representatives of the trade unions sitting in the House of Commons.) Secondly, sitting Members may be approached and asked to take an interest in the affairs of the group. This relationship between Members and outside interests was referred to by Winston Churchill when he said: 'Everybody here has private interests: some are directors of companies, some own property. ... Then there are those people who come to represent particular bodies, particular groups of a non-political character and there again we must recognize that as one of the conditions of our varied life. We are not supposed to be an assembly of gentlemen

14. In *Public Administration and the Public Interest*, p. 192, quoted Beer, *Modern British Politics*, p. 321.
15. Blondel, *Voters, Parties, and Leaders*, p. 224.

who have no interests of any kind and no association of any kind. That might happen in heaven but not, happily, here.'[16] R. H. S. Crossman, in similar vein, wrote that 'a considerable number of MPs on both sides of the Commons act as the paid political agents of outside bodies – whether trade unions, churches, business companies or pressure groups – lobbying Ministers on their behalf and sometimes, when they rise to speak, reading aloud almost verbatim the brief they have received from the body which retains their services'.[17] Such a relation Crossman did not consider unethical so long as the connection was openly acknowledged and so long as the outside organization did not attempt to bring improper pressure to bear in order to influence the way a Member voted. On the other hand, James Callaghan, as Chancellor of the Exchequer in 1965, appeared to be concerned about these relations between MPs and outside interests when he said: 'When I look at some Members discussing the Finance Bill I do not think of them as the Hon. Member for X, Y or Z. I look at them and say "investment trusts", "capital speculators" or "that is the fellow who is the Stock Exchange man who makes a profit on gilt-edged". I have almost forgotten their constituencies, but I shall never forget their interests. I wonder sometimes whom they represent, the constituents' or their own or their friends' particular interests.'[18] Not surprisingly, exception was taken to Mr Callaghan's remarks and the matter was referred to the Committee on Privilege. The Committee held that it was generally recognized that MPs represented more than just their constituencies and consequently that no breach of Parliamentary privilege had been committed.

The influence of MPs as group spokesmen is, however, strictly limited. The dominance of party, and the tight control that the executive exerts over the legislature, ensure that on no important issue is it likely that a Government decision will be *successfully* challenged. Group links take second place to party loyalty, and should a clash arise between group interest and party interest the latter will, in most circumstances, prevail. Thus it is reported that when asked if 'he would vote for a Conservative or Liberal uni-

16. To the Committee of Privileges of the House of Commons 1947. Quoted Guttsman, *British Political Elite*, p. 319.
17. Quoted Beer, *Modern British Politics*, p. 24, n. 4.
18. See *The Times*, 7 July 1965. Callaghan was himself a spokesman for the police interests. It is also interesting that he ignored the Union connections of so many of the PLP.

lateralist if the Labour candidate in his constituency supported the Bomb', Michael Foot, a leading supporter of the Campaign for Nuclear Disarmament, replied 'certainly not'.[19] Such subordination of private belief to party loyalty entails that, unlike their American counterparts, British Members of Parliament cannot usually 'deliver their votes' to an individual cause. As members of a parliamentary party they usually have certain access to the leaders, the decision-takers of the party, that may ensure a hearing for the views of the groups they seek to represent. It is unlikely, however, that they will translate that representation into votes that run counter to declared party policy if such action would imperil the Government. (John Mackintosh has pointed out that when, in January 1968, a group of Labour Party backbenchers abstained on a motion of confidence in the Government, they were careful to keep the numbers down 'in order that the existence of the Government should not be endangered'.)[20] Indeed, it may also be the case that they do not always have even this access, and Mackintosh has cited the negotiations over the Annual Price Review as a case in point. 'During the two months when the critical decisions are being taken the Minister, as one holder of the office has put it, "goes into purdah". He virtually refuses to see any MPs, even from agricultural constituencies, in case it should bias his view or spoil his negotiations with the NFU.' During this period he must not appear to be listening to any '"extraneous influences",' but the '"Minister would be delighted to see [MPs] at any time in the year other than the two months when farm policy was being determined".'[21] In this particular instance we have, on the one hand, a demonstration of the limited role of MPs as group spokesmen, and, on the other, an illustration of the accepted place of a group in the policy-making processes. Interestingly, in spite of its own influence as a group well-entrenched in the Government's decision-making process, the Farmers' Union would appear to be suspicious of group activity. In July 1973 a move was afoot in the House of Commons to ban the export of live animals (on the grounds of the cruelty involved) and the NFU, which was opposed to such a move, immediately

19. C. Driver, *The Disarmers* (Hodder 1964), p. 70. We should note however, that Mr Enoch Powell, while a Conservative Member of Parliament, advocated support for a Labour Government if it were prepared to detach Britain from the Common Market.

20. Mackintosh, *British Cabinet*, p. 585.

21. See the *Westminster Bank Review*, May 1968, pp. 31–2, and *The Times*, 30 Nov. 1968.

upbraided the Commons for relying on evidence presented by pressure groups.)

This situation contrasts sharply with that in the United States, where a Congressman or Senator, free from party discipline as it is known in Britain, is in a position to dispose of his vote in the legislature according to his own judgment, and such freedom renders him a vital factor in group strategy. Groups appreciate that persuasion can be translated into direct action and Congressmen are, consequently, subject to much greater importuning than are Members of the House of Commons. It would appear that in Britain the large business organizations have come to realize that 'the House of Commons is no longer as necessary, nor indeed as useful, as its constitutional importance suggests that it should be',[22] and that the critical centres of power are to be found in the Civil Service.

Appeals to the 'grass roots' have not been an over-popular method employed by the 'partial' groups in Britain to augment their other channels of influence, and, indeed, resort to them may usually be taken to indicate a breakdown in the usual processes of negotiation. Nevertheless, from time to time nation-wide campaigns are mounted. Widespread use may be made of press and hoarding advertising; leaflets and stickers may be distributed, like those of the Road Hauliers' Association which exhorted the population to 'kill Transport Bill'; mass meetings and the lobbying of MPs may also be resorted to. Radio and TV are not directly available as propaganda media for groups, with the apparent long-standing exception of the relationship that exists between the National Farmers' Union and the never-ending soap opera, 'The Archers'. Time on the air cannot be purchased to present a case. However, a skilful group will direct its activities in such a way that it receives full, and free, publicity from news coverage or discussion-type programmes.

The value of these methods that seek to exert public pressure on Governments is open to doubt when matters of what might be deemed party political interest are involved, for in normal circumstances Governments are assured of their majorities in the House of Commons and can afford to stand by previous decisions. Indeed, it may be that in many cases public appeals have a disutility, so far as the groups are concerned, in that relations with the Government and the administration, through the 'normal channels', may thus be worsened.

22. Blondel, *Voters, Parties*, p. 217.

Most of the foregoing applies to the role of 'partial' groups in the Governmental process. The promotional, or 'exclusive', and the one-issue groups are not, by and large, so institutionalized and the emphasis they place upon the different access points to Government is perforce of a different order. Most are unable to rely upon a continuous exchange of ideas and information with Government departments, but are dependent upon their success in persuading the public and Members of Parliament of the merits of the cause they are promoting. The potential of these groups for securing action depends to a great extent upon the non-political nature of their aims. Thus, if their objectives are not of programmatic concern to the major parties they are unlikely to encounter a 'whipped' party reaction. Alternatively, in these days when more and more areas are being made the subject of party whipping, and when free votes are becoming more and more rare in the House of Commons, the path to success may, on occasions, lie in party adoption of group aims.

It is important to note here that while there is little competition among the partial groups for members – the occasional trade union demarcation dispute, the rivalry between the Automobile Association and the Royal Automobile Club come most readily to mind – many promotional or one-issue groups face opposition from groups advocating the contrary cause. For instance, those who seek the abolition of blood sports find themselves opposed by those who like to hunt, shoot, and fish: recent attempts to abolish live-hare coursing met with well-organized support for the 'sport'. The anti-capital punishment lobby has long been challenged by those who believe in the value of an 'ultimate deterrent', and now that it has been abolished there is much being done with the aim of securing its reintroduction.

The 'exclusive' and one-issue groups within British society have importance as a means whereby 'moral issues' receive a hearing and a public consideration that might otherwise be denied them (political parties tending to steer clear of 'controversial' matters that may lose them votes); as an avenue for special pleading; and as an outlet for the energies of those whom Professor Finer has described, rather unkindly, as 'little better than cranks and bores'.[23] Undoubtedly the most publicized of such groups in recent years has been the Campaign for Nuclear Disarmament. Founded in 1958 it represented the 'most spontaneous, virile, and sincere political movement' to be produced in Britain for many years

23. Finer, *Anonymous Empire*, p. 28.

Indeed, its extreme moralism, its crusading spirit, the mass rallies and the intensive lobbying, evoked memories of that great nineteenth-century crusade, the Anti-Corn Law League. Other groups, their activities less dramatic than those of the CND, have been responsible for significant social reforms, which in recent times have included the abolition of capital punishment, the reform of the law relating to homosexuality, and the changes in the abortion law. At other times, as with the proposal that the third London airport should be developed at Stanstead, Government threats to local amenities may be averted or delayed through the efforts of defensive ad hoc groups that spring into being over the particular issue and then disappear when the matter has been resolved. Finally, 'eccentrics', to soften Professor Finer's terminology, buzz around the fringes of Government activity, having little effect except to offer further demonstration of the all-embracing character of groups in Britain.

There is, then, a 'vast, untidy system of functional representation that has grown up alongside the older system of parliamentary representation'[24] – a system that has not escaped criticism. Critics claim that unfair advantages accrue to the large, the wealthy, and the easily-mobilized groups, and also that oligarchic tendencies at work within the group organizations render their leaders remote from and unrepresentative of the rank and file. Such criticism has a certain weight. Many trade unions and manufacturers' organizations, large, wealthy, and cohesive, have close, friendly, and continuing links with Government, while consumer, one-issue and promotional groups, generally small, poor and difficult to mobilize, are a much less integral part of the Governmental process. Further, the active membership of many groups is so small that policy determination has become largely a matter for paid officials who are subject to little check from the rank and file. Consequently, those who claim to speak for a group may be speaking mainly for themselves.

This dual criticism offers superficial justification for the claim that group practices tend to pervert the democratic processes. This is, however, to exaggerate their role and to ignore the very real safeguards that exist against such dangers.

First and foremost, of course, there is the check offered by the representative and responsible nature of British political life. Governments in Britain cannot easily shrug off responsibility for action or inaction. When they face the electorate they

24. Beer, *Modern British Politics*, p. 337.

do so with a record upon which judgment will be passed. Overt bias in policies, undue favour to one section of the community at the expense of another, involves electoral liabilities as well as assets which must be weighed carefully before decisions are taken. That access to Government and administration is easier for the larger, better organized groups is to be expected; for, as we have already observed, Governments need the information and the co-operation that they can provide. But having said this, it must be recognized that there is still an obligation upon Governments to seek out other, possibly conflicting viewpoints before action is taken. It is usually suggested that the Government has a special responsibility to the consumer interests as, *vis-à-vis* the producer groups, these are poorly-organized and inarticulate. However, the use of the blanket term 'consumer interests' tends to disguise the fact that most consumers are also either producers themselves or are related to producers. Thus, for many, what is lost on the consumer swings is largely recouped on the producer roundabout. Nevertheless, there still remain those who have little or no 'producer' interest and who must, therefore, look to the Government for protection.

In addition to the checks upon politicians occasioned by their responsibility to the electorate, there are the constraints upon the executive that arise from its responsibility to the legislature. Although, as we have seen, the increasing scope of Government activity has made it more and more difficult for Parliament to engage in close, detailed criticism of much of the work of Whitehall, the doctrine of Ministerial responsibility and the possibility of parliamentary enquiry, through questions, debates, or committees, provide a further check on Governments which might be prepared to yield to unjustified group demands.

Finally, there are the checks offered by the nature and role of party organization. Party leaders sift through the competing claims made upon them, accepting or rejecting in the light of party philosophies and political necessity. But their task is much more than that of mere brokerage. As Professor Beer has written: 'Where party government is as highly developed as in Britain . . . party does not merely aggregate the opinions of groups, it goes a long way towards creating those opinions by fixing the framework of public thinking about policy and the voters' sense of the alternatives and the possibilities'.[25] Indeed, it may well be that when parties or governments appear to respond to group pressures

25. Ibid. p. 347.

they are responding, as Beer suggests,[26] to demands which they 'have themselves framed and elicited'.

The allegation that too often group spokesmen are unrepresentative of an apathetic membership should also not be exaggerated. It is a fact of organizational life that control falls into the hands of activists who constitute but a small percentage of total membership. This does not necessarily mean, however, that group policies will be out of line with the wishes of the rank and file. Non-involvement by the majority may merely reflect satisfaction with the work of the leadership. Certainly it is unlikely that any serious divergence between leadership policies and membership interests would long be permitted to continue. In addition to the internal checks against abuses that exist, there is also an obligation on the part of Governments, of Civil Servants, and of Party leaders, to assure themselves of the credentials of those who claim to speak on behalf of a group.

Interest groups have been described as occupying the 'critical centres of power in the political process',[27] and while this may be an overstatement of their role they certainly do have an important part to play in keeping Governments and parties in touch with the electorate. As 'one of the great moving forces of politics', groups permit the dialogue between governors and governed to be a continuing process. Group membership permits the citizen greater expression of his interests and needs than does a blanket vote cast for one of the political parties. That some group spokesmen inadequately represent, or even mis-represent, the views of their members is in large part a function of the apathy of those who join a group and then leave policy formulation to a few activists and the group bureaucracy. That some sections of society are more amenable to organization than others, and find readier acceptance by Governments, is a fact of life in all political systems. The test of a representative system concerns the extent to which it affords protection to its weaker, less articulate parts.

Robert Lane has written that a defect of interest groups is that they 'tend to fractionate a person so that he cannot, through these narrower vehicles, find representation as a whole man'.[28] He regards this as a defect because, in the American political context, group activity is often seen as a substitute for party

26. Ibid. p. 347.
27. S. J. Eldersveld in 'American Interest Groups', a paper given to the International Political Science Association 1957.
28. Robert E. Lane, *Political Life* (Free Press 1964), p. 320.

activity. The absence of clear lines of political responsibility, the diffusion of power throughout the various parts of the federal system, the failure of political parties to draw together that which is separated by the Constitution, have left groups in possession of much of the field. The 'fractionated' man is in the ascendant at the expense of the 'whole man'. In such a system the strong have prospered at the expense of the weak.

In Britain, on the other hand, group activity is seen as complementary to party activity. The strong, centralized, two-party system makes for clear lines of responsibility and offers representation to the 'whole man'. At the same time, within this general context, groups provide myriad opportunities for the display of the many sides of the 'fractionated' citizen. Democratic government demands that both the 'whole' and the 'fractionated' man be served. So long, then, as the political parties, the bodies that are electorally responsible to the nation as a whole, can 'make up their minds and live up to their commitments',[29] and so long as they recognize their responsibilities towards minorities as well as towards majorities, group activity, far from being the serious problem that some would have it, becomes a necessary and important part of political life. Indeed, it is possible to argue that, like God, if groups did not exist they would have to be invented.

29. General Interim Report of the Buchanan Committee on Lobbying, 20 Oct. 1950 (pursuant to HR 298 of United States 81st Congress 1st Session) p. 66.

Part III

New Bottles

Chapter 8

Ad Hoc Agencies

In this chapter we move on from the regular Government departments, staffed by civil servants, to the less regular agencies, now so numerous, that are variously known as 'ad hoc' bodies and 'statutory authorities for special purposes'. These are characterized by specialization of function, varying degrees of autonomy, and whole or partial exemption from the normal processes of accountability to Parliament, through Ministers. The nationalized industries are the best-known examples, and on these we shall be concentrating most of our attention; but there are many others so variously constituted and so heterogeneous in purpose that one has the utmost difficulty in classifying them functionally or typologically. If they do not constitute what Dr Harold Seidman (speaking of analogous institutions in the USA) has called a 'headless fourth branch of government', they at least present us with a series of apparent constitutional anomalies.

Although most of the institutions with which we shall be dealing are comparatively recent creations, the ad hoc agency is not in itself a new phenomenon. There was a comparable sprawling of 'irregular' administrative, judicial and quasi-judicial institutions during two previous periods, the Tudor period and that of the Industrial Revolution, both of them characterized by deep and rapid social change (see Chapter 1, pp. 15, 24). The first crop, the prerogative 'courts' abolished by the Long Parliament, were irregular from the standpoint of the Common Law; the second, exemplified by Improvement Commissioners, Turnpike Trusts, Boards of Health, Poor Law Boards, etc. irregular *vis-à-vis* the stereotype of responsible departmental administration. Most of the latter were eventually absorbed by the regular departments or by newly-created local authorities, responsible to local electorates. The third, and present, crop is also irregular from this point of view, but the agencies concerned are so numerous and important that the adjective 'irregular' has ceased to be intelligibly applicable to them. Moreover, there is every indication that although their constitutional position and impact on current constitutional doctrines are still unsettled, they are unlikely to disappear, either by a process of withering away or by one of absorption.

In the 1930s, Sir Ivor Jennings drew attention in the following words to the importance of these so-called autonomous bodies in the British system of administration:

The administrative system has become far more complicated than is generally recognized. The simple dichotomy of central departments responsible to Parliament through ministers and local authorities responsible to a local electorate no longer exists. The twenty-four ministers are not leaders of columns which march behind them in regular ranks, for the columns now have outriders on their flanks and a relatively unorganized mass of camp followers trailing behind. . . . Equally false is it to assume that for every act that is done by a public authority someone is responsible to Parliament.[1]

Since then the situation has become steadily more complex, particularly during the post-war period. Through the proliferation of ad hoc agencies, the structure of the administrative system has departed further and further from the principles enunciated by the Haldane Committee in 1918, when it gave the comparatively few agencies of this kind then existing a cursory examination. Referring to these and to the new ones that the Government was proposing to establish, it wrote:

We are so far from thinking that the importance of a service to the community is prima facie a reason for making those who administer it immune from ordinary Parliamentary criticism, that we feel that all such proposals should be most carefully scrutinized, and that there should be no omission, in the case of any particular service, of those safeguards that Ministerial responsibility to Parliament alone provides.[2]

The Haldane Committee believed in tidy administration, grouped in ten main divisions, each under the control of a Minister or (in some cases) of several Ministers. Today, we have become convinced by experience that this kind of tidiness is impossible. The Committee also accepted the sufficiency of Ministerial responsibility as a means of ensuring the probity of the administration

1. W. Ivor Jennings: *Cabinet Government* (1st Edn, Cambridge 1936), p. 80.

2. 'Report of the Committee on the Machinery of Government', 1918, p. 11, para. 33. This recommendation was really a repetition of what had been said on the subject by the 'MacDonnell' Commission on the Civil Service (1912), which demanded the 'regularization' of recruitment to the Road Board and the Development Commission (two contemporary ad hoc agencies) and regarded 'with apprehension' the creation of 'any authority having large funds at its disposal which is outside effective ministerial control and parliamentary criticism'.

and its responsiveness to public opinion. Today, our acceptance of this panacea is bound to be more qualified. As for the 'importance to the community' of a service as the main alleged justification for its de-politicization, one may agree that this is insufficient – indeed, it is irrelevant; but there are now a whole number of *specific* reasons for the adoption of the ad hoc principle, only one of which, viz. the existence of 'certain functions of government which require for their exercise a judicial temper and a position of independence that cannot be maintained by a Minister who is constantly exposed to criticism in Parliament',[3] was mentioned by the Haldane Committee.

By the 1930s five major circumstances under which the adoption of 'semi-autonomous' forms of administration, non-responsible or only partly responsible to a Minister, might be justified were elucidated by Jennings. The first was the need to provide a service, of a cultural or personal kind, which might be seriously distorted or even corrupted by having to run the gamut of political responsibility. The examples he quoted were the British Broadcasting Corporation and the Unemployment Assistance Board. Secondly, there was the need to devise institutions which would enable producers to market their products in an organized way but with a minimum of political interference. Contemporary examples, then very much in the news, were the various Agricultural Marketing Boards, the Herring Industry Board and the Flour Millers' Corporation. Thirdly, there was the need to regulate professions, such as medicine and the law, by means of corporate bodies subject only to 'slight political supervision'. Fourthly there was the need to organize a number of 'technical services', such as those provided by the Crown Lands Commission, the Forestry Commission and the Central Electricity Board, which required 'little political control'. Fifthly, there was the desirability of 'de-politicizing', as far as possible, authorities of a quasi-judicial type, such as those set up 'to deal with wages, the licensing of transport undertakings, the determination of unemployment insurance benefit, unemployment assistance, war pensions, liability to national and local taxation, and so on.'[4]

3. Ibid. p. 11, para. 32. The reference was to what we now call 'administrative jurisidictions', which are dealt with in Chapter 11.

4. W. I. Jennings, *Cabinet Government* (1st Edn, 1936), pp. 75–6. Jennings actually distinguished four reasons, but listed five, unless his intention was to include the General Medical Council and the Potato Marketing Board in the same category.

Although these five major justifications continue both to apply and to overlap, the kind of autonomy which seemed so important in the 1930s no longer receives the degree of emphasis that Jennings places on it. Today, there is less stress on the relative absence of 'political interference', except in respect of authorities performing quasi-judicial functions (see below, Chapter 11), and more on the need for the use of administrative or managerial techniques allegedly difficult for the officials of a normal Government department to acquire and apply, because of their civil service status, their subjection to Treasury Control and their total answerability to Parliament through Ministerial chiefs. It is now recognized that the important thing is not to try to abolish political controls, but to use them selectively, in such a way that the operations of the so-called autonomous agency are kept in line with general Governmental strategy, without undue interference in the technical or 'day-to-day' aspects of its work. This distinction between general policy and day-to-day administration, as we shall see, has tended to dominate discussion – at least until very recently – about the role in the British system of government played by the nationalized industries, which hardly existed (except in the form of the London Passenger Transport Board, the Port of London Authority and the Central Electricity Board) at the time when Jennings was writing.

With the continued increase, since the 1930s, in the number, complexity and importance of these semi-autonomous bodies, the difficulty of reducing them to classificatory order, based upon the reasons for their creation, has also increased. While the nationalized industries represent the most important addition to the list (as measured by the number of people they employ, the extent of their financial resources, and their impact on the shape and growth of the national economy), it is constantly being lengthened by other ad hoc creations of the most varying kinds, both functionally and typologically.

To illustrate this, we will attempt a classification of the major ad hoc bodies (other than those of a judicial or purely advisory character) brought into existence since the beginning of the 1960s. A few of these are purely commercial in character, such as the National (now British) Steel Corporation, appointed to manage the nationalized steel firms, and the National Airports Authority (established by the Wilson government and wound up by the Heath Administration), which has been given the job of running the nationally-owned airports on business principles. To these may be added the five transport boards (viz. Railways, London Transport, Docks, Waterways and the Transport Holding Company) among which the responsibilities formerly discharged by the British Transport Commission have been divided by the Act of 1962.

A second group, while engaged in the performance of certain commercial functions, might most appropriately be classified as promotional. It includes the Industrial Reorganization Commission, which has been given the job of searching 'for opportunities to promote rationalization schemes which could yield substantial benefits to the national economy', and the General Practice Finance Corporation, which exists to facilitate the financing of premises and equipment used by National Health Service practitioners. Promotional bodies in other fields include the Industrial Training Boards and the three Research Councils (Science, Natural Environment and Social Science) created by the division and extension of the functions previously performed by the Department of Scientific and Industrial Research.

Of purely regulatory bodies, there are at least two new examples: the Air Transport Licensing Board (which issues licences to operators, both public and private, of airline routes) and the Boards for the Professions supplementary to Medicine (e.g. chiropodists, dieticians, medical laboratory technicians, occupational therapists, physiotherapists, radiographers and remedial gymnasts), co-ordinated by a Council.

Another series of new ad hoc bodies is concerned with what might be described as the distribution of uncovenanted social benefits. The most important of these is the Supplementary Benefits Commission, which, on the creation of the Ministry of Social Security, took over most of the functions of the former National Assistance Board. Rather more doubtfully to be included in the same category is the Criminal Injuries Compensation Board.

Others, some of them of great importance, perform a mixture of functions. The Land Commission, possessing wide powers to acquire, manage and dispose of land for development, might be described as commercial, promotional and regulatory. So might the River Authorities and the Commission for New Towns, which holds and manages the assets previously owned by discontinued New Town Development Corporations. The Independent Television Authority (now the Independent Broadcasting Authority) also combines commercial and regulatory responsibilities.

To these one should add bodies which, while formally of advisory status, in fact perform important regulatory functions, sometimes by dint of the conciliatory procedures they operate (e.g. Race Relations Board), sometimes, as in the case of the Prices and Incomes Board, by virtue of the fact that the Government will normally act on their advice. At the time of writing two further bodies of a similar character, both concerned with industrial relations, are about to be created.

The relations between these heterogeneous institutions and their 'relevant' Ministries vary according to constituting legislation and developing conventions. There is nothing that can be described as a 'system'. New agencies have been created, without much advance planning, as new needs, allegedly or apparently unsuitable for provision by normal administrative departments, have made themselves evident.

There is nothing inherently unhealthy about this development of a complex network of boards, commissions and authorities. If, according to contemporary criteria, adequate standards of efficiency are achieved, if the consumer or client receives civilized treatment and reasonable satisfaction of his needs, and if ultimate democratic responsibility is safeguarded, and operations are openly conducted and subjected to external disciplines designed to prevent abuses and injustices, it is of no importance that the overall structure has an untidy appearance. But can one say that these desiderata are being properly satisfied? The means of satisfying some of them (e.g. the prevention of abuses and injustices) will be discussed in a later chapter. As for the others, there is neither sufficient time nor adequate information to deal with them here, even in a general way. What is clear, however, is that the role and rationale of ad hoc agencies will have to be given close and continuous attention by the persons conducting the enquiries into the machinery of government that now seem to be contemplated. To that extent, the remarks of the Haldane Committee about the need for 'careful scrutiny' are as valid as when they were originally published.

We here select for special examination one more-or-less coherent group of ad hoc agencies – the nationalized industries. The reason for this selection is threefold. First, all the agencies that come within the scope of this expression are charged with commercial or at least technical services; secondly their role in the British system of public administration has been thoroughly and on the whole productively discussed; and thirdly, the contribution that they make to the national economy is of very great importance. That importance is adequately illustrated by the facts that the annual investment of the nationalized industries is equal to that of the whole of private manufacturing industry, and that they account for 11 per cent of the gross domestic product and 8 per cent of total employment. 'When the Government's proposals for further nationalization of the docks are implemented,' said the White Paper of November 1967, the nationalized industries 'will provide most of the economy's basic needs for energy, transport, communications, steel and export facilities; and the efficiency with which so large a sector operates will have a significant impact on the evolution and rate of growth of the whole economy'.[5]

The desirable extent of nationalization is still of course a controversial subject, though considerably less so than at one time; while both the performance of the nationalized industries and their internal organization are still continuously and sometimes acrimoniously discussed in the newspapers and other organs of public opinion. These matters are of no concern to us here, except peripherally to our main discussion, which is about the way Britain has attempted and is still attempting to fit the nationalized industries into its politico-administrative system, by a process of two-way adjustment.

The major problem in this field is a familiar one – how to give the nationalized industries adequate commercial freedom, yet simultaneously to maintain those forms of public control necessary to ensure that they follow the Government's overall economic strategy and social objectives. The ideal aimed at was classically expressed by President Roosevelt when he opened the Tennessee Valley Authority, which he described as 'clothed with the power of government, but possessed of the initiative and flexibility of private enterprise'. Taken literally, this is an unattainable ideal. The attempt to get as near to it as possible has taken the form of a series of shifting compromises of which we have certainly not yet seen the end.

Most of Britain's present nationalized industries date from the period 1946–50, when the third Labour Government was in power; but the form of nationalization then adopted, the public corporation, dates from the inter-war period, when Conservative, or predominantly Conservative, Governments set up the British

5. 'Nationalised Industries, A Review of Economic and Financial Obectives.' Cmnd 3437, p. 4, para. 5.

Broadcasting Corporation, the Central Electricity Board, the London Passenger Transport Board and British Imperial Airways. Indeed, the origins of the public corporation in Britain can be traced back even further – at least to the creation of the Port of London Authority (1908) which displays many of the features of the public corporation which are now so familiar.

The aim of the public corporation is to provide an organizational form through which the reconciliation of commercial freedom with public control may best be facilitated. It is strongly associated with the name of Herbert Morrison, Minister of Transport in the Labour Government of 1929–31 and later Lord Morrison of Lambeth, who drafted the legislation under which the London Passenger Transport Board was created by the Government that followed. In his *Socialism and Transport* (1933) he developed a theory of the public corporation still accepted in its broad outlines by those whose views on public enterprise might be described as orthodox; it was Morrison, too, who converted the Labour Party to the public corporation as a vehicle for its nationalization programme. (Previously the party had thought of nationalization in terms of setting up new Government departments on the Post Office model, modified only to the extent necessary to ensure a measure of workers' participation at the various levels of management.)

The major characteristics of the public corporation are as follows:

(a) it is wholly owned by the state, even though it may raise all or some of its capital by the issue of bonds to the public;

(b) it is created by special law and is not subject – except to such extent as may be prescribed – to the ordinary company law;

(c) it is a body corporate, i.e. a separate legal entity which can sue and be sued, enter into contracts, and acquire property in its own name;

(d) it is independently financed, obtaining its funds by borrowing, either from the Treasury or from the public, and deriving its revenues from the sale of its goods and services;

(e) it is exempt from the forms of parliamentary financial control applicable to government departments;

(f) its employees are not civil servants and are recruited and remunerated on terms and conditions that the corporation itself determines.[6]

6. A. H. Hanson, *Nationalisation* (Allen & Unwin 1963), p. 13.

It is obvious that the emphasis in this characterization is on the immunities enjoyed by the corporation, which are intended to give it a business flexibility denied to the normal Government department. The general Government control within the framework of which these immunities are supposed to exist is ensured by conferring statutory powers on the relevant Minister. It is he who appoints the board of the corporation and, within whatever statutory limitations may be prescribed, determines its conditions of service. It is the Minister whose approval is required for the corporation's capital investment programmes and proposals for research, training and education. It is he, together with the Chancellor of the Exchequer, who has to sanction the raising of capital finance from external sources (e.g. the Treasury or the public), who prescribes the corporation's form of accounts and appoints qualified commercial auditors to report on them annually. The Minister, moreover, can require the Board to provide him with any information he may wish to have. Perhaps most important of all, he is empowered, after consultation with the board, to give it any 'directions of a general character as to the exercise of performance by the Board of their functions in relation to matters appearing to the Minister to affect the public interest'. These are the powers that the Minister exercises over most of the nationalized industries today. It should be noted that they are considerably more extensive than the powers granted to him by the inter-war nationalization statutes.

The 'general directions' clause, which has been the subject of so much dispute, was intended by the Labour Government that introduced it as a kind of holdall to provide sanction for any policy interventions by the Government that could not be covered by the more specific powers contained in the statute. Its inclusion in the post-war nationalization legislation was the product of two main factors: the great importance of the post-war nationalized industries in the development of the British economy; and the belief – strong, if not very effectively implemented – of the Labour Government in economic planning. However, only on one or two occasions has it ever been used for any important purpose; since the Minister, by virtue of his *appointing* powers, can ensure through informal methods that, in the last resort, the Government's views about the way in which a nationalized industry should behave shall prevail.

The quality, qualifications and experience of board members, and particularly those of the chairman, are obviously of key importance. The appointment of members and chairmen in fact can be regarded as the most vital of the Minister's powers. In making appointments he has an almost entirely free hand, the relevant statutes laying down only the most general of rules to guide him. Apart from the universal provision that Members of Parliament and Ministers themselves shall be excluded from board membership, the kind of statutory guidance provided is typified by the clause in the Gas Act of 1948 which provides that members of the Area Gas Boards shall be

> appointed by the Minister from among persons appearing to him to be qualified as having had experience of, and shown capacity in gas supply, local government, industrial, commercial or financial matters, applied science, administration or the organization of workers.

The general aim, both statutory and ministerial, is to provide the industry with the best possible collective leadership and not, as in the case of comparable boards in certain other countries, to secure the representation of certain interests, such as those of workers and consumers. In the British nationalized industries workers and consumers are allowed a consultative voice only, through joint consultative machinery and consumers' councils, both statutorily prescribed.

The number of board members varies from one nationalized industry to another, without much rhyme or reason. At present the Coal Board has twelve members, while the Electricity Generating Board, with a broadly comparable range of responsibilities, has only nine. Usually the Minister may vary the number of appointees within certain limits, which in some cases are very wide indeed. Membership of the British Steel Corporation, for instance, may vary from eight to twenty-one and that of the British Railways Board from eleven to nineteen. Remuneration of board members tends to vary with their responsibilities, but in general is smaller than that for similar appointments on boards of private industries comparable in size – a feature of the present pattern of nationalization which has evoked criticism on the grounds that it tends to deny to the nationalized industries their fair share of talent at the top level.

All boards contain part-time as well as full-time members. The balance between the two varies according to the way in which a particular board is organized. The reason, for instance, why the Coal Board has six full-time members (in addition to a full-time

Chairman and Deputy Chairman) and only four part-time members is that the 'functional' principle of board organization has here been strongly emphasized. Each of the six full-timers exercises general supervision over some aspect of the organization's work. In British European Airways (now merged with BOAC as British Airways), which had only three full-timers in addition to the Chairman but up to seven part-timers (including the Deputy Chairman), the functional principle was adopted only to the extent of appointing to board membership three heads of departments. The reason why the Transport Holding Company has only one full-timer (the Deputy Chairman and Managing Director) is that the Company's work lies mainly in the control of its subsidiaries, which are the main operational units. In all cases the function of the part-timer is not to manage or even supervise the management of any division of a board's organization, or any aspect of its work, but to bring to bear his knowledge and experience on the major problems with which the enterprise is confronted.

Internal organization varies even more widely. In some cases the broad layout of the industry is determined by statute. Responsibility for the Electricity Supply Industry, for instance, is divided between a Generating Board, twelve Area Boards with distributary functions, and an Electricity Council with co-ordinating and common service responsibilities. Members of the Generating Board and of Area Boards are all appointed directly by the Minister of Power, who also directly appoints six members of the Electricity Council (including the Chairman and the two Deputy Chairmen), the others being three members of the Generating Board and the twelve chairmen of the Area Boards. In the coal industry, on the other hand, the Minister appoints only the members of the National Coal Board, which is statutorily free to devise its own 'lower level' organization, which consisted until very recently of divisions, areas, groups and collieries. With the progress of nationalization, however, the general tendency has been for the statutes to become organizationally more specific, perhaps partly due to the fact that the somewhat uncertain debut of the nationalized coal industry created widespread criticism of the conferment of generalized responsibility on a central board. The tendency towards increasing statutory specificity may be illustrated by the break-up of the former Transport Commission through the formation of entirely independent statutory boards for railways, docks, waterways, London Transport, and for the miscellaneous undertakings gathered together under the Transport Holding Company.[7]

The two specific problems of the nationalized industries here to be examined are, first, the balance between autonomy and control, and the nature of the ever-changing relationship between the relevant Minister and the boards under his supervision; and secondly, the role of Parliament *vis-à-vis* the industries, in the light of the degree of Ministerial responsibility prescribed by statute and the amount of control exercised by the Minister de facto. The reason for this concentration is that these are the two features of greatest interest to students of British government as distinct from students concerned with the more economic aspects of the nationalized industries.

As we have already remarked, in pre-war days there was no granting of generalized Ministerial powers. What the Minister could and could not do was then clearly specified, although necessarily varying with the nature of the undertaking concerned. According to the views then prevailing, the main task of the Government was to find a number of people with suitable industrial and commercial experience to man the board, and then let them 'get on with the job' with the minimum of interference on the part of those whom Mr Frank Pick, formerly Vice-Chairman of the London Passenger Transport Board, rather rudely described as 'inquisitive and irresponsible guardians of the public interest'. Public enterprises in fact were regarded as purely business concerns which, for specific reasons, had to be brought – unfortunately from the standpoint of most Conservatives – into what is now described as the 'public sector'. The desire for depoliticization expressed itself in one instance (that of the London Passenger Transport Board) in the extreme form of refusing to the Minister powers of appointment, which were placed in the hands of a miscellaneous collection of 'appointing trustees'.

As might be expected, the Labour Party, when it first got the opportunity to put its nationalization policies into effect, showed

7. The fluctuations in transport organization, however, cannot be said to follow a particularly rational pattern. By the 1947 Act the Transport Commission acted through a series of separately appointed 'Executives' for Railways, Docks and Inland Waterways, Road Transport, London Transport and Hotels. By the Transport Act of 1953, these Executives were abolished except for London Transport. The latest Transport Act of 1962 in effect restores the Executives (although not the same ones) and abolishes the Commission. Co-ordination is now provided, if at all, at the ministerial level.

less confidence in the inherent wisdom and capacity of business men. The social as distinct from the purely commercial responsibilities of the nationalized industry tended to be emphasized; indeed the industry was even given a statutory obligation to 'serve the public interest in all respects.' Moreover, the need for rapid economic reconstruction, in which the newly-nationalized industries would obviously have to play a key role, together with the commitment of the Labour Party to economic planning, were incompatible with the conferment of a degree of 'autonomy' such as the pre-war nationalized industries had enjoyed. Consequently there were more extensive grants of Ministerial powers, and an attempt was made to distinguish the functions of the Minister from those of the board by way of conferring on the former responsibility for 'general policy' and on the latter responsibility for 'day-to-day administration'. This distinction, however, was never very successful, partly because the respective responsibilities could not be clearly defined, but mainly because so close and so informal a day-to-day contact developed between the Ministers and 'their' Boards that it became impossible to say at which of the two levels any particular decision had been taken. As we shall see, consequent blurring of the dividing line between Ministerial responsibility and board autonomy caused great dissatisfaction, particularly among Members of Parliament.

With the advent to power of the Conservative Government in 1951 some attempt was made to sort out this confusion. The distinction between day-to-day matters and policy matters tended to be replaced by one between 'purely commercial' considerations and those involving the 'public interest'. This view, which became the new orthodoxy of the 1950s, was most clearly expressed by the Herbert Report on the Electricity Supply Industry, which held that the nationalized industry could best make its contribution to the development of the economy by pursuing its own self-interest as a commercial concern. If it was to act non-commercially in any particular matter, it should do so only at the specific behest of the responsible Minister, who would give the industry 'precise instructions' as to what it was required to do

> The less the principle of commercial operation is invaded the better it will be for the efficiency of the industry [wrote the Committee]. Taking the long view, we believe this to be of the greatest importance to the success of nationalization, but it must be recognized that unless Parliament and Government are prepared to deny themselves the power always and in every particular to require the industry to act purely on

economic considerations, the Minister must be armed with the necessary authority. We would, however, urge that the lines of demarcation between the industry and the Minister should be clear. There should be no doubt as to where the responsibility lies, when the industry is acting on other than purely economic considerations.[8]

It must be admitted, however, that little more than lip-service was given to these principles, which were hardly less ambiguous than the previous ones. There was indeed an almost insuperable difficulty in defining the 'principles of commercial operation' for industries which were not subject to the normal commercial incentives, which obtained their capital (either directly or by way of permission to issue stock) from the Government, which enjoyed some degree of monopoly (although in all cases a diminishing one), whose operations affected the whole of the national economy and whose social obligations existed in close interpenetration with their purely economic ones.

The already established relationship between the Minister and the board therefore underwent little change. The Government could not give up the attempt to formulate and apply, in collaboration with the industries concerned, a coherent fuel policy or transport policy; nor could it cease to take an active and continuous interest in the administration and management of British Railways or the National Coal Board, both of which, for different reasons, were undergoing financial and organizational crises. Moreover it chose in two important matters deliberately to flout certain specific recommendations of the Herbert Report. Without any specific statutory authority it persistently 'influenced' the pricing decisions of certain nationalized industries, particularly the National Coal Board and Transport Commission, and in 1956 it decided that all the nationalized industries should raise their capital from the Exchequer and not from the public by way of the issue of fixed interest bonds. (Previously, with the exception of the NCB, the industries had been authorized to issue stock and the Herbert Committee recommended that the Electricity Supply Industry, at least, should be required to 'fight for its capital by going to the market'.[9]) Ministers responsible for the nationalized industries also firmly resisted the demands voiced by the Select Committee on Nationalized Industries (see below, p. 185) that the informal or 'dinner-table' relationships that had developed

8. 'Report of the Committee of Enquiry into the Electricity Supply Industry', Jan. 1956. Cmnd 9672, para. 497.

9. Ibid. para. 345.

between Minister and board should be replaced by more formal ones.

By the early 1960s, therefore, it was clear that neither the dichotomy of 'general policy' and 'day-to-day' nor the distinction between 'commercial' and 'non-commercial' considerations offered any adequate guide to the division of powers. There could be no doubt that the nationalized industries, as instruments for the implementation of public economic policies, could not be allowed to possess the large measure of autonomy that many had claimed for them. The important thing was that the public policies applicable to them should from time to time be clearly defined by the Government, so that the industries could receive a degree of managerial freedom that was genuine precisely because the long and medium-term objectives they were required to pursue and the limitations within which they were required to operate had been clearly specified in advance.

The first attempt to define a relationship of this type in general terms was made by the White Paper entitled *Financial and Economic Obligations of the Nationalized Industries*[10] in April 1961.

> The Nationalized Industries [said this document] cannot . . . be regarded only as very large commercial concerns which may be judged mainly on their commercial results; all have, although in varying degrees, wider obligations than commercial concerns in the private sector.

The statutory provision requiring them to balance their current accounts 'taking one year with another' (which had been included in most of the nationalization acts) was given the precision of a five-year period, during the course of which each industry would be required to make a contribution out of profits towards its own capital investment. The industry was to be given a target expressed as a rate of return on its total assets, taking into consideration the social obligations it was required to fulfil as well as its expected performance as a commercial concern. By such methods it was hoped to improve the 'performance and morale' of the nationalized industries, to 'reduce the occasion and need for outside intervention' in their affairs and 'enable them to make the maximum contribution to their own development and the wellbeing of the community as a whole'.[11] Accordingly targets were set for a series of five-year periods. The Electricity Boards, for instance, were expected to produce an average return of 12.4 per cent gross

10. Cmnd 1337.
11. Ibid. para. 33.

for the period 1962–63 to 1966–67; the Gas Boards an average of 10.2 per cent gross over the same period; the British Overseas Airways Corporation, 12.5 per cent net for the period 1966–67 to 1969–70; British European Airways, 6 per cent net for the period 1963–64 to 1967–68. The Coal Board was required 'to break even after interest and depreciation, including £10 million a year to cover the difference between depreciation at historic cost and replacement cost'; the Railways Board was given, by statute and without much confidence, the obligation of reducing its deficit and breaking even as soon as possible. These targets may have been crude and generalized, but they facilitated a more rational relationship between Minister and enterprise. A much more refined attempt at 'targeting' (the results of which cannot as yet be judged) was made by a further White Paper entitled *Nationalized Industries, a review of Economic and Financial Objectives*, issued in November 1967.[12] Generalized financial targets were retained as a 'convenient rule of thumb for management';[13] but each target was henceforward to be based on pricing and investment policies worked out according to much more sophisticated criteria than those habitually used in the past. 'Discounted cash flow techniques' (employing an 8 per cent rate of discount) were to be used to determine *prima facie* whether the new investments proposed by the industry would justify their initial cost, while pricing policy was to be related to the concept of marginal cost, both short-term and long-term.

These changes brought the Minister and the industry nearer together rather than pushing them further apart, Contact between the two has been intensified rather than diminished, despite the government statement that it did not intend 'to interfere in the day-to-day management of the industries'.[14] For, as the White Paper itself said, 'the whole system of financial objectives within which the industries operate is a very flexible instrument'.[15] changes in economic circumstances, the development of new social objectives and a whole number of other factors demand that the targets should be kept under continuous review. (Thus, in its efforts to deal with the deteriorating economic situation of the early 1970s, the Conservative Government interfered directly with the pricing policies of the various industries, holding in-

12. Cmnd 3437.
13. *The Times*, 3 Nov. 1967.
14. Cmnd 3437, para. 38.
15. Ibid. para. 24.

creases to levels much below those that had been sought.) Consequently, even if one eliminates all considerations other than the formulation and application of targets, consultation between board and ministers is not likely to be any less continuous than in the past. However, it is hoped that a closer definition of the points at which the Government may (and indeed must) intervene and the development of more sophisticated techniques for the formulation of objectives may render the Minister–Board relationship more fruitful and reduce interference in the pejorative sense (i.e. of the kind that reduces management's independent responsibility for the achievement of specific results) to a minimum.

All this means that the whole question of the extent of the Minister's *constitutional* responsibility for the nationalized industries has been given an imperfect answer. Such imperfection is probably in the nature of things, but its existence raises issues which have been vigorously discussed and which cannot even now be regarded as settled. Perhaps the most important of these is the degree and kind of parliamentary responsibility for the nationalized industries, a subject which is being debated almost as actively today as it was during the early days of nationalization.

During the post war period there have been at least in theory wide opportunities for the exercise of what is sometimes misnamed parliamentary 'control'. If it wishes to do so the House of Commons can debate the annual reports and accounts of a nationalized industry when they are laid on the table by the responsible Minister. It also has opportunities for discussion on supply days or when new legislation relating to a nationalized industry is presented to it, or on the fairly regular occasions when the Minister comes forward with a proposal to raise the limits on the industry's borrowing powers and on a variety of other occasions. Questions can be put to the Minister about the exercise (or non-exercise) of his statutory responsibilities and if the Member who has asked such a question finds the Minister's reply unsatisfactory, he can give notice that he will raise the matter on the Adjournment and hence, if he is lucky in the ballot or selected by the Speaker, can initiate a half-hour's debate on whatever grievance has been brought to his attention or whatever anomaly he claims to have discovered. In practice, however, owing to the limitations on parliamentary time, the affairs of a nationalized industry rarely receive a very thorough parliamentary discussion, except on occasions when (as a result, possibly, of a strike, or a report revealing heavy losses) the industry concerned happens to have hit the headlines. On Questions there are certain limitations arising from the (theoretically) limited scope of Ministerial responsibility.

It was over Questions that Members first began to express their lack of ease about Parliament's role *vis-à-vis* the nationalized industries. No sooner had the coal industry been nationalized in 1946 than it began to be obvious that the Minister was *de facto* exercising more responsibility than he was prepared to acknowledge at Question Time. The rejection of Questions of certain types (i.e. relating to so-called day-to-day matters), first by the Minister himself and then, on the basis of precedent, by the Clerks at the Table, caused widespread frustration among backbenchers. This was not entirely removed by the Speaker's ruling (June 1948) somewhat extending the scope of matters about which Questions could be asked, nor cimcumvented by the ingenuity of Members in framing Questions about 'day to day' matters in ways that made it difficult for the Minister to disclaim responsibility. Such frustration, however, is much less evident today than in the early days of nationalization, and Members have realized that, in any case, the Question is rather a blunt instrument and that they need better ways of informing themselves about the affairs of the nationalized industries which arouse their concern, so that such control as they are able to exert through the Minister shall be more meaningful.

The provision of greater opportunities for parliamentary 'inquisitiveness', demanded by backbenchers on both sides of the House at first encountered strong ministerial resistance. Such proposals were regarded by the Labour Government, and by Herbert Morrison in particular, as incompatible with the autonomy which the nationalization statutes had affected to confer on the industries, and as inevitably bringing in their train an unwarrantable extension of ministerial responsibility. The Conservative Governments after 1951, however, proved more sympathetic towards the backbenchers' views and in 1955 a Select Committee on Nationalized Industries was established, at first with terms of reference so narrow as to be virtually unworkable, but in the following year with terms wide enough to encompass almost any kind of enquiry which its members might wish to pursue. The new Committee in fact was authorized 'to examine the Reports and Accounts of the Nationalized Industries established by

Statute, whose controlling Boards are appointed by Ministers of the Crown and whose annual receipts are not wholly or mainly derived from monies provided by Parliament or advance from the Exchequer'. Since 1956 the Committee has been in continuous existence and has had its terms of reference widened to enable it to investigate the Post Office, certain government-owned companies, and some of the Bank of England's responsibilities, as well as the statutory corporations.

Although the demand that it should be equipped with an expert investigator similar in status to the Controller and Auditor General was rejected, the Select Committee, with the help of the House of Commons Clerks attached to it (supplemented, more recently, by that of temporarily-employed 'experts'), has succeeded in making a series of remarkably informative and thorough reports on the nationalized industries, useful to interested Members of the House, invaluable to students of nationalization, and generally recognized by the industries themselves as constructively critical. Indeed, against all expectations the new body has proved an effective defender of the industries against ill-informed attacks, and a firm advocate of greater clarity and formality in the allocation of responsibilities between Minister and board. It cannot be said to have been responsible for taking some of the political sting out of debates about the nationalized industries, but it has certainly been influential in raising the discussion of outstanding and current issues, both inside Parliament and outside, to a new and higher level.

Until comparatively recently the Committee investigated the nationalized industries one by one, concentrating on those questions most likely to be of interest and concern to members of Parliament, in the light of their ultimate responsibility for questions of policy, finance and organizational efficiency. In 1968, however, it produced a massive 'across the board' document on the subject of ministerial control, the product of a prolonged and thorough investigation.

With the widening of its terms of reference and the increase in the scope and depth of its enquiries, it now has a strong case for demanding expert assistance on a scale not yet made available to it. Indeed, the whole question of equipping both the Committee and the Government with some type of efficiency-auditing agency comparable with the *Commission de Vérification* in France is acquiring a new urgency.

The short-lived Prices and Incomes Board, set up under the

Wilson Government, was given the machinery to examine the organization and performance of the Nationalized Industries as a consequence of the power it received to advise the Government on any price-raising proposals made by them. But there was considerable doubt, shared by the Select Committee on Nationalized Industries itself, whether the PIB was the right body to conduct such an examination. In its Report on 'Ministerial Control of the Nationalized Industries', the Committee made a rather surprising proposal for the establishment of a Ministry of Nationalized Industries, many of whose functions would be comparable with those performed by the *Commission* in France, i.e. 'general oversight of the structure and organization of the industries with regard to their efficiency including the spread of new management techniques (e.g. critical path analyses, comterization and the use of efficiency study units)' and the 'undertaking or making arrangements for efficiency studies'.[16] Whatever decision is eventually taken on this matter, it seems likely that the Select Committee, which has developed a considerable reputation for impartiality and competence, will continue to improve the quality of its investigations.

With the policies announced by the two White Papers and the successful establishment of the Select Committee, much of the bitterness was removed from the continuing controversy about the delimitation of ministerial powers and the provision of adequate parliamentary 'control'. But while bitterness may have been reduced controversy has certainly not vanished as is demonstrated by the clashes between the British Steel Corporation and the Department of Trade and Industry, brought to light by the 1st. report of the Select Committee on Nationalized Industries for the Session 1972–73. The poor state of relations between the Corporation and the Department led the Committee to raise once more the question of how far Ministers should go in exercising general supervision over State-owned enterprises. 'Outside' interference in market appraisal (surely well within the sphere of Corporation responsibility) and in the fixing of prices (five times in less than six years) had led to a situation in which Lord Melchett, late chairman of the board of BSC, had suggested that, having been appointed to manage, he and his board should be allowed normal managerial freedom or be replaced. While Lord Melchett's demand for freedom could not be accepted in full, for fairly

16. First Report from the Select Committee on Nationalized Industries, Session 1967–68. Vol. 1, pp. 193–4.

obvious economic and political reasons, the Select Committee did suggest there was room for a much greater sense of partnership to be developed than had prevailed in the past.[17] As it wrote: 'perpetual interference, even if accompanied by reductions in debt and compensation, must reduce the morale of the Corporation in its competitive environment. Nevertheless, institutional innovation and the development of new conventions have gone a long way towards fitting those awkward bodies, the nationalized industries, more comfortably into the British politico-administrative system. There are those, including the authors of this book, who hold that the situation has been reached where limitations on ministerial responsibility and consequently on legitimate parliamentary interest might well be dispensed with; others, at present a majority, hold that so radical an innovation would destroy the valuable distinctiveness of the public corporation as a form of organization. It seems likely, however, that although these old controversies will continue, they will become less acute than certain new ones arising from more recent forms of government intervention in the economy by way of ownership and control of industrial and commercial assets. It is to such problems that we finally turn.

There are three ways in which the Government may exercise rights of ownership. One of them, departmentalization, may be regarded as obsolete, although the Ministry of Defence still runs industrial establishments such as the Royal Ordnance Factories and the Admiralty Dockyards. The classical example of a departmentally-run enterprise, the Post Office, acquired many of the characteristics of a public corporation and has now been formally transformed into one. The second vehicle for nationalization, the public corporation itself, has proved a valuable institution and is likely to remain the form of organization regarded as most suitable for the major industries nationalized during the immediate post-war period. A third possible method, the creation of a limited liability company in which the Government has an interest, total or partial, has so far been much less widely used in Britain than in many other countries; but may well become a prominent feature of the industrial and commercial landscape during the last quarter of the twentieth century, particularly if the Labour Party or another party of radical complexion enjoys substantial periods of office.

17. The fact that during the six years of Lord Melchett's chairmanship there had been five Ministers cannot have helped relations.

Already there are more examples of state shareholding than the general public realizes. The British Government participates, for instance, in the British Petroleum Co., the British Sugar Corporation and in the engineering firm of Short Bros. and Harland. In Cable and Wireless Ltd, nationalized in 1946, it is the sole shareholder. A possibly more significant development, however, is the use of public corporation itself as an agency for the control of a number of nationalized or partly nationalized undertakings, each of which maintains its separate identity. Thus the Transport Holding Company (now superseded in respect of its major functions, by the National Freight Corporation) exercised supervision over no fewer than 156 subsidiaries, including Pickfords, Thos. Cook & Son Ltd, Scottish Bus and the 'Tilling' group. The Coal Board itself has a large number both of wholly-owned and partly-owned subsidiaries engaged in activities as various as brick-making, boiler manufacturing, the production of ventilation equipment, tar distillation, search for natural gas, the manufacture of central heating and building materials, pre-cast concrete products and chemicals, the proofing of timber against rot and fire and the promotion of district heating.[18] BOAC[19] has participations, varying from 10 per cent to 100 per cent and managed by a body known as BOAC Associated Companies Ltd, in nine foreign airways undertakings. It also participates directly in the Beaufort Catering Co. Ltd (100 per cent), International Aeradio Ltd (66 per cent) and the Airways Housing Trust Ltd (67 per cent). More significantly still, it has joined with the famous private shipping line to form the company known as BOAC-Cunard Ltd, in which it has an investment of £19,600,000. The Gas Council, too, is associated with a private partnership, known as the Amoco Group, for the exploitation of the natural gas resources of the North Sea. The creation of subsidiary companies either wholly or partly owned by public corporations is therefore by no means unknown in Britain; neither is the association of public corporations with private partners in joint ventures. However, the highly miscellaneous assets of which examples are given above have been acquired at various times for various pur-

18. The Heath Government sought to disencumber itself of some of these enterprises by selling them off to the public. Among the most well-known of those disposed of were Thomas Cook & Son and the State-owned public houses of Carlisle and Gretna.

19. As mentioned above, now in association with BEA as British Airways.

poses, and without the benefit of any consistent plan or 'philosophy'. All one can say is that the public sector has become less tidy in structure and more flexible in organization than at the time when the great post-war nationalizations were being made.

Two developments in the 1960s suggested that the device of state shareholding, direct or indirect, complete or partial, might become more widely used. The first was the establishment of the Industrial Reorganization Corporation, with a capital of £200 million and the duty of seeking opportunities to promote industrial rationalization schemes which could yield substantial benefits to the national economy. This experiment was, however, brought to an end by the Heath Government which took office in 1970.

The second development was the assumption by the Wilson Government, through the Industrial Development Act, of wide powers to buy shares in private industry. This was condemned by the Confederation of British Industry as a form of 'nationalization by stealth', and it could not be said to enjoy the unanimous support of the Labour Party itself, since there are socialists who regard the public underwriting of capitalist institutions as illegitimate. The intention of the Government appeared to be to use share-holding power to promote new techniques, to strengthen firms of national importance, to modernize those with high but unrealized potential in the export market, and to rescue those in both categories that were running into trouble through lack of finance.

Despite the actions of the Heath Government in shedding some of the 'peripheral' (but profitable) enterprises that had come, one way or another, under national ownership, it seems likely that the trend, over time, will be for increasing interpenetration of the public and private sectors of the economy. Such interpenetration, already exemplified by the subsidization of certain private firms and the granting of massive state assistance to farmers, raises political and constitutional issues even more tricky than those arising from the existence of the nationalized industries. To cope with these issues further institutional innovation and the development of new constitutional conventions will almost certainly be required. Indeed, at the time of writing (winter, 1974) we await the creation of the National Enterprise Board promised by the Wilson Government – a Board which, it seems, will not only perform the functions of the old I.R.C. but will go even further in facilitating state intervention in industry.

Nationalized Industries 1966–67

	Average Net Assets	*Net Income*	*Net Income as a Percentage of Assets*	*Fixed Investment in the U.K.*	*Exchequer Loans*	*Exchequer Loans as a Percentage of fixed Investment*[1]	*Total Employees at March 1967*
	£m.	£m.	%	£m.	£m.	%	000s
Post Office	1,584	126.5	8.0	166.4[2]	130.0	48.8	422
National Coal Board[3]	794[4]	29.0	3.7	89.9	37.7	41.9	492
Electricity Council and Boards in England and Wales	3,876	200.4	5.1	664.8	397.0	59.7	229
North of Scotland Hydro-Electric Board	258	12.8	5.0	9.9	21.3[5]	215.2	4
South of Scotland Electricity Board	316	14.7	4.6	47.1	21.4	45.4	16
Gas Council and Area Gas Boards	966	46.5	4.8	215.0	164.4	76.5	124
British Overseas Airways Corporation	134	29.0	21.7	11.8	−2.8	−23.7	19
British European Airways	102	4.8	4.8	17.1	5.6	32.7	20
British Airports Authority	54	5.6	10.3	7.0	—	—	3
British Railways Board[6]	1,931	−70.2	−3.6	106.8	5.0[1]	4.7	361
London Transport Board[6]	218	1.1	0.5	22.1	19.5[1]	88.2	74
British Transport Docks Board[6]	95	5.1	5.4	9.8	3.3	33.7	11
British Waterways Board[6]	13	−0.6	−4.9	1.0	0.2[1]	20.0	3
Transport Holding Company[6]	175	14.3	8.2	23.3	10.0	42.9	103
Total, all industries	10,516	419.0	3.9	1,492.0	812.6	54.4	1,881

Notes

1. These figures exclude deficit grants of £134.7 million for British Railways, £5.9 million for LTB and £1.5 million for British Waterways, but even so do not give directly a self-financing ratio as borrowings may be affected by changes in working capital requirements.

2. Includes Giro Developmental Expenses of £0.4 million financed from Exchequer advances.

3. The NCB's financial year ran from 27 March 1966 to 25 March 1967.

4. Reflects only part of the capital construction under the Coal Industry Act 1965. Approximately £156.5 million remained at 25 March 1967, to be written off from the Reserve Fund.

5. Includes £14.8 million advanced to finance both market purchases of the Board's own stock for cancellation, and the redemption of £13.2 million of the Board's 4½% 1965–66 stock.

6. For the Calendar year 1966.

Source: Nationalized Industries. A Review of Economic and Financial Objectives. Cmnd 3437, HMSO 1967.

Chapter 9

The Management of the Economy

In the last chapter we examined the institutional consequences and political implications of government intervention in specific areas of the economy, through direct ownership. The present chapter will look at economic intervention – or, as its critics are sometimes inclined to call it, 'interference' – in the economy as a whole. We shall be concerned in fact with what is generally known as economic planning but sometimes denoted by the less politically-loaded expression 'economic management'. As one of the newer functions of government, it has already had a very considerable effect on the British institutional set-up, and is likely to have even profounder effects.

The history of government intervention in the economy is long and chequered. During the hey-day of laissez-faire in the nineteenth century each act of government intervention, whether to protect female and child labour from exploitation or to regulate the behaviour of monopolies, was regarded as requiring special justification. In the previous century however – at least before the full intellectual impact of the gospel preached by Adam Smith in his *Wealth of Nations* was felt – few people had any doubt about the responsibility of government for promoting what today we would call the growth of the economy. By the various doctrines we now group together under the name of mercantilism, the promotional and regulatory aspects of government were strongly stressed. It had the duty of ensuring a favourable balance of trade, of encouraging industry and maximizing employment, and of seeing that British shipping was properly protected against foreign competition. During the period that followed, however, most interventionism characteristic of the mercantilist period was gradually eliminated, in theory if not always in practice. The economic responsibilities of government became largely confined to the preservation of monetary stability, the raising of taxes to meet its own very moderate expenses, and the provision of a legal framework (by laws of contract, company laws etc.) favourable for the development of free enterprise.

The end of laissez-faire and the transition to the 'neo-mercantilism' of modern times are difficult to date, but there can be little doubt that the later years of the nineteenth century and the early ones of the twentieth constituted a watershed. They saw a reversion – very hesitant at first – to protectionist policies, the adoption of measures to assist British exporters to compete in overseas markets, and a wide extension of previous laws for the protection of labour and the provision of social services. These developments were greatly speeded up by the First World War, during the course of which the Government was compelled by sheer force of circumstances to exercise unprecedentedly stringent controls over the national economy. Although most of these were rapidly dismantled after 1918, interventionism continued and, in some respects, underwent reinforcement during the inter-war period. This was hardly a matter of political choice; it was made necessary by the continuing crises of the British economy (which reached its most intense point during the years (1929–32) and by the enhanced strength and status of a Labour movement committed to interventionist policies to secure what it regarded as adequate protection for the interests of the working class.

In the techniques of interventionism important developments occurred during the later 1930s. As a result of the theoretical work of John Maynard Keynes, progressive economists and politicians came to regard monetary and fiscal policies as more than a means of securing peripheral adjustments of the economy. They could be used to smooth out the trade cycle, to minimize unemployment and to stimulate desirable and discourage undesirable economic activities. Before the full impact of the Keynesian revolution could be felt, however, the Second World War broke out. During the course of it the Government had to exercise comprehensive controls over every aspect of economic life, predominantly by physical rather than by fiscal and monetary methods. The controls which it then imposed were mostly maintained during the post-war reconstruction period, when for the first time a Labour Government was in office with a clear parliamentary majority. Then, as before, intervention was largely a matter of necessity; but it also began to reflect certain deliberate policy choices. This was partly due to the Labour Government's commitment to democratic socialism, which involved not only extending the public sector of the economy but engaging in economic planning. One should remember, however, that it was not a Labour Government but a wartime coalition Government that had published the famous White Paper of 1944, which said that any future Government had a responsibility to maintain full employment – by means of the Keynesian techniques which by that time had become well known and accepted. Such an objective necessarily committed any government, whatever its ideology, to a degree of interventionism previously unknown except in wartime. Since then, although Governments with attitudes very different from those held by Labour have been in office for most of the time (1951–64 and since 1970–74), they have continued to accept an ultimate political responsibility for economic welfare. Moreover, public expenditure has become so vast that the influence of governmental policies on the shape of the economy and on the direction and pace of its growth has become decisive. Today public expenditure accounts for about 40 per cent of the gross national product (excluding debt interest but including transfer payments). The situation, it should be noted, is not fundamentally different in the other countries of western Europe, where taxation absorbs between one-quarter and one-third of the gross national product and directly state-controlled investment accounts for between 40 per cent and 60 per cent of total investment.

Our interest here lies in the institutions themselves rather than in the specific policies that Governments have followed. Intensified economic intervention has demanded a considerable adaptation of institutions. As we have seen, new duties have been imposed on old ministries, new ministries have been created by the familiar fusion/fission process and government intervention in the economy has been responsible for the creation of a large number of new ad hoc agencies. Already, in the 1930s, policies of economic promotion and regulation had spawned a fair number of these. In addition to the few nationalized industries, there were the Coal Mines Reorganization Commission (1930), the Wheat Commission (1932), the Import Duties Advisory Board (1933), the Herring Industry Board (1935), the Sugar Commission (1936), the Livestock Commission (1937) and the White Fish Commission (1938). Since then there has been a remarkable proliferation of such bodies: the Pay Board and the Price Commission, established as part of the Conservative Government's counter-inflation policies, being but two of the more recent examples.

It is clear that intervention has grown very rapidly of recent years, in response to new needs and changing conceptions of policy, and that it has resulted in the creation of new institutions and the revamping of old ones in a somewhat chaotic fashion. The demand that it should become more coherent, co-ordinated and purposeful was first heard in the 1930s, when progressive conservatives as well as socialists found the courage to use the dreaded word 'planning'. This demand was satisfied during the Second World War, when the Government had a mandate to manage the economy for one single purpose – winning the war with Germany, Japan and their allies. The remarkable degree of success achieved by the managed economy of the war years naturally strengthened the view (which was particularly attractive to socialists) that a similar purposefulness should be displayed in peace time, i.e. that the Government, having won the war, should use its new-found powers to strengthen the British economy in such a way as to enable it to support a rising standard of living. Although doubts were expressed whether wartime techniques of control could or should be used in peacetime, when unity of will and purpose was by no means so evident, economic planning had become a central political issue, which brought with it the problems of establishing permanent machinery for its realization.

Labour's effort in this direction between 1945 and 1951 has been regarded by most students as rather feeble. At the beginning, Herbert Morrison, as Lord President of the Council, was given overall responsibility, and the familiar forms of co-ordination through cabinet committees, inter-departmental committees and the Treasury were used more or less as before; but very soon these were seen to be insufficient. The politicians and administrators concerned were overburdened by other duties. Hence the decision was taken to establish a *Ministry of Economic Affairs*, under the political leadership of Sir Stafford Cripps, and to equip it with a specialized agency, the Central Economic Planning Staff, for the provision of information and advice. Simultaneously the Central Statistical Office and the Economic Section of the Cabinet (both wartime creations) were strengthened. Together they played an important part in the production of the Annual Economic Surveys which, apart from the Four Year Plan prepared for OEEC in connection with 'Marshall Aid', were the nearest approximations to overall planning documents that the Labour Government ever published.

The new ministerial set-up was, however, short-lived. After the resignation of Mr Hugh Dalton in 1947, Sir Stafford Cripps became Chancellor and took both Economic Affairs and the CEPS with him into the Treasury, where they tended to play a rather subordinate role, largely as a result of the hand to month existence that the pressure of immediate economic problems forced the Government to live. When the Conservatives came to office in 1951 and abolished the CEPS, there were few to mourn it. Nor did the discontinuation of the publication of the annual Economic Surveys cause any very violent criticism. As in the latter days of the Labour Government, the Treasury had no competitor as chief economic co-ordinator, although it did now appear to be rather less well equipped for the performance of this function. In 1953 it absorbed the Economic Section of the Cabinet Office.

The dismantling of the Central Economic Planning Staff was partly the result of the hostility of the Conservative Party at that period to the very idea of economic planning. In giving expression to this hostility the Conservatives struck a responsive chord in public opinion; for by this time many citizens had come to identify planning with unwelcome physical controls and the persistence of war-time and post-war shortages of consumer goods. Hence no alternative machinery was created. Indeed, during their first eight or nine years of power the Conservatives tended to place more faith in the stimulation of competition than in the regulation of the economy. This bias was reflected in their policies for the nationalized industries, in their partial dismantlement of rent control, in their abandonment of Labour's attempt to set up development councils for individual industries and in the legislation they passed in 1956 to limit restrictive practices – a far stronger measure than the Act of 1948 which represented Labour's contribution to this purpose. It would be absurd to suggest that there was no economic management during these years; but the techniques employed were mainly of the short-term variety, relying mainly on the powerful but clumsy tools of credit control and taxation, and being predominantly concerned with the preservation of stability, i.e. the rectification of the balance of payments and the containment of inflation, rather than with the promotion of growth. Little remained of the apparatus which Labour had attempted to use, apart from an advisory Economic Planning Board consisting of a mixture of official and non-official members all appointed by the Chancellor of the Exchequer. This Board, the major consultative committee on economic policy, did not attempt and was not intended to direct or supervise the planning of the economy. At best it provided senior officials with the means of testing the reactions of the major interested groups to economic proposals that were in the course of formulation. Indeed, its lack of any specialized assistance prevented it from functioning as more than a sounding board.

Not until the late 1950s did any change become apparent in the Conservative attitude towards economic planning. By that time the fundamental unsoundness of Britain's economic position could no longer be disregarded. The slow rate of growth, the sluggishness of exports, the increasing seriousness of balance of payments crises, the persistence of inflationary trends, the intensification of regional imbalances and the growing inadequacy of the economic infrastructure – all these dictated a fundamental rethinking of policy. The need was 'to make rational choices about the development of various sectors of the economy and to devise policies which would operate on individual parts of the economy in addition to the more traditional means of influencing the level of economic activity as a whole'. This meant 'deliberately and carefully working out the priorities in the development of the economy within the resources likely to be available; endeavouring to ensure for example that productive investment in certain sectors would grow faster than in others', and 'reducing regional imbalances' – so that more resources were 'called into employment without giving rise to undue inflationary pressures'.[1]

The announcement that a new approach was to be adopted came in Mr Selwyn Lloyd's parliamentary statement of 26 July 1961. After references to the Economic Planning Board and 'various other advisory councils' he said:

> I want something more purposeful than that. I envisage a joint examination of the economic prospects of the country stretching five or more years into the future. It would cover the growth of national production and distribution of our resources between the main uses, consumption, Government expenditure, investment, and so on. Above all, it would try to establish what are the essential conditions for realising potential growth . . . I want both sides of industry to share with the Government the task of relating plans to the resources likely to be available.[2]

Towards the end of the following month, the Chancellor held meetings with employers' and workers' representatives to obtain their views about what economic planning involved and how it should be organized. Two proposals appear to have received serious consideration. The first was for the establishment of an independent planning body charged with the production of economic forecasts and projections; the second envisaged a 'two-

1. Sir Eric Roll, 'The Machinery for Economic Planning: 1. The Department of Economic Affairs' in *Public Administration*, Vol. 44, Spring 1966.
2. *HC Debates*, Vol. 645, Col. 439.

tier' body of which the top, policy-making tier would consist of representatives of the employers, trade unions and nationalized industries, together with some 'outsiders', meeting under the chairmanship of the Chancellor, while the lower tier would consist of an 'office' of experts. The latter proposal had the support of the employers and was eventually adopted by the Chancellor, who in a letter of 23 September, addressed to the Trade Union Congress, the Federation of British Industries, the British Employers Federation, the Association of British Chambers of Commerce and the National Union of Manufacturers, proposed the formation of a National Economic Development Council (NEDC), intended to be advisory in role but powerful in influence. It would be assisted by a full time Office (NEDO) for which the staff would be recruited on temporary secondment from the Civil Service, industry, commerce and the universities. The Office's duties would be to examine the development plans of the main industries in the private sector, and in the light of such examination and of discussions with government departments about other sectors of the economy, such as the nationalized industries, prepare studies for the Council's consideration.

The employers' representatives accepted these proposals almost immediately, but the trade unionists demanded time for consideration. Annoyed by the Government's wage pause policy and sceptical of the reality of its conversion to economic planning, they required certain assurances as a condition for their participation. It was not until January 1962 that the General Council of the Trade Union Congress, by a majority of 21 to 8, agreed to nominate representatives. One of the most powerful of British trade union leaders, Mr Frank Cousins, voted with the minority.

In the meantime, without waiting for trade union support, the Chancellor began to recruit staff, appointing as Director General of the NEDO Sir Robert Shone, who had been an executive member of the Iron and Steel Board since its establishment in 1953, and as Economic Director the economist Sir Donald MacDougall, of Nuffield College, Oxford.

The Council as eventually established consisted of six representatives of the private employers, six of the trade unions, two of the nationalized industries (Transport and Coal), two academics with wide experience of public affairs, three Ministers (the Chancellor of the Exchequer, the President of the Board of Trade and the Minister of Labour) and the Director of the Office.

By this time the fairly widespread scepticism about the seriousness of the Government's intentions had been considerably allayed by its acceptance of the Plowden Report on public expenditure,[3] and by its issue of a White Paper entitled 'Incomes Policy, the Next Step'[4] in which it announced its intention of setting annual targets for increases in national production and of collecting together and publishing at regular intervals factual information for the benefit of wage negotiators and arbitrators about the extent to which the targets had been hit.

The first meeting of NEDC took place in March 1962, and by May 1962 its modus operandi had been publicly announced. Sir Robert Shone and his team were to draw up by the end of the year a report which would examine the implications and work out the statistical projections for a 4 per cent per annum expansion programme for the years 1961–66. This percentage figure was described as 'a reasonably ambitious figure likely to bring out the problems that have to be solved if faster economic growth is to be achieved and as a help in focusing thinking on problems of faster economic growth'.

More specifically NEDC was to examine the potential contribution of government services, to initiate a special study of the distributive trades, and to seek from individual industries factual information about the likely implications for them of the 4 per cent annual growth rate. It would also continue studies already in hand to identify the major obstacles to growth.

For these purposes the Office was organized into two main divisions, one to study general economic issues and major obstacles to growth, the other to concern itself with the problems and programmes of individual industries and broad sections of the economy.

Concern with industrial programmes very soon led to the establishment of formal machinery for consultation with individual industries, as part of NEDC's own structure. Thus in 1963 it was decided to create Economic Development Committees (which became popularly known as 'Little Neddies') consisting of representatives of employers and trade unions sitting together with members of the relevant government departments. In stressing the importance of these bodies, Sir Robert Shone has written:

> Consultation and involvement of industry is essential if a National Plan is to have a real chance of influencing attitudes particularly of

3. See above, pp. 126–7.
4. Cmnd 1626.

> firms and industries. To put it at its minimum, the planning operation is a valuable way of getting industry to consider development in relation to the growth of the economy over a period of at least five years ahead. But since the achievement of better performance depends on more efficient use of man power and capital, on better export performance and on other matters to which private industry has a major contribution to make it is of great value in achieving these objectives if industry can be effectively involved. The work of preparing estimates in practical quantitative terms on matters such as the expected productivity is of importance not only in providing basic data for the Plan but in focusing the directions in which action is needed. The importance of this function is demonstrated by the fact that the check-list in the National Plan requires the E.D.C.s to take action on a vast range of problems concerned with the competitive strength of their industry.[5]

This new set-up was powerfully influenced by the already existing machinery for economic planning in France. The National Economic Development Council was in many ways similar to the French Economic and Social Council. The Office corresponded with the Commissariat du Plan while the Little Neddies were obviously inspired by the French Commissions de Modernisation. The lively interest in these French institutions displayed by the politicians and administrators engaged in constructing Britain's new planning machinery showed the development of the hitherto uncharacteristic willingness to learn from foreign experience – a willingness which, as we have seen, was also reflected in Fulton Committee proposals for the reorganization of the Civil Service.

So far the Little Neddies have proved the most useful part of this machinery. They have increased in number and done a great deal of business. However, major changes in the planning set-up, made by the Labour Government which came into office in 1964 and shortly to be described, have put NEDC itself in a somewhat ambiguous position, where its role is perhaps only marginally more important than that of its predecessor, the Economic Planning Board.[7] Even its most publicized achievement, the Plan published as *Growth of the United Kingdom Economy to 1966*, was rapidly superseded by a new National Plan covering the years 1966–70. In the formulation of this famous or notorious

5. 'The Machinery for Economic Planning: 2. The National Economic Development Council' in *Public Administration*, Vol. 44, Spring 1966, pp. 19–20.

6. See above, p. 138 passim.

7. See above, p. 196.

document NEDC's help was certainly enlisted and services of its Office were employed, but the main work of preparation was undertaken by a new government department, the Ministry of Economic Affairs.

The decision to revamp the machinery so soon after its initial establishment was a product of the desire of the Labour Government for a stronger and more authoritative form of planning than could be provided by an essentially advisory body acting as an aide for a reorganized Treasury.[8] The essential reform was the creation of the Ministry of Economic Affairs – a new type of government department without direct executive responsibilities and drawing its authority from the leadership provided by a very senior Minister (initially Mr George Brown) who, as was only natural, took over from the Chancellor the Chairmanship of the NEDC. Its duties, 'responsibility for the management of the National Economy as a whole', were essentially the same as those of the economic staff of the Treasury, most of whose members were transferred to it. Specifically it had to

> formulate the general objectives of economic policy in its totality and act as the coordinator of the policies of individual departments towards the achievement of these objectives.

In order to do this it was required

> 1. To relate each department's activities and requirements to the general objective of national economic policy, to the prospective availability of economic resources and to the total claims upon them;
> 2. To provide informed advice to departments, as partners in a joint enterprise, on all aspects of economic policy, and to help them to fulfil their departmental responsibilities efficiently and economically.[9]

This takeover was justified by the need to give these duties a degree of emphasis which it was considered the Treasury was unable or unwilling to give. Special stress was laid on the fact that the new department stood 'for the interests of the economy as a whole' and had no narrow 'departmental interest to defend'.[10] It was divided into three groups, dealing respectively with Economic Planning and Public Expenditure, Regional Planning and

8. See above, p. 129 passim.
9. Sir Eric Roll, 'The Department of Economic Affairs' in *Public Administration*, Vol. 44, Spring 1966, p. 4.
10. ibid. p. 5.

Industrial Policies, and Prices and Incomes.[11] Its staff, part of which was taken over from the NEDO, had a higher proportion of professional economists in senior posts than is to be found in any other department.

Almost immediately this major governmental innovation ran into difficulties. Relations with the Treasury were uneasy, since whereas the DEA was thinking in terms of stimulating steady, long-term economic growth, the Treasury remained mainly concerned with the search for internal and external stability. As the creation of the new ministry was followed by a series of major economic crises, culminating in the devaluation of November 1967, the Treasury inevitably emerged victor from the contest and the National Economic Plan produced by the DEA in 1965 was soon recognized as obsolete and to all intents and purposes discarded. Ministerial changes also accentuated the growing uncertainty about DEA's future. Mr George Brown, whose disagreements with the Chancellor of the Exchequer, Mr James Callaghan, became notorious, was replaced by a less dynamic although no less senior personality, Mr Michael Stewart. In August 1967, as part of the Cabinet reshuffle in which Mr Stewart became Foreign Secretary, it was announced that the Prime Minister himself would take over responsibility for the DEA with the assistance of an up-and-coming Labour politician, Mr Peter Shore, who had special knowledge of economic policy matters. Mr Shore was appointed Secretary of State for Economic Affairs with a seat in the Cabinet. One of his major duties was to prepare a new Economic Plan, which was published early in 1969. Later in the year, however, as a part of Mr Wilson's major ministerial organization, the Department was abolished and the economic planning function restored to the Treasury.

Throughout its brief life the Department of Economic Affairs was the centre of acute controversy. Whether either its creation or its abolition can be justified is a moot point. Here we will look at it simply as an example of the institutional problems raised by the recently-adopted economic planning functions of government, and for this purpose briefly examine the pros and cons of its existence, as advanced by two of the most distinguished and well-informed protagonists in the controversy.

Sir Douglas Allen, formerly the Permanent Undersecretary of the Department, produced a moderately worded and thoughtful

11. Its 'External Policies' group was transferred to the Board of Trade by the reorganization of August 1967 (see below).

apologia.[12] His first argument in favour of a separate ministry, distinct from the Treasury, rested on the distinction between the budget, which provided a 'natural focus' for the Treasury's work, and the 'succession of medium term economic plans', which provided the natural focus for that of the DEA. For medium term purposes, he held the Treasury was an unsuitable instrument, owing to the heavy involvement of its personnel in other kinds of work, and the danger that the adoption of extra responsibilities might impair its 'more traditional . . . responsibilities'. The former division of functions between Treasury and DEA, he considered, 'ensures that both aspects (i.e. the short term and the medium term) are given adequate consideration when important policy decisions are taken'. Lastly, in rebuttal of the criticism that the proved irrelevance of the 1966–70 plan had exposed the futility of the DEA's activities, he took issue with the belief that there was 'no future for planning unless it can bring about a visible acceleration in the rate of growth'. Much of the work done by the DEA 'to improve our industrial efficiency, or international position and our balance of payments' did not depend on the accuracy of these 'detailed numerical projections' which popular opinion tended to regard as the department's peculiar province. Moreover, even though former numerical projections had proved unrealistic, the continued undertaking of such mathematical and statistical work was essential if the Government's decisions about priorities were to be realistic and its responses to the changing economic situation adequate. Indeed, he added, 'the need for numerical projection of this kind would in fact be even greater if the economy were not growing'.

The last of these arguments is on a different level from the others. Essentially, it is directed against 'Powellite' views to the effect that attempts to plan the economy, at least of the kind so far made, are inherently futile. It does not necessarily reinforce the case for a DEA, whose planning functions might well be as successfully or more successfully performed elsewhere. Indeed, Sir Douglas showed a tendency to throw away his arguments for the administrative rationality of the DEA as such when he said:

> Decisions to set up new Departments or redistribute functions are essentially political decisions. There are no objective rules for deciding how many Departments there should be, or how wide should be the

12. 'The Department of Economic Affairs' in *Political Quarterly*, Oct.–Dec. 1967.

responsibility of a single departmental Minister. Indeed, changes are necessary from time to time as either problems or Government objectives change. Similarly whether or not a Department is fulfilling the purposes for which it is created is largely a political judgment.[13]

That the DEA was *both* irrational administratively and ill-advised politically was argued by Mr Douglas Jay, a politician whose experience of economic administration entitles his views to be treated with respect.[14]

His view was that experience had shown that the only sound organizational approach to economic planning was 'to place supreme authority firmly on one senior economic Minister clearly responsible for the balance of payments, the Budget, planning, prices and incomes, investment, the currency reserve and the inter-relations of these, with as many supporting junior Ministers or departments as the subject matter requires'. 'All the elements in the economy', he continued, 'interplay so actively with one another that, in the absence of one clearly responsible co-ordinating Minister, you will necessarily get blurred responsibility, indecision, delay and finally, in the economic circumstances of post-war Britain, sooner or later (usually in about two years) crisis'. In the light of these principles he considered that the absorption of the Ministry of Economic Affairs by the Treasury in 1947[15] was the result of the correct decision 'based on the lessons of numerous mistakes and experiments through the 1930s and 1940s'.

Of his two major examples of such mistakes, the first was the 'competitive chaos that reigned between the major war production departments' in 1940 and 1941. Fortunately the lesson had been learned before it was too late and the chaos brought to an end by the creation of the Ministry of Production which successfully accomplished a herculean task of co-ordination. The second mistake was Labour's initial division of responsibility for economic affairs between Herbert Morrison as Senior Economic co-

13. In this respect Sir Douglas is in agreement with the views that we have expressed above; see pp. 123–4.

14. See his 'Government Control of the Economy' in *Political Quarterly*, April–June 1968. Mr Jay was Economic Secretary to the Treasury between 1947 and 1950 and Financial Secretary to the Treasury between 1950 and 1951. He served for a period as President of the Board of Trade in the Labour Government which came into the office in 1964. During the Second World War he was a member of the Civil Service.

15. See above, p. 131.

ordinating Minister and Hugh Dalton as Chancellor (1945 to 1947). Although at the time this division seemed to have much to recommend it, it soon became clear that 'the problem was the United Kingdom balance of payments and the fashioning of our whole economic policy so as to achieve solvency and repay debts' – a problem which could be solved only if 'one Minister and one department bore the clear prime responsibility'. Again the lesson was learned and the 'one Minister' solution adopted in 1947 when Sir Stafford Cripps went to the Exchequer.

Justifying the 1947–51 arrangements, against which so much criticism had been directed, Mr Jay wrote:

> The essentials of this set up were: union of the planning and financial departments under the Chancellor in almost hourly contact; the small size of the planning and coordinating sections; scrupulous concentration on coordination rather than interference; and adherence to the principle that contact with outside industry, public or private, was left to the sponsoring department and not duplicated by the coordinator.

Alleging that 'for the four years 1947–51 – when this essential machinery was in force – our success in coming to terms with our balance of payments difficulties was probably greater than in any other post-war years before or since', he attributed this very largely to the system of economic co-ordination then in force, although admitting that personalities, both at the political and civil service levels, also had an important beneficial influence.

The return by Labour to dual control in 1964 he considered disastrous. Wrong in principle, its vices were accentuated by behaviour of the Ministry of Economic Affairs, which he held to be very different from that attributed to it by Sir Eric Roll.[16] The Ministry, he considered,

> never learnt the crucial difference between coordination and interference; and it never understood the distinction between a sponsoring department directly in contact with industry and a planning department working through other Ministries.

His recommended solution was the one eventually accepted: to wind up the Ministry and transfer its 'genuinely competent staff' – among whom he apparently included few economists – 'to a planning unit separate from the Treasury but under the authority of the Chancellor'. Under this new set up the National Economic

16. See above pp. 201–2.

Development Council would be kept as a consultative body but deprived of the staff which has already become largely redundant. The servicing of NEDC would be provided mainly by the Chancellor's Office, to which the Council itself should, as before, be attached.

Mr Jay's case, like Sir Douglas Allen's, is wide open to criticism. It may be questioned, for instance, whether there is an appropriate parallel between the role that Mr Jay would give the Chancellor of the Exchequer and that played by the Minister of Production in wartime. There is also considerable doubt whether the 1947 to 1951 set-up worked as smoothly as he claims. His involvement in it, first as Economic Secretary to the Treasury and then as Financial Secretary, may conceivably have prejudiced him in its favour; indeed his whole case seems to express a nostalgic desire to return to what he evidently regarded as the good old days of Sir Stafford Cripps. He also tends to weaken his own argument by placing such heavy emphasis on short term adjustment as against medium and long term growth. This is a typical Treasury man's bias, which the creation of the Ministry of Economic Affairs was intended to offset. Cripps, like subsequent Chancellors, was overwhelmingly concerned with getting the economy on to an even keel and it was the very limitations of this policy that created the demand for the establishment of a growth-minded Ministry. The appeal to experience, moreover, is partial and insular rather than general and universal and there are few apart from Mr Jay who would now argue that the lessons of the past point clearly and unmistakably to the desirability of concentrating planning powers in the hands of the Minister who is primarily concerned with the management of the nation's finances. Lastly there is the question of the role that the Ministry of Economic Affairs actually played during its short life. Was it really, as Mr Jay alleged, a persistent meddler in other people's business? We have neither the knowledge nor the experience to provide answers to these questions, nor is it our responsibility to take up a position in the controversy. If Sir Douglas Allen and Mr Jay have been quoted at length, it is simply because their rival views illustrate the dilemmas confronting the institutional innovator.

Of the innovations of the 1960s, the DEA was perhaps the most important, and the projecting and coordinating functions it attempted are now almost universally recognized as vital. But we should not overlook the contribution that continues to be made by the little Neddies. Through their efforts, management, union and government bodies are brought together in an attempt to create the conditions necessary for economic development. Leslie Metcalfe and Dean F. Berry, in an article in *The Times* of 1 December 1972, highlight three roles of the EDCs in the 1970s: *Diffusion* – identifying problems common to a group of firms, disseminating possible solutions, compiling statistics; *Representation* – presenting the views of industry to the government, particularly when the firms themselves are poorly organized for the task; *Consultancy* – encouraging active collaboration by all the representative organizations in a particular industry in diagnosing collective problems and working out acceptable policies. As Metcalfe and Berry wrote: 'The common threat that runs through the problems [of the economy] is increasing organizational interdependence due to the growth in scale of business operations and the involvement of trade unions and government in industrial decision-making'. Therefore any major changes in the management of the economy 'will have to be based on the fact of organizational interdependence in an essentially *pluralistic* economic system'.

Neither, in this talk of innovations, should we ignore the Central Policy Review Staff to which we referred when discussing the Cabinet. The CPRS was established to fulfil part of the role originally envisaged for the Department of Economic Affairs; that is, to act as a central planning unit which would enable decisions on the allocation of resources to be taken in a more rational manner. Lack of knowledge of Whitehall procedures, departmental hostility and ministerial suspicions have so far combined to limit its effectiveness, but its position within the orbit of Number Ten and the access of its chairman to the ear of the Prime Minister give it potential as a major element in any future development of the machinery for planning.

With all three major political parties today positively committed to planning, the problem for any government is to discover the right institutions for its purposes and to fit them into the existing machinery of government. The nature of the solution depends initially on what kind of planning it has decided to adopt, i.e. where on the scale between the two ideal types, the 'indicative' on the one hand and the 'command' on the other, a given national planning system is to be located; but whatever variety is chosen it is essential to find institutional means of coordination (which is the essence of any kind of planning) that operate effectively as such. This involves locating the supreme planning agency at a sufficiently exalted level in the hierarchy of government to enable it to exercise the necessary authority, yet at the same time ensuring that it does not interfere unnecessarily and harmfully with the efficient discharge by other agencies of their distinctive responsibilities. (Thus, those who advocate the creation of a Prime Minister's Department, out of, say, the Civil Service Department, the Cabinet Office and the Central Policy Review Staff, fall foul of certain constitutional purists who see such a projected move as a threat to ministerial responsibility, both individual and collective, and as a dangerous step towards a Presidential style of Government.) This problem of administrative machine-building is by no means straightforward, for its solution is dependent on both personal and political factors that can either facilitate the smooth working of the machine or bring it to an abrupt halt. Administrative arrangements which work well with one set of people may work very badly with another. Much depends too on the nature of the political objectives which are built into the planning exercise; the machine must be constructed in a way that ensures their realization. Hence there is no final solution to this or to any other problem of administrative construction. All one can reasonably demand is a *relative* degree of organizational stability; for an adequate period of trial is obviously necessary before judgment can be passed on the virtues and vices, capacities and incapacities of any chosen set-up.

Chapter 10

Regionalism and Decentralization

To proceed from problems relating to the management of the economy to those concerned with the decentralization of administrative resources and responsibilities is to make a natural transition; for one of the outstanding features of the new planning machinery is its decentralized regional agencies: the Regional Economic Planning Boards and Planning Councils.

In making this transition, however, a word of caution is necessary; for 'decentralization' is one of the most ambiguous words in the political scientist's vocabulary. Moreover, it is a word with rather powerful emotional overtones, particularly at the present time, when it tends to be associated with politically controversial demands for greater popular participation in the running of public affairs. Generally speaking, 'decentralization' awakens favourable responses. It is taken as denoting a decision-making process characterized by speed, human understanding and responsiveness to grass-roots initiative. 'Centralization', on the other hand, has an emotional penumbra which embraces, at the very least, the pejorative characteristics of unimaginative bureaucracy, delay, red tape and the erosion of local liberties.

By an extension of this associative process, 'regionalism' has also tended to become a good word. 'More power to the regions' is a slogan that has acquired a certain popularity. It is heard with particular frequency in those areas of England, such as Yorkshire, Tyneside, Merseyside and Devon and Cornwall, where some degree of regional consciousness exists, whether vestigially or embryonically. It makes an even stronger appeal in Scotland and Wales, where it is linked with strong feelings of resentment against Westminster and Whitehall 'dictatorship' and increasing demands for a greater measure of national autonomy. On the other hand, it is sometimes regarded with a certain suspicion by people who believe that *small* units of local government are essential for true popular participation, and particularly by local councillors and officials who fear that their favourite parish pumps are doomed to suffer replacement by larger and more powerful engines of administration, whether democratic or bureaucratic in their mode of operation. As a preliminary to discussing the subject-matter of this chapter, therefore, some attempt to achieve semantic clarity must be made.

Interpreted in its widest possible sense, decentralization can be functional or geographical or both; it can also be bureaucratic or democratic or some combination of the two. Certain examples of purely functional decentralization of administrative responsibilities have already been dealt with, in our chapter on the ad hoc agencies. Here we are concerned entirely with forms of decentralization which have a geographical connotation: the delegation or devolution of decision-taking duties to outstations of various kinds, whether they be bureaucratically controlled offices – of the central departments or democratically-elected authorities of the kind that constitute the British system of local government. As 'decentralization' can mean so many different things, however, we propose to use the word 'deconcentration' for the purely bureaucratic phenomenon. The ordinary citizen is familiar enough with deconcentration when, for instance, he is informed by an officer of the Ministry of Social Services that his claim to benefit has been allowed or disallowed, or by a local Post Office controller that he can or cannot be supplied with a telephone. In such cases, formal responsibility remains with the central Minister, but the taking of the actual decision (within the ambit of centrally-determined rules and procedures and subject to appeal either to a bureaucratically superior authority or to an administrative tribunal or both)[1] is confined to the 'outstationed' official.

The terms 'local' and 'regional' also require some elucidation. For most people, 'local' refers to the town, village, neighbourhood, or – at most – county. But today the most important deconcentrations of decision-taking powers by central government departments are made in favour of agencies that cover, not merely several towns, villages and neighbourhoods but usually several counties. This larger area of administration is what is usually known as a region; and regionalism is normally taken to refer to the practice of conferring responsibilities on persons or bodies, whether bureaucratically-appointed or democratically-elected, enjoying jurisdiction over areas of such dimensions. The reason why regionalism, of recent year has become such a significant feature of the British system of government is that economies of scale indicate the region as the area over which certain important governmental functions may be most efficiently organized. With the increasing complexity of the functions and

1. See below, Chapter 11, p. 251 passim.

responsibilities of the central government departments, the delegation of information-collecting and decision-taking responsibilities to sub-national units has become inevitable, and the region has been found, by experiment, to provide the unit to which the more significant forms of such delegation may be made most conveniently. Most of the Ministries engaged in the provision of services or the regulation of activities, e.g. Trade and Industry, Environment, Social Services, Agriculture, Fisheries and Food, have spawned regional outstations. The regional principle has also been applied to the administration of hospitals and the distribution of gas and electricity.

Regionalism, therefore, is at present very strongly associated with that form of bureaucratic, geographical decentralization that we have termed 'deconcentration'. Although the regional agencies we have mentioned work in collaboration (to varying degrees) with elected local government authorities, the latter cover areas which are usually smaller than those delimited by regional boundaries. At the regional level, there are no authorities which *both* exercise powers conferred on them by parliamentary statute *and* are responsible, wholly or partly, to a distinct electorate for the manner in which they discharge those responsibilities. Many people think that there ought to be such authorities; but that is a question to be discussed later in this chapter.

Regional Authorities

From the point of view of the central administration, regional deconcentration poses three problems: (1) how to define and delimit the regions; (2) how much decision-taking authority to confer on them; and (3) how to co-ordinate the operations of various regional agencies whose activities impinge on one another.

These three problems are, of course, closely interconnected. In particular, delimitation and co-ordination figure as almost inseparable companions. If each agency were a law unto itself, the problem of determining the optimum catchment area for purposes of regional administration would be purely technical; and as there is a different optimum for each service there would be as many regions as agencies. Indeed, the actual tendency for different agencies to create different regional units has been strong and persistent, as the accompanying maps show. (See maps 1–3.) But if inter-agency co-ordination is to be effectively organized at the regional level, the adoption of common bound-

Map 1 Ministry of Transport Division

aries, if not absolutely essential, is at least highly desirable. Such standardization means that someone has to effect a compromise between the various optima, which also means that no branch of the administration, except by happy accident, is entirely satisfied with the shape and size of its regional sub-units. Standardization, however, becomes increasingly important as, with the development of regional planning, both economic and physical, the coordination of services below the Whitehall level becomes an essential precondition for the avoidance of the familiar phenomenon of apoplexy at the centre and anaemia at the extremities.

Map 2 Hospital Regions

Even so, it is by no means a new idea. It was first mooted at the beginning of this century by that erratic prophet, H. G. Wells, and first worked out as a practical plan in 1905 by a Fabian pamphleteer named W. Saunders, who suggested that a new 'heptarchy' should be created, 'with seven or eight provinces under *ad hoc* boards elected by local authorities to deal with each of the functions requiring large-scale administration'.[2] This idea, with various modifications, subsequently enlisted the support of

2. Brian Smith, *Regionalism in England* (Acton Society Trust 1965), Vol. II, pp. 7–8.

Map 3 Gas Board Areas

town and country planners such as Patrick Geddes and guild socialists such as G. D. H. Cole, and received fullest and most publicized expression in a work, published in 1916, called *The Provinces of England*, by the geographer, C. B. Fawcett.

All these schemes, however, may be said to have started from the Town Hall rather than from the Whitehall end of the spectrum, in that they were plans for reorganizing and simultaneously strengthening the apparatus of *elected* authorities. In any case nothing came of them except the sowing of seeds which, after having lain dormant for many years, sprouted with some vigour during the 1960s.

As a means of imposing regional coherence on the activities of central government departments, as distinct from raising local government to the regional level, the first major attempt at standardization was a product of the war-time emergency of 1939–45, when England was divided into ten regions, each under a Regional Commissioner. Primarily responsible for the co-ordination of civil defence arrangements, the Commissioner was also endowed with authority to exercise the full powers of government in the event of any breakdown of communications with London. Both to facilitate these emergency plans (which fortunately never had to come into force) and to cope with vastly expanded responsibilities, the relevant central government departments regionalized themselves and became involved in a plethora of regionally-based co-ordinating boards and committees, mainly concerned with the production, distribution and rationing of scarce goods, both military and civilian.

The Regional Commissioners disappeared after the end of the war, partly because they were no longer regarded as necessary but mainly because the local authorities were prepared to tolerate them and co-operate with them only for the duration of the emergency. As Professor Fesler has pointed out, the 'prefectorial' type of regional co-ordination of which the Commissioners were an expression invariably generates tensions in a democratic polity, particularly in one where a high value is placed on the institutions of democratic local government.[3] The regional organizations of Ministries and other agencies of central government, however, continued to flourish during the immediate post-war period, when reconstructon, reform and planning were the watchwords. To prevent a chaotic proliferation of regional patterns and thereby strengthen co-ordination, the Treasury in 1946 devised Standard Regions (see Map 4) to which departments were required to conform unless they could show good reasons for not doing so. This standardization, although it did not apply to

3. See James Fesler, 'Centralisation and Decentralisation' in *International Encyclopaedia of the Social Sciences*, 1968, p. 374. Mr Smith writes: 'When local government is well-developed and capable of introducing into public administration the flexibility made necessary by local needs and problems there is correspondingly less demand for multipurpose field agents of the central government to communicate with the decision-makers in the centre on behalf of local communities and sectional interests. The technical services of government concentrate on perfecting administrative performance rather than on moulding administration to provincial circumstances.' (*Field Administration*, London 1967, pp. 24–5.)

Map 4 The Standard Regions

the *ad hoc* agencies, such as those responsible for electricity, gas and hospitals, was of real value. Organizationally, it operated through the bringing together of senior regional officials in a series of co-ordination committees, e.g. Regional Building Committees, Distribution of Industry Panels, Physical Planning Committees, etc.

With the advent to power of the Conservatives in the 1950s, less emphasis was placed on this regional apparatus, and some of it was allowed to atrophy. Most of the regional committees were discarded and some of the regional offices were closed down. Between 1956 and 1958, for instance, the Ministry of Housing and

Local Government – the very Ministry for which regionalization might have seemed, at first sight, most appropriate – disembarrassed itself of all its regional outstations. Even those departments which persisted in the regionalization of their activities were no longer required to adhere to the standard areas formerly prescribed by the Treasury. Nevertheless, this reaction against regionalism did not really go very far: not nearly as far as was hoped by some of its advocates, among whom were to be found the economy-minded, the enemies of planning and the enthusiasts for local liberty of the more traditional kind. No reduction was effected in the number of outstationed civil servants, which actually increased from 354,970 in 1950 to 432,464 in 1960, despite the deregionalization of the Ministries of Power, Supply and Housing and Local Government and a considerable cutting down of the regional staff employed by the Ministry of Public Building and Works.[4] The reason for the maintenance or expansion of regional organization by most of the other relevant departments was obvious: they could not discharge their duties in any other way. The main effects of the 'reaction', therefore were (a) a de-emphasis on regional planning and co-ordination, (b) some degree of reversion to ad hoc as distinct from standard regions, and (c) less delegation of decision-taking powers to region-based officials, who became more concerned with inspection, supervision and liaison than with the exercise of executive authority. These tendencies, as we shall see, were sharply reversed in the 1960s, partly as a result of the reconversion of British Governments to the idea of planning and partly of an upsurge of regional consciousness, particularly in those areas which felt themselves to be suffering from economic neglect.

Experience has now shown that regional standardization, despite its disadvantages for individual services, is essential if ordinary inter-departmental and inter-agency co-ordination is to be achieved at an administrative level lower than that of Whitehall. Still more essential is such standardization if activities in the regions are to be governed by a coherent plan that involves all departments and agencies in the formulation and implementation of interlinked priorities. But standardization of areas, to achieve

4. Figures for outstationed civil servants, however, should not be taken as a reliable index of the degree of regional deconcentration, which depends on the location of decision-making powers rather than on the distribution of staff between Whitehall and the outstations. (On this point, see Fesler, *Encyclopaedia of Social Sciences* p. 373.)

its full effect, must also be accompanied by at least a substantial standardization of delegated powers; for if the officials of Ministries A, B and C are less well-endowed with decision-taking authority than those of Ministries X, Y and Z, the implementation of regionally-agreed policies must wait until the least 'responsible' representative on the relevant inter-departmental committee has received the go-ahead from his boss in Whitehall. In the absence of a pattern of delegation common to all departments, 'the tendency to limit the powers of officials outside Whitehall is to some extent self-perpetuating', as Professors Mackenzie and Grove have pointed out; since 'one of the advantages of a decentralized system is lost if one Department insists on referring to headquarters problems that others settle locally, and this means that all must conform to the practice of the most cautious'.[5]

Although some progress towards the standardization of both areas and powers has been achieved, it cannot be said that British regional organization has as yet met the more obvious requirements in either respect.

Regionalism and Planning

The current revival of interest in regional administrative organization, as a co-ordinating device, is partly a product of the new emphasis since 1960 on economic and physical planning and of a growing recognition that the two forms of planning, as they are both concerned with the most efficient use of Britain's scarcest resource, land, cannot be conceptually or practically separated. As Mr Sharpe has said, it was the National Economic Development Council's report of 1963, entitled *Conditions Favourable to Faster Growth*, that set the stage 'for the reorientation of national economic planning in a regional direction'.[6] Even before the publication of this document, important gestures towards the regional co-ordination of economic growth were being made, for the benefit of areas suffering from an unusually high incidence of unemployment. Special investment programmes were devised for Scotland, Merseyside and the North-East; a Development Department for Scotland was set up; a Cabinet Minister was commissioned to make a study of the problems of the North-East; and Mr Edward Heath received, as part of his Ministerial title, responsibility for *regional development* as well as for industry and

5. W. J. M. Mackenzie and J. W. Grove, *Central Administration in Britain* (Longmans 1957), p. 272.

6. *British Politics and the Two Regionalisms* (mimeographed paper), p. 7.

trade. It was left to the Labour Government of 1964, however, to establish an entirely new regional planning machinery covering the entire country.

The essence of that machinery was the division of the country into planning regions, each equipped with an executive Planning Board, consisting of the regional departmental officials entrusted by their Whitehall masters with the control of their respective 'outstations', and with an advisory Planning Council, ministerially appointed from among people qualified by expert knowledge or by the capacity to speak on behalf of regional interest groups (e.g. industrialists, trade unionists, local councillors etc.). For economic planning, therefore, Britain is now equipped with co-ordinating and advisory machinery at a level higher than that of local government but lower than that of Whitehall, and if regionalism, as a device for administrative co-ordination, is here to stay, its further growth will be from this base. Even if economic planning, as at present understood, falls once again into the doldrums, a repetition of the 'dismantling' experience of the 1950s is unlikely for two reasons – the one functional, the other political. The functional reason is that Britain *needs* 'the interposition of an agent of the central government responsible for the oversight of central government services for an area wider than individual local authorities' – an agent that will not only plan, co-ordinate and take some of the burden of decision-taking and approval-giving from Whitehall's drooping shoulders, but 'reflect back to the centre the particular interests and problems' of the area for which it is responsible.[7] The political reason is the product of what Mr Sharpe calls a 'sense of relative deprivation'. By this he means the violation done to the Britishers' belief in equality of opportunity by the existence of backward regions. Although he does not attribute the recent growth of regional sentiment entirely to this sense, he clearly considers it a factor strong enough 'to sustain a regional dimension in British politics whatever happens in the short run to economic planning'. When one adds such political influences to the incontrovertible needs of administrative rationality, the likelihood of a further development of Britain's embryonic 'middle tier' becomes rather more than merely speculative.

7. ibid. pp. 12–13. Mr Sharpe also says that 'we are possibly unique among the advanced counties in not having' – at least until recently and in embryo – 'an intermediate tier of government between local and central government'.

Regional and Local Government

From administration we have passed to politics and have thereby added, by implication, the concept of *decentralization*, as understood in the democratic sense, to that of administrative *deconcentration*. For today Britain is confronted not merely by an organizational need for a middle tier where the policies of central departments and agencies may be sub-planned and sub-co-ordinated with reference to special area needs, but by a demand, varying in strength and coherence, for *regional self-government*. This is obviously strongest in Scotland and Wales but by no means absent elsewhere. As we have already remarked, the views of the early regionalists, who started from the local government end and thought in terms of elected assemblies, are enjoying a revived popularity. If democracy is to flourish and a capacity for participation in public affairs be stimulated, why should the new regional organizations be solely responsible to Whitehall? Do we not need an upward extension of local democracy rather than a downward extension of central bureaucracy? Can a regional organization function effectively even as an eye of the central government unless it is truly representative of regional opinion? And can this be effected otherwise than by making it wholly or partly responsible to an elected council, whether this be a 'maxi' version of a local authority or a 'mini' version of the Westminster Parliament? To deal with these questions we must first look, very briefly, at the structure and functions of local authorities in England and Wales,[8] as it was established prior to the Local Government Act of 1972 coming into operation.

Contrary to popular impression, that system of local government was not ancient. The curious patchwork of administrative counties, county boroughs, municipal boroughs, urban districts, rural districts, and parishes dated from the nineteenth century. It was the combined product of a variety of political and social reform movements which had their first major impact on local government in the Municipal Reform Act of 1835 and their last (at least during the nineteenth century) in the Local Government Act of 1894, which established the urban and rural district councils as a second tier and the parish councils as a third to the administrative counties set up six years before. Until the 1972 Local Government Act, which came into effect on April 1st 1974,

8. 'England and Wales' rather than 'Britain' are here specified because Scotland has a separate and distinct system of local government.

there was no radical reform of the areas of local government (although a considerable amount of tinkering with them) not of its financial basis. Areas, originally the product of a combination of traditional, political and administrative factors,[9] were never rationally delimited, in accordance with economic, demographic or functional criteria. The main source of finance, to the extent that the local authorities met the cost of their activities from their own funds, was and is still the property tax, dating back to Elizabethan times, known as the rate.

As to the responsibilities of the local authorities, these were increased spectacularly in many fields, sharply decreased in others, and also redistributed as between the various tiers. Originally concerned mainly with law and order and with environmental health, they acquired welfare, housing, educational, physical planning and amenity function of the highest importance, the greater part of which were concentrated in the hands of the upper tier councils in those areas under the two-tier system (county and district) and of the all-purpose county borough councils in those, mainly highly-urbanized, where the one-tier system prevailed. But losses of functions, usually as a result of the establishment of regionally-based ad hoc authorities such as area gas and electricity boards and regional hospital boards, were equally significant, particularly in those fields of administration where the diseconomies of confiding responsibility to a disorderly collection of authorities of widely differing sizes and resources were most obvious.[10] Attempts to prevent such losses by dint of voluntary or compulsory co-operation between adjoining authorities, through Joint Boards and Joint Committees, achieved only limited success. Furthermore, the growing demand for substantial uniformity of service, as between people living in different areas,

9. It was tradition, or 'sentiment' that dictated, for instance, that the ancient counties, many of them far too small in area and population to provide viable units even for the limited range of services they were originally empowered or required to organize, should be preserved; likewise that certain ancient towns (one of them with a population as low as 24,000) should be accorded county borough (i.e. 'all-purpose') status. See William Hampton, 'The County as a Political Unit' in *Parliamentary Affairs*, Vol. XIX, No. 4, Autumn 1966, pp. 462–4, and the references there quoted.

10. The *reductio ad absurdum* of lilliputianism to be found in Scotland, where housing functions was confined to 175 'small burghs'. Of these '56 have under 2,000 inhabitants and yet each . . . constitutes a housing authority several of which have an annual programme of one house, while many are in the 5–10 house bracket'. (John P. Mackintosh, 'Devolution and Regionalism, the Scottish Case' in *Public Law*, Spring 1964, p. 23.)

combined with the regressiveness of the rate as a source of funds to make local authorities more and more dependent on central government grants.

Such dependence was held to imply subordination, on the principle that he who pays the piper calls the tune. Whether the very real subordination that existed however, was a product of financial relationships cannot be simply answered: for the central government possessed legal powers over local authorities which were quite independent of the grant system and which would have been retained even had the authorities acquired greater financial autonomy. But whatever the cause, the multiplicity of central directions and approvals, enforced by inspection and audit, had a strong tendency to convert them into decentralized agencies of Whitehall. While there were countervailing forces, mainly of a political kind, while commonsense limited the amount of back-seat driving that the central government was prepared to attempt, and while it would be wrong to present central–local relationships as mainly antagonistic rather than collaborative, the position occupied by the local authorities nevertheless reminds one of Metternich's famous saying that co-operation between a man and his horse is highly desirable, provided one is the man and not the horse.

Something was done, particularly after the 1920s, to rationalize the areas and strengthen the powers of the local authorities. In particular, the pattern of London government was completely transformed. But the effort was comparatively weak and sporadic, and certainly did not produce a set-up which was significantly more rational, in relation to the expansion of needs and diversification of functions, than that originally established in the late nineteenth century.

These well-known facts about British local government, so briefly summarized, have been described and illustrated in many scholarly works.[11] It therefore became *de rigueur* to speak in terms of the 'decline' of local government and to issue warnings that, unless it were radically reformed, it would gradually wither away, like the State in Marxian theory. Whether this somewhat lurid prediction could be justified or not, there can be no doubt that, prior to the 1972 Local Government Act, British local

11. The books of Professor William A. Robson on this subject are of particular importance. See his *The Development of Local Government* (3rd Edn, Allen & Unwin 1954), and *Local Government in Crisis* (Allen & Unwin 2nd Edn, 1969).

government was in a state of crisis; nor can one doubt that the citizen's interest in his local councils, as measured by his readiness to vote in local government elections, was lacking in vigour, despite the intimacy and ubiquity with which the services they provided impinged on his everyday life.

In the middle 1960s, then, it became apparent that reform, so long delayed by the central government's unwillingness to offend local vested interests whose support or opposition had been regarded (rightly or wrongly) as of major political importance, could not be put off any further. That the Labour Government, elected in 1965, was of this view was indicated by its appointment of a Royal Commission, under the chairmanship of Lord Redcliffe-Maud, with the following terms of reference:

To consider the structure of Local Government in England, outside Greater London, in relation to its existing functions; and to make recommendations for authorities and boundaries, and for functions and their division, having regard to the size and character of areas in which these can be most effectively exercised and the need to sustain a viable system of local democracy.

The Maud Report, which appeared in June 1969, made radical proposals, which became the subject of widespread discussion. The acceptability of these proposals, summarised later in this chapter, and of the new system which has at last emerged, depends on one's view of the potential role of elected councils in the British political system. To this we now turn.

Among the advocates of reform, there were wide areas of disagreement. Such disagreement did not normally extend to a calling into question of the elective principle itself – although some critics suggested, if only tentatively, that Britain might be as well or as ill administered if locally elected councils were replaced by deconcentrated agencies of the central government, perhaps assisted by advisory bodies.[12] Most students of govern-

12. 'The institutions of central government are a necessary part of every nation state, but although local administration is also a necessity, local institutions are not, and if local authorities are created, their nature may be of many kinds and certainly they need not have statutory powers directly conferred upon them by the legislature. And there is no reason why they should be elected bodies.

'In other words, it would be a workable system of government in England and Wales, if, under the central departments, there existed, for example, administrative regions governed by Boards nominated by Ministers. The system might be less efficient; it might be (though not by its nature) less

ment would agree that some form of grass roots democracy is essential, if only because it helps to persuade people, by the addition of example to precept, that politics is the art of the possible.[13] Whether this is so or not, the increasing demand for popular participation in the political decision-taking process would of itself ensure that no proposal for *abolishing* local self-governing institutions would get a tolerant hearing. Where *serious* disagreement has arisen has been on questions about (a) the levels at which locally elected authorities should operate, (b) the relations that should be established between them and the central government, and (c) the manner in which they should organize themselves for the performance of their functions.

It is at this point that we must refer back to the distinction, made at the beginning of this chapter, between decentralization and deconcentration. Many reformers held the view that, as it was at the regional level that most of the important 'local' decisions were made, and as the region provided the most viable administrative sub-division for the provision of an increasing variety of services, and as there were signs – albeit sometimes ambiguous ones – of the growth of a sense of regional identity, local government itself should be regionalized. This would involve the replacement of deconcentration by decentralization, through the establishment of elected councils or assemblies for regions of approximately the size and shape of the existing planning regions (see Map 5) and the total or partial devolution to these councils or assemblies, by parliamentary enactment, of the control and co-ordination of most of the services at present administered by the outstations of the central government departments and other central agencies. As, by comparison with the present local authorities, such councils or assemblies would be strong bodies, supported by their own corps of adequately specialized and diversified officials, they could not only regain many of the functions (such as hospital administration) previously taken away from local administration, but assume responsibilities never hitherto

---

humane and less responsive to the needs of the community. But there is no reason why it should not be wholly workable without tyranny.

'... it is important to recognize that the system does not carry within itself its own justification. Mayers and aldermen and councillors are not necessary political animals. We could do without them.' J. A. G. Griffith, *Central Departments and Local Authorities* (Allen & Unwin 1966), p. 542.

13. See C. H. Wilson (ed), *Essays on Local Government* (Blackwell 1948) pp. 18–19.

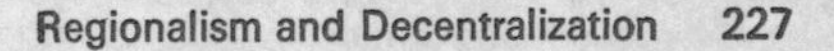

Map 5 Economic Planning Regions

confided to elected bodies. Moreover, in the performance of these duties, they could be permitted a degree of freedom from central control inconceivable in the present set-up, and hence enabled to frame policies uniquely adapted to the needs and even the prejudices of the people within the areas of their jurisdiction. It was also argued that authorities possessing responsibilities on this scale would be able to find elected members with abilities superior to those possessed by many of the present County, County Borough and County District Councillors, who were alleged to lack both the power and the prestige necessary to make their jobs attractive to people of high intelligence and marked originality. To the argument that authorities of such size would no longer be meaningfully 'local', it was replied (a) that, with the increase in spatial mobility through modern transport and communications, the 'locality' had undergone expansion, and (b) that the new regional units would not need to monopolize all decentralized functions, but could be, and ought to be, associated with smaller second-tier authorities, which would not only enjoy sub-delegated responsibilities but receive, as of right, certain responsibilities that did not require, for their efficient performance, a catchment area of regional size.

Obviously, such a scheme was fraught with problems. What powers were to be devolved on the regional authorities? How much central control was to be exercised, of what kind and by what methods? Were region-based civil servants concerned with the devolved functions to be transferred to the new regional authorities, or merely lent to them and simultaneously continue to exercise the powers, both of direct administration and of control, that Whitehall still retained? What divergencies from nationally-approved standards of service were to be permitted, and how much discretion was there to be in respect of the division of financial resources as between the various services claiming attention (e.g. roads, education, health, etc.)? How far were the regional authorities to combine fiscal with administrative responsibilities, through being given a tax-base sufficiently wide and flexible to finance the services devolved on them? If they were to depend on regionally-raised rather than centrally-provided financial resources, what mechanism could be devised (comparable with the rate-deficiency grant) to ensure that the poorer of them would not be confronted with the unenviable alternative of providing second-class services or imposing excessive taxation? If, on the other hand, they were to get the greater part of their money from the Exchequer, how could it be guaranteed that they would behave in a financially responsible manner?

To these vital questions different writers gave different answers. At one end of the scale, there were those for whom the regional council would be essentially a county council writ large; at the other, those for whom it would be the Westminster parliament writ small. The most extreme proposals for regional decentralization came from Mr John P. Mackintosh, MP, who would give his regional councils all the powers at present exercised by what he termed 'intermediate government', including powers of economic planning.

Of the eleven councils envisaged in his scheme (see Map 6), two would cover Scotland and Wales, and the remaining nine account for the North, North-West, Yorkshire and Humberside, East Midlands, West Midlands, 'Anglia', South East (including London), South Central and South West. 'Of considerable power in terms of population and resources', each would be able to perform a wide variety of functions and to engage staffs comparable in quality with that of the central civil service. Regional Councils (and Scottish and Welsh Assemblies) would be directly elected for a fixed term of three years, and would organize themselves on the parliamentary pattern, with Ministers responsible for departments, and not on the familiar local government pattern whereby executive duties are confided to committees; for Mackintosh believed that the committee system has 'debilitating effects' and that regional governments 'as large and complex' as those he recommended 'could not be run by groups of elected members deciding both policy and administrative detail'. Each council or assembly would have 'a prime minister and a cabinet, the latter consisting of about eight ministers, a possible division of portfolios being development, finance, health, housing, agriculture, education, police and fire services and the arts and amenities'. Each, moreoever, would recruit its own officials, subject to certain central regulations designed to ensure that 'there should be equivalence of ranks and pay so that training could be provided in common for all regional and the central civil services and that cross-pointings and transfers between the central and regional services could be easy and frequent'.

To provide the councils and assemblies with an independent source of revenue, rates could be supplemented by local income taxes; but most of the funds required would be allocated among the regions by central government from the proceeds of national taxation, on the basis of annual negotiations between the regional governments and the Treasury. Once the regions had received the money, however, they would be free to spend it as they thought fit, subject only to a centrally-imposed obligation to 'meet certain minimum standards such as free compulsory education to a certain age, a free health service, certain levels of pay for certain employees and so on'.

As for second-tier authorities, the pattern of these would be

Map 6 Proposed Eleven Regions

freely devised by the regional governments themselves, and would vary from region to region in accordance with need, opinion and – presumably – tradition.[14]

One of us has questioned both the practicability and the necessity of so thoroughgoing a reorganization; but there can be no doubt that, although Mackintosh's proposals are wide open to criticism, the reformer who believes that all intermediate government should be made democratically responsible to a regional electorate is compelled to think big. Perhaps the most serious flaw in the scheme is its implicit assumption that regional democracy equipped with such wide powers would be compatible with the formulation and implementation of a coherent national economic plan. For planning involves forms of regional *discrimination*, such as the selection of growth-points, that would provoke the strongest possible opposition from those regions discriminated *against*, with the result that central–regional tensions could easily mount to a point of crisis, where they would have to be resolved, quite arbitrarily, by someone's fiat – and that fiat, one may reasonably suppose, would be the central government's.

As Sharpe has written, 'the overriding purpose of regional planning' has so far been that 'of redistributing economic resources between regions. Some regions stand to gain from this process in that they will get more than they would have got were there no planning. But equally some regions must lose, growth or no growth. This process requires that there is some higher common superior to do the redistributing. In a nut shell, centralist regionalism is an instrument for strengthening central government . . .'[15]

Sir William Hart, formerly Clerk to the Greater London Council, put the same point even more forcibly. The regional machinery for economic planning, he wrote,

is the means by which the Government seeks to inform itself of the respective needs and possibilities of the regions and to secure that the means available to it for influencing economic growth are so used as to carry out the differential policy which it determines. In other words, the . . . machinery can be regarded as related to the preparation of the capital investment programme – or, to lengthen its effect, the National Plan – and to implement it by coordinating Government action in the regions. It operates on a different plane from that in which local authori-

14. John P. Mackintosh, *The Devolution of Power* (Penguin and Chatto & Windus 1968), Chap. 9.

15. *British Politics and the Two Regionalisms*, p. 8.

ties act: it creates the framework within which local government exists, rather than seeking to enter into competition with it.[16]

It was all this, of course, that Mackintosh and his fellow-thinkers wanted to change. Through replacing deconcentration by decentralization they would ensure that the national plan, instead of being *imposed* by the central government, would *emerge* from a complex process of negotiation between democratically-responsible authorities at both levels, the central and the regional. And it may well be that this is a preferable method of economic planning to the one that Britain is now attempting, despite the critical disputes that it might produce. But the implications of the change of system must be faced, and it is an illusion to imagine that elected regional councils would be interested in doing the *same* sorts of jobs as the regional Planning Board are trying to do – only more efficiently, less bureaucratically, and more democratically.

We do not say, however, that Mackintosh-type regional councils are necessarily to be condemned as a possible solution to the problems here under discussion; for it can be argued that Great Britain is moving towards a situation in which political diversity, along regional lines, is gaining ground over political homogeneity, that this will have to be institutionally recognized and the necessary sacrifices of coherence in national economic policy consciously made. We merely wish to point out that there *are* such sacrifices, and to indicate certain consequences of a transition to democratic regionalism of which its advocates are not always sufficiently aware.

Reformers who continued to stress national homogeneity and who believed that there was still a need for regional deconcentration of governmental powers to 'little Whitehalls' tended to envisage the future of local government in more modest terms. If one simply wished local authorities to exercise their present range of powers (together with a few new ones) more competently and more comparatively free from the multifarious controls of which the bigger and better councils so persistently complained, then rationalization at a level lower than that of the big region appeared to be the solution. Among students who thought along these lines, many advocated the adoption of the so-called 'city region' as the standard pattern. The city region, as its name implies, is 'an area consisting of a large town and much of the sur-

16. 'The Conurbations and the Regions' in *Political Quarterly*, Vol. 37, No. 2, April–June 1966, p. 136.

rounding countryside as feels its pull, in employment, marketing, shopping, entertainment, professional services and so on'.[17] Mr Derek Senior, the dissident member of the Maud Commission, whose name is prominently associated with this proposal, originally suggested the creation of 42 such city-regions as the basic units of local government. Using demographic, economic and cultural criteria, he classified them into mature, emergent, embryonic and potential (see Map 7). With minimum populations of 250,000, they would, in his view,

> be ideally equipped in catchment area, case-load and financial resources to be responsible for the management of a unified, positive health service (including health centres and hospitals), of traffic, commuter transport and regional motorways, of seaports and airports, land drainage and water supply; for all higher education short of university standard; for organizing the demand for housebuilding components . . ., for the comprehensive renewal of city centres; for the abatement of air and river pollution and the reclamation of derelict land; for crime squads and multi-purpose sports centres; for the promotion of regional development – and for the making of development plans.[18]

This was clearly local government, as we know it, reorganized to enable it to exercise its existing powers more effectively and with greater autonomy and to acquire a limited number of new powers justified by the criteria of adequacy of catchment area and abundance of financial resources. Mr Senior, indeed, was fully conscious of the implications of what he was proposing; for he specifically denied to his new authorities those broader

17. William Hampton, 'The County as a Political Unit' in *Parliamentary Affairs*, Vol. XIX, pp. 468–9, quoting *The Times* leader of 23 Aug. 1965.

18. *Political Quarterly*, Vol. 36, No. 1, Jan.–Mar. 1965, pp. 89–90.

The distinction between the region as conceived by Mr Mackintosh as the basic area of local government and the City region as conceived by Messrs Senior, Sharpe and others is thus illustrated by Professor Self:

'The main alternatives lie between basing the new regions on major centres or adopting broader units having some general resemblance to the present standard departmental regions. Simply to illustrate this point, the North of England might be divided (under the first method) into about ten regions based upon Tyneside, Teesside, Leeds, Sheffield, York, Hull, Merseyside, Manchester, Preston and Carlisle; while under the second method it would fall into four broader regions (the North-East Coast, Yorkshire, Lancashire–Cheshire, Westmorland–Cumberland.'

He considers that 'in general the first approach would coincide best with the facts of human geography, the needs of effective planning, and the desirability of manageable and intelligible democratic units'. ('Regional Planning and the Machinery of Government' in *Public Administration*, Vol. 42, Autumn 1964, pp. 232–3.)

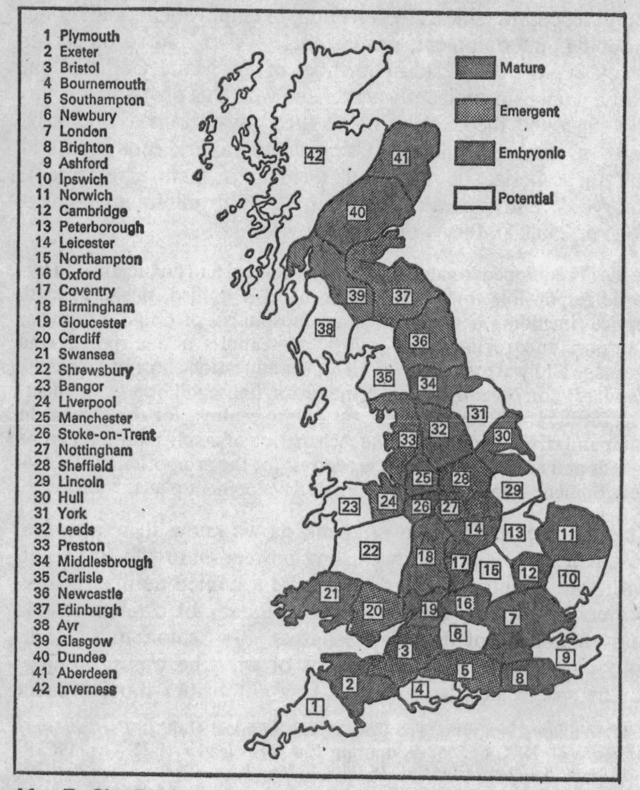

Map 7 City Regions

functions that Mr Mackintosh would give to his regional councils and assemblies. Planning, he said,

> can make no headway unless central government does organize itself to think with one mind about all aspects of physical development and takes the initiative in formulating regional *strategies*, on whatever scale it finds convenient, for the timing and relative location of major residential, industrial, commercial and recreational developments and of the communications between them.[19]

The job of the city-region, in fact, was not to engage in the kind of overall planning which must necessarily be concentrated at the

19. *Political Quarterly*, Vol. 36, No. 1, Jan.–Mar. 1965, p. 83.

national and regional levels, but to *implement* plans by translating them into strictly local terms, with special reference to land-use.

As far as England was concerned, discussions of the subject inevitably took as their starting point the Maud proposals, which were the product of the most thorough and penetrating investigation of the country's local government system ever to have been undertaken. These proposals, although extremely radical, were somewhat eclectic, in that they did not derive exclusive inspiration from either of the main schemes of reform outlined above. The 'city-region' pattern was only *partly* reflected in the suggestion that England (outside London) should be divided into 61 new local government areas, of which all but three[20] should be equipped with a council responsible for the full range of local services since only *some* of the proposed areas are focused on a single urban centre. The Commission, although stating as one of its principles that 'areas must be used on the interdependence of town and country', nevertheless concluded that 'the city region was not an idea which could be applied uniformly all over England', since it provided the 'clue' only for a limited number of areas, such as 'the great urban concentrations of Birmingham, Liverpool and Manchester' and those areas 'where a big town is the natural centre for a wide area of surrounding countryside and small towns'.[21] Likewise, in its acceptance of the need to combine these operational authorities with planning authorities at the 'big region' level, it went only a short distance towards satisfying the demands of the advocates of regional mini-parliaments. In recommending the creation of 'eight provinces, each with its own provincial council', it specified that the councils (apart from their officially appointed members should be elected, not directly by the citizens of each province, but indirectly by the members of the sixty-one area councils, and that the 'key function' of the

20. The three are the great conurbations of Birmingham, Liverpool and Manchester, where 'responsibility for services should be divided in each case between a metropolitan authority whose key functions would be planning transportation and major development, and a number of metropolitan district authorities whose key functions would be education, the personal social services, health and housing'. For the new areas proposed by the Maud Report, See Map 8.

21. For the record, it should be added that the Commission also made the much-criticized proposal that at the grass roots level there must be elected 'local councils, not to provide main services, but to promote and watch over the particular interests of communities in city, town and village throughout England'. The dissident Mr Senior makes a similar proposal (see below, p. 236).

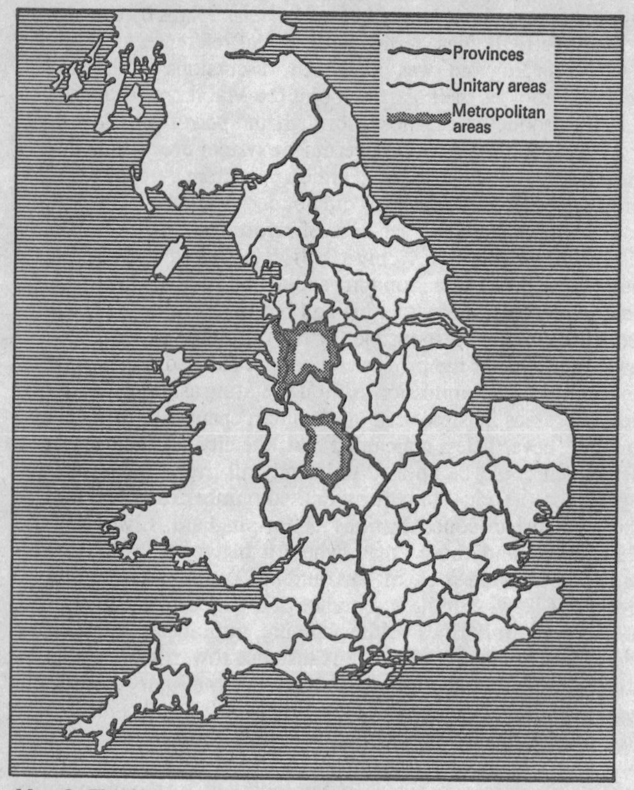

Map 8 The New Areas and the Old

provincial body should be, not the direct provision of services, but the determination, in collaboration with the central government, of 'the provincial strategy and planning framework within which the main (i.e. the sixty-one) authorities must operate'. The provincial councils, therefore, were to be little more than the present Regional Economic Planning Councils fortified by elected members representing the regional (or provincial) electorate at one remove. Thus, at the big region level, power would continue to flow from the top downwards, even though the upward flow of *advice* might be significantly strengthened.

The Commission justified these proposals on the grounds that their implementation would greatly improve the capacity of local government to do the four main things required of it – 'to perform efficiently a wide range of profoundly important tasks concerned with the safety, health and well-being of people in different localities; to attract and hold the interest of its citizens; to develop enough inherent strength to deal with the national government in a valid partnership; and to adapt itself continuously to the unprecedented changes that are going on in the way people live, work, move, shop and enjoy themselves'. So far as the impact of these proposals on the central government is concerned, the Committee envisaged that the provincial councils would give it 'new opportunities for decentralizing power' and that the area councils would be strong enough to encourage it 'to trust them with increased responsibility and substantially relax the present detailed supervision'. The Commission was also of the view that with reorganized and strengthened *general* authorities at the two sub-national levels, the need to create ad hoc authorities (i.e. 'unrepresentative machinery for special purposes') would be reduced.

All this was well argued in great detail – but not sufficiently well to convince one of the Commission's most enterprising and hard-working members, Mr Derek Senior, who produced a minority report, equal in length to the main one, in which he recommended, as a preferable alternative, 'a predominantly two-level system of service-running local government, comprising 35 directly elected regional authorities, responsible for the planning/transportation/development complex of functions . . ., for capital investment programming and for police, fire and education; and 148 directly elected district authorities responsible for the health service, the personal social services, housing management, consumer protection and all other functions involving personal contact with the citizen'. These would be complemented, at the grass roots level, by 'directly elected common councils, . . . representing existing parishes and towns or parts of towns small enough to have a real feeling of community', and at the upper level by 'five appointed provincial councils with members predominantly nominated by the regional authorities within their areas'. The former would have discretionary power to provide local amenities, while the latter would be mainly responsible for 'long-term strategic planning'.

The Maud Report, therefore, did not produce a solution to the problems of regional and local government likely to win unanimous support, even among those who had no vested interest in

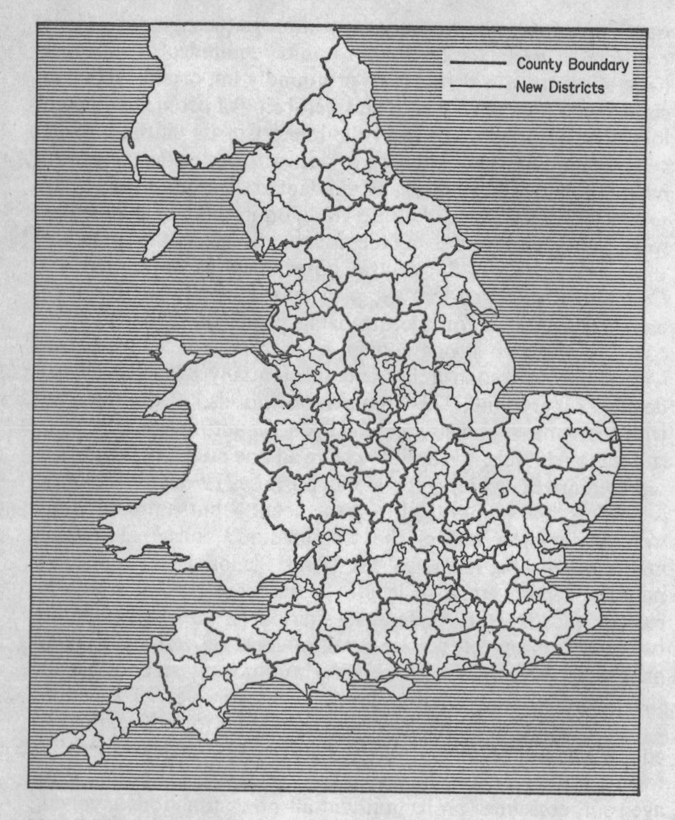

Map 9 The new system

maintaining the status quo or something very much like it. Nevertheless, it was a constitutional document of the highest importance, presenting the national government with a challenge which, sooner or later, it would have to meet.[22]

Action, in fact, was not too far away. Declining to wait the report of the Commission on the Constitution (appointed in 1969 to consider the relations between the national government and the 'several countries, nations and regions of the United Kingdom'), the Conservative Government published, in February 1971, its White Paper on Local Government in England,[23] which presaged the Local Government Act of the following year. Both the White Paper and the subsequent Act fully recognized the basic conflict that existed between the claims of efficiency and the demands of representative democracy – the former generally calling for larger units of government which are, perforce, more remote from the electorate, while the latter, seeking to maintain some element of government relatively close to the people, calls for smaller units. The system that came into effect on 1 April 1974 represents the Conservative Government's answer – (some would say very imperfect answer) to that problem. The basis of this new system rests on the division of functions between two tiers of authorities – counties and districts. At the same time, however, a distinction has been drawn between Metropolitan areas (the large conurbations) and non-Metropolitan areas (mixed urban and rural communities). Thus, in England and Wales, outside London, there are now six Metropolitan Counties (Greater Manchester, Merseyside, South Yorkshire, West Yorkshire, West Midlands and Tyne and Wear) and forty-seven non-Metropolitan counties. These counties in turn embrace 35 Metropolitan Districts and 333 non-Metropolitan districts.

The table at the end of the chapter illustrates the allocation of functions among the various authorities, and two points might be made here which illustrate the thinking behind the allocations. First, the Counties were considered the more appropriate bodies for over-all planning and the provision of services where uniformity was considered desirable (for example Police, Fire Brigades, Consumer Protection), while the Districts provided the details for the plans and services more closely related to local knowledge and local needs. Secondly, while the non-Metropolitan Counties were given responsibility for Education, Libraries and Social Services, in the conurbations these were made the responsibility of the Districts, as the Metropolitan Counties were thought too large for the effective organisation of those functions.

It is, of course, far too early to offer any judgment of the new system in action, but we can essay a few comments about the structure itself and the degree to which it represents an acceptable resolution of the efficiency/democracy dichotomy. First, the application of a 'Greater London' style to the larger conurba-

22. The quotations in the above paragraphs are taken from the 'short version of the Maud Report (Cmnd 4039). The full Report is published as Cmnd 4040, and Mr Senior's Memorandum of Dissent as Cmnd 4040–I.

23. Cmnd 4584.

tions is a timely recognition that for too long sensible and coherent planning had been hampered by boundaries that no longer had relevance to indiscriminate urban sprawl and its accompanying problems. Secondly, in similar manner, but on a smaller scale, there has been the sweeping aside of many of the anomolous borders that perpetuated artificial barriers between town and country, borough and county. These amalgamations are seen as the answer to the demands for greater efficiency but many feel, with some considerable justification, that the price for that efficiency is remoteness – the average population of the Metropolitan counties is almost two million and of the non-Metropolitan counties close to 700,000. It was in order to mitigate these fears that the Districts were created. They, it was hoped, would maintain closer links with the electorate and enhance the degree of popular participation in local affairs. However, even here it is quite apparent that for many people the Authority will seem much more distant than in the past. The reduction in the number of local authorities by something like two-thirds has inevitably entailed an increase in the size of the new districts. (Thus the average population of the 35 Metropolitan Districts or Boroughs is about a quarter of a million, and of the 296 non-Metropolitan Districts or Boroughs about 100,000.[24]) Furthermore, the number of locally elected officials has been almost halved as a result of these amalgamations, and this is almost certain to add to the sense of remoteness.

While this new structure is then much less local than hitherto, this need not in itself occasion greater electoral apathy, for if voters are persuaded that the new Authorities are creatures of substance they may well feel that the changes are for the better. However, it seems unlikely that the electorate will be so persuaded for, apart from the confusing allocation of functions apparent from the Table, other Acts of the Conservative Government were surely destined to erode still further the authority and responsibilities of Local Government bodies. The Housing Finance Act of 1972, for instance, took from the Local Authorities the right to determine Council House rents in their areas; the National Health Service Reorganization Act involved the replacement of

24. These bald averages disguise considerable variations in size: the range of population in the Metropolitan Districts is from 174,000 to 1,096,000 and of the non-Metropolitan Districts from 24,000 to 425,000. N.B. All figures in this paragraph and footnote refer to the English Counties and Districts outside Greater London.

Hospital Management Committees and Local Authority health services by fourteen Regional and ninety Area Health Authorities; the Water Act swept aside local water undertakings in favour of ten regional water authorities.(The Water Act did at least provide for a majority of local politicians on each Authority although the chairmen were appointed by the Minister, but the Health Service Act provided that the Minister shall appoint the fourteen regional authorities and the chairmen of the ninety area authorities, while the regional authorities appoint the members of the area authorities – with a token four seats reserved to local politicians.) While one cannot yet assess the effect of these changes on the morale and image of the new local authorities, it is evident that if such developments are extended into other spheres then Local Government, as the British have known it, will atrophy and eventually die.

Scotland, Wales and Northern Ireland

When we turn to the so-called Celtic fringe, the nature of the problem changes, owing to the comparative exemption of these areas from the political homogeneity still characteristic of England. One of the consequences of nationalistic feelings and demands, now making themselves more and more evident in both Scotland and Wales, is that administrative problems in these parts of the British Isles cannot be isolated, as to some degree they still can be in England, from political ones. The man who first said that 'mere administrative rationality will have to yield to strict political prejudice' was probably a civil servant located in Edinburgh.

First, we must examine the already-distinctive characteristics of regional organization in these troublesome areas. Scotland has long been treated in many ways as a separate political and administrative unit. She has her own distinctive legal, educational and local government systems, and her own Established Church. At Westminster, there are few English MPs who would dare to participate in debates on purely Scottish matters.[25] Much of the business relating to Scotland is transacted by a Scottish Grand Committee which meets at least twelve times a year. There is also a Scottish Standing Committee to deal with the committee stages of Scottish Bills. Since 1895 Scotland has had a separate Secretary of State, who invariably occupies a seat in the British Cabinet. Both before and after the creation of this office, there took place a progressive devolution of administrative responsibilities to Edinburgh, culminating in the creation of a Scottish Development Department in 1962. Today, the Scottish Office comprises four departments in St Andrew's House, all responsible to the Secretary of State: Development, Home and Health, Agriculture and Fisheries, and Education. Of the UK Departments whose responsibilities extend to Scotland (e.g. Trade and Industry, Employment, Social Services, Defence, Inland Revenue and Customs and Excise) most have Scottish offices; and several of the UK ad hoc authorities, such as the Forestry Commission, the Herring Industry Board, the White Fish Authority and the Crown Lands Commission, report to the Secretary of State for Scotland in respect of their Scottish activities.

Wales also has a Grand Committee, together with a Standing Committee, at Westminster, but did not acquire a separate Secretary of State until 1964. His duties are more limited than those of the Secretary of State for Scotland, and the Principality, although possessing a 'little Whitehall' at Cardiff, does not have the advantage – if advantage it be – of a series of separate departments comparable with those at St Andrew's House. However, a nominated Welsh Council, with executive duties, has replaced the former advisory Council for Wales, and is now responsible for the duties formerly performed by the Welsh Economic Council, Welsh Arts Council, the Development Corporation for Wales and the Welsh Tourist Board.

These arrangements give little satisfaction to the Scottish and Welsh nationalists, many of whom envisage a degree of autonomy within the Commonwealth amounting to independence. How serious a force Scottish and Welsh nationalism is capable of becoming cannot as yet be judged. There are two major unknowns: first, the measure of popular support that the nationalists are capable of mobilizing and maintaining at General Elections;[26] second, the extent to which nationalism is more than a reflection of a sense of relative deprivation and hence diminishable by centrally-formulated schemes to improve the economic position and prospects of the two predominantly Celtic areas. On either issue, prediction would be foolhardy.

There seems to be some evidence that alleged relative deprivation is more sensitive an issue in Scotland than in Wales. 'In the

25. On any stage of a Scottish Bill, 'any English MP who might have the temerity to speak would be regarded with a mixture of horror and fury by Scots MPs on both sides'. (J. P. Mackintosh, 'Scottish Nationalism' in *Political Quarterly*, Vol. 38, No. 4, Oct.–Dec. 1967, p. 391.)

statement of basic aims of Plaid Cymru,' write M. P. Grant and R. J. C. Preece, 'the safeguarding of the culture, language and traditions of Wales is given precedence before the protection of its economy. SNP literature places more emphasis on the alleged economic deprivation of Scotland . . .'[27]
What one can say with confidence is that, to the extent that deprivation is equated with failure to receive a fair share of public services, the nationalist claim that Scotland is deprived does not accord with the facts. Indeed, as John P. Mackintosh points out, 'there is much evidence that Scotland (quite rightly) gets specially favoured treatment'.[28] The same is probably true of Wales. But it should be remembered that both countries *are* backward in comparison with England *as a whole* and it is at England as a whole rather than at comparable areas of England (e.g. the North-East or Merseyside) that the nationalists tend to look. Even this type of comparison, however, does not necessarily support the nationalist case; since it is very improbable that independence would bring any economic improvement, whatever provisions for economic and fiscal relationships with England were incorporated in the Acts of Disunion although, of course, the disposition of the North Sea oil revenues will undoubtedly have significance here. 'Relative deprivation' then, does not offer to the outsider any very convincing argument for independence. If it appears to convince many Scots and Welshmen, this simply provides additional evidence that in Great Britain, as elsewhere in the world, natoinal sentiment is never the product of rational

26. The spectacular successes of the SNP and Plaid Cymru at by-elections in 1966–68 do not provide reliable indicators, for well-known reasons. See Iain McLean, 'Scottish Nationalists' and Alan Butt Philip, 'Plaid Cymru' in *New Society*, No. 328, 9 Jan. 1969. The 1974 general elections saw a dramatic increase in electoral support for the national parties. It is yet to be seen whether this support will be maintained.

27. 'Welsh and Scottish Nationalism' in *Parliamentary Affairs*, Vol. XXI, No. 3, Summer 1968, p. 258. Of Welsh nationalism. Mr E. Hudson Davies (Labour MP for Conway since 1966) says: 'So firmly has a desire to preserve the language been intertwined with nationalism, that many Welshmen have expressed surprise that a serious nationalist movement could exist in Scotland where there was no viable living language to preserve.' Nevertheless, the need for the Welsh nationalists to appeal simultaneously to those who emphasize cultural discrimination (as in the Welsh-speaking areas of North Wales) and those whose major concern is with economic deprivation (as in the predominantly English-speaking areas of South Wales) is giving rise to a certain 'schizophrenia' in the movement. ('Welsh Nationalism' in *Political Quarterly*, Vol. 39, July–Sept. 1968, pp. 324, 331.)

28. *The Devolution of Power*, p. 157; and see tables on pp. 158–61.

economic calculation. Despite dire warnings about the consequences of 'balkanization', mini-nationalisms are growing everywhere. There is more than a possibility, therefore, that the Westminster government may be compelled to extend the limited degree of autonomy that Scotland and Wales now enjoy.[29] If this comes to pass, the pattern of Scottish and Welsh autonomy might well follow, in some respects, that already granted to Northern Ireland, which enjoyed a form of devolution which has certain affinities with federalism.

The 'Stormont model' was itself forced on the British Government by a political necessity: the unwillingness of a predominantly and militantly Protestant majority in the Six Counties to join with the rest of Ireland first in Home Rule and then in full independence, and their determination simultaneously to maintain the British connection and enjoy the maximum possible degree of regional self-government. Northern Ireland, while continuing to be represented at Westminster, had its own parliament and cabinet which wielded extensive powers devolved by 'imperial' legislation.[30] That these arrangements worked with reasonable satisfaction both to the English and at least to the Protestant majority of the Northern Irish is sometimes attributed to the determination of the ruling Unionist Party at Stormont to keep closely in step with England in all matters of importance; but, as Mr Mackintosh points out in arguing against 'the notion that an element of devolution must lead to an immediate rush towards total separation', there are 'other squally important forces pressing in the same direction'.[31] Being a poor area, Northern Ireland cannot maintain standards of public service even roughly equivalent to those in Britain without either imposing penal rates of

29. Cornish nationalism is a less serious and more purely romantic phenomenon; since Cornwall could hardly maintain a separate political existence, except possibly as a unit of a Cornish–Breton–Channel Islands Federation – a solution to her 'problem' which would hardly appeal to the French government, and might not get much support from the Bretons and the Channel Islanders.

30. It should be noted that the 'Stormont' ministries perform duties imposed on them by the Westminster parliament as well as by the Northern Ireland parliament. For instance, 'it is estimated that the Ministry of Agriculture . . . spends five-eighths of its time administering Imperial services on behalf of the Whitehall Ministry of Agriculture: mainly the guaranteed prices and market clauses of the 1947 Agriculture Act'. Thus 'the Northern Ireland situation is essentially a form of local government in that permission to handle certain problems for a given area is granted by the central parliament'. (John P. Mackintosh: 'Devolution, Regionalism: the Scottish Case' in *Public Law*, Spring, 1964, p. 20.)

taxation or accepting a subsidy. As a result of a series of financial arrangements of some complexity, Westminster has agreed to subsidize Stormont and Stormont has agreed to be subsidized. Without such assistance, which naturally has certain strings attached to it, the British connection would be of little value except as an institutional expression of a sentimental attachment; with such assistance, the initial desire to keep in step is perpetually reinforced. Hence, 'whether Stormont was controlled by the Unionists or not, the pressure for a high degree of uniformity and co-operation would remain'.[32]

It has been suggested that for similar reasons the Scots and the Welsh would find this form of devolution equally acceptable, even though it is strongly rejected both by the SNP and by Plaid Cymru. On at least two occasions, Liberals have introduced into the British House of Commons Private Members' bills designed to provide precisely such a quasi-federal solution. The whole matter was one of the main talking points of the Constitutional Commission which published its report on October 31st 1973 and recommended the devolution of some central government powers to Scotland and, to a lesser extent, Wales, in an effort to reduce discontent with the present system of Government and as a response to national feeling in Scotland and Wales.

Conclusion

As we have seen, the issues of deconcentration, decentralization, local and regional democracy, and devolution are closely interlinked. Nevertheless they must be kept conceptually separate, for reasons that have been explained.

It is quite sensible, for instance, to advocate a greater degree of regional administrative deconcentration without simultaneously insisting that the deconcentrated departments and agencies should also be decentralized, in the sense of becoming responsible to elected assemblies. Indeed, as has been suggested, the respective demands for deconcentration and decentralization may in certain important respects prove incompatible. It is equally sensible to advocate the 'raising of local government to the regional level' as a means of facilitating or enhancing participatory forms of democracy, provided that one realizes that this may have unfavourable as well as favourable political and administrative consequences. If, on the other hand, one

31. Mackintosh, *The Devolution of Power*, p. 181.
32. ibid. p. 181.

plumps for the 'city-region' concept, one must accept the disadvantage – if disadvantage it be – that the resultant democratic institutions cannot undertake a whole number of important functions with which, on purely 'participatory' grounds, one might well wish to endow them. Finally, one can advocate greater autonomy, by way of devolution, to Scotland and Wales, without wishing to confer even a more limited autonomy on a series of English regions, and without disregarding the likelihood that a whole new collection of politico-administrative problems will thereby be created.

As we have repeatedly stressed, our task in this book is to define the problems and explain the implications of the solutions that have been proposed for them. While we can hardly avoid suggesting solutions where these seem obvious to us, we are concerned with institutional analysis rather than with prescription. There is no aspect of British government where such analysis is more urgent than that which has been so briefly surveyed in this chapter.

Major Local Government Functions from 1 April 1974

Counties:
Education*
Personal social services*
Libraries
Planning (structure plans, development control
[strategic and reserved decisions],
acquisiton and disposal of land, development and re-development)
Highways and related subjects – traffic and transport co-ordination.
Housing (certain reserve powers, e.g. overspill)
Consumer protection
Refuse disposal
Museums and art galleries
Parks and open spaces
Playing fields and swimming baths
Police
Fire

** In the Metropolitan Areas these functions are administered by the District and not the County Authority, but the Metropolitan County does have the additional task of Passenger Transport Authority.*

Districts:
Planning (local plans, most development control,
acquisition and disposal of land,
development and redevelopment)
Maintenance of unclassified roads in urban areas
Public Transport – operation
Housing and town development
Building regulations
Environmental health and services
Refuse collection
Museums and art galleries
Parks and open spaces
Playing fields and swimming baths
Cemeteries and crematoria

Chapter 11

Delegated Legislation and Administrative Tribunals

In this chapter we deal with a collection of institutional innovations as important as those described in Chapter 8. Indeed, the major part of our subject, administrative jurisdiction, is concerned with a series of ad hoc agencies of a special type – those which dispense a form of justice different from that provided by the ordinary courts of law.

The title of this chapter indicates how far we have moved from the separation of powers regarded by Montesquieu – although falsely so – in the eighteenth century as one of the major and most valuable characteristics of the British Constitution. The advent of big government has made it less and less possible to separate, in distinct bodies of institutions, the respective functions of legislation, administration and justice. With the growth of bureaucracy, the general tendency has been for the administration to invade the provinces of the other two powers, thereby, as some would have it, shifting the constitutional centre of gravity away from Westminster and the Temple and towards Whitehall. Not unnaturally, such developments have caused alarm and despondency, and not only among those constitutional lawyers who believe the ancient principles of the sovereignty of Parliament and the rule of law, as clasically described by Dicey in his *Law of the Constitution*, to be the essential foundation stones of our political way of life. 'Is British Liberty in Danger from Administrative Encroachments?', the title of an Oxford Prize essay in the 1930s, was a real question then, and remains so today. Since the 1930s, however, the British have taken a number of important steps to try and ensure that bureaucratic 'encroachment' is controlled in such a way as to preserve – and in some cases to enhance – those liberties of the subject which they continue to regard as of paramount importance. In the present chapter it is with these steps that we shall be mainly concerned.

Delegated Legislation

By 'delegated legislation' we mean the delegation by Parliament, through statutory enactment, of rule-making powers to administrative agencies – principally Ministries and local authorities.

The practice is by no means a new one. Indeed, a number of very early examples are quoted in the Report of the Committee on Ministers' Powers of 1932, which was established 'to consider the powers exercised by or under the direction of (or by persons or bodies appointed specially by) Ministers of the Crown by way of (a) delegated legislation and (b) judicial or quasi-judicial decision . . .' Thus, in 1785, the Commissioners for Stamp Duties were given 'power to do acts necessary for putting into force the duties imposed on horses and carriages, and in certain cases to make regulations for effectively securing the duty on such carriages', while the Mutiny Act of 1717 gave the Crown 'express authority to make and constitute under His Sign Manual, articles for the better government of His Majesty's forces as well *within* the kingdoms of Great Britain and Ireland as beyond the seas . . .' Even earlier instances of the delegation of legislative powers were quoted from statutes passed in the reign of Henry VIII and Edward VI. All these, however, were sufficiently exceptional to be noteworthy. More usually, Parliament chose to couch its public statutory enactments in highly specific terms which left very little scope for the exercise of rule-making discretion on the part of the administrative authorities.[1] This was fully possible so long as public laws were comparatively rare and their content simple. With the advent of the regulatory and social-service-providing state, the possibilities of legislative specificity steadily diminished. As a result the nineteenth and twentieth centuries saw delegated legislation swell to a great flood. Confronted with any matter of real complexity, Parliament took refuge in passing what became known as 'skeleton' legislation, in which it confused itself to the enunciation of certain principles and policies and confided the application of these to the rules and orders which it authorized the appropriate administrative agencies to promulgate.[2]

1. See Report, Cmnd 4060, particularly pp. 11–15. A frequently quoted – and very late – example is the Thames Navigation Act of 1866, which contained 'saving clauses' concerning 'the trees at Temple Lock' and 'George Cherry's Land'.

2. As early as 1877, Thring. a Parliamentary Counsel, in his *Practical Legislation*, expressed the view that 'the adoption of the system of confining the attention of Parliament to material provisions only, and leaving details to be settled departmentally is probably the only mode in which parliamentary government, as respects its legislative functions, can be carried on'. Eighty years earlier, Jeremy Bentham had prophetically envisaged the possibility of extensive delegation, 'the legislator sketching out a sort of imperfect mandate which it leaves to the subordinate power-holder to fill up'. According to Sir Cecil Carr, the first statement of the principles behind

As with so many things in British Government the practice grew up 'gradually, as and when the need arose in Parliament, without any logical system'.

'The power has been delegated by Parliament', wrote the Committee on Ministers' Powers, 'for various reasons, because for instance, the topic involved much detail, or because it was technical, or because the pressure of other demands upon Parliamentary time did not allow the necessary time to be devoted by the House of Commons to a particular Bill.'[3] A more recent and fuller summary of the reasons for delegation has been provided by Mr Speaker's Counsel in his Memorandum to the Select Committee on Procedure of 1966–67, viz:

(a) The normal justification is its value in relieving Parliament of the minor details of law making. The province of Parliament is to decide material questions affecting the public interest; and the more procedural and subordinate matters can be withdrawn from their cognizance the greater will be the time afforded for the consideration of more serious questions involved in legislation.

(b) Another advantage is speed of action. Action can be taken at once in a crisis without public notice which might prejudice the object of the exercise. For instance an increase in import duties would lose some of its effect if prior notice was given and importers were able to import large quantities of goods at the old lower rate of duty.

(c) Another advantage is in dealing with technical subjects. Ministers and Members of Parliament are not experts in the variety of subjects on which legislation is passed e.g. trade marks, patents, designs, diseases, poison, legal procedure and so on. The details of such technical legislation need the assistance of experts and can be regulated after a Bill passes into an Act by delegated legislation with greater care and minuteness and with better adaptation to local and other special circumstances than they can be in the passage of a Bill through Parliament.

(d) Another is that it enables the Department to deal with unforeseen circumstances that may arise during the introduction of large and complicated schemes of reform. It is not possible when drafting legis-

---

delegated legislation was made by Plato, about 2,300 years ago, viz. 'In all matters involving a mass of petty detail the lawgiver must leave gaps; rules and up-to-date amendments must be made from year to year by persons who have constant experience from year to year in these things, and who are taught by practice until a satisfactory code is finally agreed upon to regulate such proceedings.' (See Sixth Report of the Select Committee on Procedure Session 1966–67. HC Paper 539, pp. 56, 58.)

3. Cmnd 4060, p. 16.

lation on a new subject, to forecast every eventuality and it is very convenient to have power to adjust matters of detail by Statutory Instrument without of course going beyond the general principles laid down in the Bill.

(e) Another is that it provides flexibility. Circumstances change and it may be desirable to take power to deal quickly with changing circumstances rather than wait for an amending Bill. This is particularly convenient in regard to economic controls, for instance exchange control and hire purchase.

(f) Finally there is the question of emergency; and in time of war it is essential to have wide powers of delegated legislation.[4]

Prima facie evidence of the growth of delegated legislation is provided by the increasing size of the annual volume of Statutory Rules and Orders, which has dwarfed in sheer bulk the Statute Book itself. Between 1894 and 1913 an average of 1,238 Rules and Orders were published annually; between 1919 and 1929 the average had risen to 1,677. The number rose to a peak, as might be expected, during the 'reconstruction' period immediately following the Second World War. The year 1948 saw the publication of no fewer than 1,858 'Statutory Instruments' (as by that time Rules and Orders had become known). Since then there has been a considerable fluctuation.[5] Numbers, however, are no indication of importance, and it can hardly be said that delegated legislation has played a decreasing role in our lives during the course of the last twenty years. Every Act creating, extending or changing a social service and every Act providing for the future regulation of the economy has equipped the relevant Minister with extensive powers to make rules, orders and regulations of wide applicability, seriously affecting the rights and duties of those who become subject to them. Even today, however, it is rare to encounter a measure of delegation as wide as that prescribed by the famous Poor Law Amendment Act of 1834, which authorized and required the newly-constituted Poor Law Commissioners, 'from Time to Time as they shall see occasion to make and issue all such Rules, Orders and Regulations for the Management of the Poor, for the Government of Workhouses and the Education of the Children therein . . . and for carrying this Act in all other respect as they think proper'. But it should be immediately added that the

4. HC Paper 539, pp. 113–14.

5. Recent annual numbers have been: 1974 – 2,102; 1965 – 2,201; 1966 – 1,641; 1967 – 1,981; 1968 – 2,079; 1969 - 1902; 1970 – 2044; 1971 – 2178; 1972 – 2077.

powers over Local Education Authorities given to the Minister of Education (now Secretary of State for Education and Science) by the Education Act of 1944, do not, in toto, fall very short of this comprehensive remit.

It is hardly surprising that the growth of delegated legislation, both quantitatively and qualitatively, should have confirmed the fears of those who were already worried about the danger of 'Civil Service dictatorship'. Clearly, the Minister himself could exercise very little effective control over the spate of rules and orders being issued in his name, while Parliament, the 'onlie begetter' of these legally-enforceable instruments, seemed to lack the time, the will and the knowledge to ensure that they accurately expressed its original intentions. The Courts, of course, could always declare ultra vires a rule or order which clearly went beyond statutory authorization, but this was not always of much help to the aggrieved citizen, even if he could afford the expense of bringing a legal action. For no court regarded itself as competent to question the reasonableness or appropriateness of an exercise of delegated powers which was within the scope of the frequently very wide authority conferred on the Minister by the relevant Statute. Moreover, there were, in a very few statutes, clauses which permitted the Minister to issue regulations modifying the terms of the statute itself 'in order to bring it into effect', and even clauses which at least appeared to remove from the courts any kind of control over vires.[6] Such clauses were, in fact, very much less objectionable than they appeared to be at first sight, but they caused great outcry among lawyers and constitutional pundits. The latter type of clause has never been used since the publication of the Report of the Committee on Ministers' Powers of 1932 – a fact which suggests that it achieved nothing apart from causing its civil servant originators to be accused of harbouring dictatorial ambitions. With one or two possible exceptions, the former type of clause is now generally regarded as necessary and harmless. Of sinister intentions on the part of the Civil Service the Committee found no evidence whatever.

It did, however, find that the existing situation had certain

6. For instance, the following clause in the Smallholdings and Allotments Act of 1908: 'An order so confirmed (by the Board of Agriculture) shall become final and have effect as if enacted in this Act, and the confirmation by the Board shall be conclusive evidence that the requirements of this Act have been complied with and that the Order has been duly made and is within the power of this Act.'

unsatisfactory features. Among these were the variations in the procedures used by Parliament to exercise 'pre-natal' control over the rules and orders issued under its authority. Most of them[7] had to be 'laid' before the House, but the period of 'laying' varied quite unconsequentially, and it was not invariably open to a Member of the House to move a resolution (technically known as a 'prayer') to the effect that a rule or order should be annulled. Nor did the House, in the Committee's view, pay sufficient attention either to the proposals for delegated legislation embodied in the Bills it was called upon to debate or to the content of the rules and orders (frequently technical in character and couched in formidable legal jargon) that were subsequently issued under the Act that Parliament had passed. To rectify these defects it proposed that each of the Houses of Parliament should appoint, at the beginning of each session, a 'small Standing Committee' for the purpose of:

(a) considering and reporting on every Bill containing a proposal to confer law-making power on a Minister:

(b) considering and reporting on every regulation and rule made in the exercise of delegated legislation power, and laid before the House in pursuance of statutory requirements.[8]

Nothing was done about this recommendation until 1944, and then only as a result of strong pressure from backbenchers on both sides of the House of Commons. The date is significant. War-time 'emergency' legislation, much of which was subsequently extended into the post-war period, had conferred on Ministers unprecedently wide powers, and it was clear that projected measures of post-war reorganization, by whichever party they might be effected, would bring in their train further extensive grants of authority to issue delegated legislation. By this time, moreover, the *necessity* of such legislation, which many Conservatives had previously been reluctant to accept, was almost universally recognized. Unless parliamentary 'sovereignty' was to be dangerously undermined, there seemed no alternative to the establishment of a House of Commons Committee such as the Report of the Committee on Ministers' Powers had recommended. Accordingly, a Select Committee on Statutory Rules and Orders (subsequently Statutory Instruments) was created with

7. With the exception of 'local' orders, in respect of which there were other safeguards comparable to those applying to private bills.
8. Report, p. 67.

powers to examine 'every Statutory Instrument laid or laid in draft before the House . . . with a view to determining whether the special attention of the House should be drawn to it on any of the following grounds:

(i) that it imposes a charge on the public revenues or contains provisions requiring payments to be made to the Exchequer or any Government Department or to any local or public authority in consideration of any licence or consent, or of any services to be rendered, or prescribes the amount of any such charge or payments;

(ii) that it is made in pursuance of an enactment containing specific provisions excluding it from challenge in the courts, either at all times or after the expiration of a specific period;

(iii) that it appears to make some unusual or unexpected use of the powers conferred by the Statute under which it was made;

(iv) that it purports to have retrospective effect when the parent Statute confers no express authority so to provide;

(v) that there appears to have been unjustifiable delay in the publication of in the laying of it before Parliament;

(vi) that for any special reasons its form or purport calls for elucidation.'[9]

The creation of this Select Committee was followed in 1946 by the passing of the Statutory Instruments Act. This not only cleaned up a rather complex muddle of rules about publicizing Instruments or otherwise ensuring that persons affected by them should be promptly informed of their existence; it also – and more importantly in the context of our present discussion – regularized the procedure for 'laying' them before the House of Commons. In respect of 'laying' procedure, Instruments had been, and still are, divided into three classes; (1) those that were simply 'laid' without any speific requirements or provision for parliamentary scrutiny or confirmation; (2) those that required a positive (or 'affirmative') Resolution of the House to give them validity or maintain their validity; and (3) those that automatically possessed or acquired validity unless they were annulled as a result of a successful 'prayer'. For the first two classes no major procedural changes were required; for the last one it was important, if Members were to know what they could 'pray' against and within what time limit, that the procedure for laying should be meticulously regu-

9. These terms of reference were subsequently added to, partly for certain technical reasons which need not concern us here, and partly to extend the Committee's powers (see below, p. 251, n. 11).

lated and that a standard period should be prescribed. The Act enabled both of these requirements to be satisfactorily met; in particular, it prescribed a rule that for instruments laid before the House and subject to the 'negative' procedure the period of laying should be forty days, exclusive of any days (apart from weekends) when the House, through prorogation or adjournment, was not in session.

These two reforms – the creation of what became known as the 'Scrutiny' Committee and the passage of the Statutory Instruments Act – were universally recognized as meeting many of the reasonable criticisms made by those who claimed that delegated legislation was escaping parliamentary control. There were some critics, however, who demanded two further reforms. Both involved an extension of the terms of reference of the Statutory Instruments Committee. Not only should the Committee be authorized, as the Select Committee on Ministers' Power had suggested (see above, p. 247), to examine *proposed* delegations of rule-making powers as embodied in bills presented to the House, in addition to the actual exercise of such powers under Acts already passed; it should concern itself with the 'merits' of Statutory Instruments as expressions of the policies prescribed by or implied in the parent Statutes, and not merely with the regularity of the procedures by which they were made, the degree of unusualness or unexpectedness they appeared to embody, the extent of their intelligibility and the other rather technical matters covered by the Committee's terms of reference. For, as the record of the Committee's proceedings soon showed, it was comparatively rare for an Instrument to fall within any of the specified categories; but it was by no means rare for a Member to take objection to an Instrument because its *content* seemed to him inappropriate or unsatisfactory. Indeed, the vast majority of 'prayers' were 'political' in this sense. Yet Members had no guidance from the Committee on the very matters in which they were most interested. To many, it seemed that despite the recent reforms, they had still to wade through a vast mass of paper, much of it covered with semi-intelligible legal jargon, to try to discover the Instruments to which they might conceivably take legitimate objection.

Neither of the two demands has been met, yet these latter-day controversies about delegated legislation no longer occupy much of Parliament's attention. Forms of delegation have become sufficiently standardized to make the scrutiny of bills by the SIC seem superfluous. Today, moreover, the demand seems to be for *more* delegation to reduce the complexity of legislation and to facilitate its application by the executive agencies, rather than for less, and hence there has been a diminution of the tendency to look at each bill with deep suspicion on the grounds that it may be conferring excessive powers on the relevant Minister. As for the detection of demerit in a Statutory Instrument, this has proved far less difficult than was previously imagined, partly as a consequence of the rise in the significance of interest groups in the British political process. In practice, the Member of Parliament does not need to spend much of his time turning over the pages of the Instruments that have been laid on the Table of the House; for, if there is anything in any one of them which might cause remediable discontent, he can be certain that some organized body claiming to represent the affected parties will bring it to his attention. It is true, of course, that the Whips are on for 'prayers' and that if the matter is pressed to a division, the Government will get its more-or-less automatic majority. Nevertheless, the possibility of unfavourable publicity arising from the debate makes the framers of Statutory Instruments particularly careful not to give unnecessary offence; and it is by no means unknown for a Government department to withdraw an instrument, with a promise of amendment and re-presentation, if the mover of the 'prayer' has put up a good case of a non-partisan kind.

Meanwhile, the Select Committee on Statutory Instruments continues its modest, poorly-publicized but useful task. The House may or may not take notice of its rare adverse reports;[10] but its very existence, together with the conscientiousness with which it has performed its task (ably assisted by the Counsel to Mr Speaker) has effected notable improvements in the form of Statutory Instruments, in their intelligibility and in the promptness with which they are made available for parliamentary inspection. It cannot be said, however, that parliamentary control of delegated legislation is incapable of further improvement. The treatment of so-called 'hybrid' Instruments, for instance might be made more satisfactory; these, which, although general in character, affect specific private interests, are at present subject to a special type of procedure in the Lords but not in the Commons. There is also some uneasiness about those Instruments whereby

10. Although one must remember that it is open to any member of the Scrutiny Committee itself to 'pray' against any Instrument on which the Committee has reported adversely.

the Minister confers rule-making powers on himself or on some outside body; for the so-called 'grandchildren' that arise from this process escape any specifically prescribed form of parliamentary control. Perhaps of more importance than either of these problems is the alleged waste of time on the floor of the House involved in the debating of 'prayers' that are neither very controversial nor, to the majority of Members, very interesting. These, it has been suggested, might be referred to a committee. All these matters were the subject of recommendations or comments by the Select Committee on Procedure of 1966–67.[11]

Of greater concern to the ordinary Member, however, is the fact that 'prayers', although 'exempted business', are not always fitted into the forty days available for them. When this happens, owing to the exigencies of the parliamentary timetable, the Government usually attempts to provide would-be 'praying' Members with other opportunities, outside the forty-day limit. Even so, it would appear that the occasions when the Members concerned fail to get a hearing are tending to increase (see table on p. 258). This potentially serious situation, which is likely to be exacerbated by the increasing frequency of delegated legislation and by the increasing congestion of the Commons' timetable (both of which may be confidently predicted) would seem to strengthen the case for using the committee device, as suggested above.

Despite these remaining problems, it cannot be said that delegated legislation today presents, as it presented some 25 years ago, any major constitutional or political issue. Now recognized as a necessary and beneficial technique of government, it is something the British have learnt to live with.

Administrative Tribunals

This cannot be said, however, of the second of the two subjects with which this chapter is concerned. Despite some very important reforms, mostly dating from the 1950s and the 1960s, few would care to allege that Britain's arrangements for the exercise of judicial and quasi-judicial functions by Ministerial departments or administrative tribunals are now in a satisfactory condition.

11. HC Paper 539, especially pp. xiii–xiv. Two other recommendations of the Procedure Committee have recently been put into effect, through an extension of the Terms of Reference of the Scrutiny Committee. Since November 1967 the latter has been able to examine 'laid' Statutory Instruments which are not subject to Negative or Affirmative Resolution and also to report on Instruments of which the drafting 'appears to be defective'.

Indeed, there is still much controversy about the very scope and meaning of 'administrative justice'; for, with the growth of the regulatory responsibilities of government, the distinction between administrative functions and judicial ones, which in former days seemed reasonably clear, has become blurred.

	7 Feb. 67 to 6 Feb. 68	*7 Feb. 68 to 6 Feb. 69*
Prayers put down	41	54
Prayers debated within 40-day period	28	21
Motions debated after expiry of 40-day period	4	12
Prayers not debated	8	19
(Official opposition motions not debated)	(7)	(6)
Prayers withdrawn	1	2

Source: Statutory Instruments List and Notice Paper of the House of Commons

This lack of precision, although not completely avoidable, is to many disturbing, since the quality of the justice dispensed by bodies other than the law courts has not always been as high as the public might expect. Simple prerequisites, such as the right to state a case fully, to criticize one's opponent's case, and to exercise both rights before an adjudicator who is not only impartial but seen to be so, have not invariably been met. Indeed, there are some who doubt whether these elementary demands of 'natural justice' can be properly satisfied unless there is an established *system* of administrative courts, such as has been advocated, as we shall see later, by Professors Robson and Mitchell.[12] This field of governmental responsibilities, therefore, presents a problem area of considerable importance to anyone seriously interested in maintaining civil liberties and ensuring fair and considerable treatment of persons adversely affected by bureaucratic regulation of their activities.

In discussion of this subject – and more particularly in students' essays – administrative justice and delegated legislation are often

12. See below, p. 275 passim.

confused with each other. This confusion has three sources. First, the two phenomena were closely, and sometimes almost inextricably, associated by Lord Hewart in that famous book, *The New Despotism*, in which he inveighed so vigorously and wildly against both. Secondly, they both represent – or seem to represent – incursions by the administrative into fields previously reserved to the other two 'powers', the legislative and the judicial. Thirdly, it frequently happens that judicial-type decisions made by Government departments or by administrative tribunals arise from the application to individual cases of rules that the administrative has itself made under delegated powers. At the outset, therefore, we must clarify the distinction between the two.

Delegated legislation, as we have already said, is a generic term referring to rules and orders made by Government departments, local authorities and other administrative agencies under powers granted by parliamentary Statute. Administrative justice, on the other hand, denotes the conferment on a public body, other than a regular court of law, of the power to decide disputes, arising from specific decisions which, for one reason or another, have been made subject to challenge on grounds that are sometimes narrowly, sometimes widely defined. Both types of power, the rule-making one and the dispute-deciding one, are 'delegated' in so far as they are both conferred on the appropriate agency by legislative authority. But they are powers of different kinds which, for both analytical and practical purposes, should be kept distinct.

In sheer size and scope, administrative justice now dwarfs justice of the more conventional and familiar kind, as provided by the regular courts of law. The ordinary citizen, in fact, is far more likely to have to appear before an administrative tribunal or to present a case to be enquired into 'by the Minister', than to find himself involved in the machinery of justice as represented by the magistrates' courts, the County Courts or the Assizes. The last count of administrative jurisdictions, done by Robert S. W. Pollard, revealed that they numbered many hundreds. Tribunals, representing the more formalized kind of administrative jurisdiction, were regarded by the Committee on Ministers, Powers of 1929–31 as 'somewhat exceptional, to be resorted to only in special circumstances and requiring strict safeguards'; but since then 'the continuing extension of governmental activity and responsibility for the general well-being of the community has greatly multiplied the occasions on which an individual may be at issue with the administration, or with another citizen or body',[13] and much of this judicial business has been confided to new tribunals or added to the responsibilities of old ones. In particular, the growth of social service and physical planning legislation during the post-war period has provoked a great increase in the number of cases annually decided by these bodies. Generalizing about the scope of administrative justice, the Franks Committee wrote:

'The general impact of decisions by tribunals and Ministers on the public today is illustrated by the fact that Rent Tribunals have in some recent years dealt with as many as 15,000 cases and that the annual number of planning appeals is about 6,000. Although the number of cases heard by National Insurance and Industrial Injuries Local Tribunals (50,000 to 60,000 annually) is smaller than the number of unemployment insurance cases heard in the years just before the war, the scheme is now on a wider basis and potentially affects nearly everyone'.[14]

A functional classification of administrative tribunals is not difficult, and one can hardly improve on that produced by the Franks Committee in 1957:

(1) Tribunals concerned with Land and Property (e.g. County Agricultural Executive Committees, Agricultural Land Tribunals, Local Valuation Courts, the Lands Tribunal, and Rent Tribunals);
(2) Tribunals concerned with National Insurance, National Assistance and Family Allowances (e.g. National Insurance and Industrial Injuries Local Tribunals, the National Insurance Commissioner, the Industrial Injuries Commissioner, National Assistance Appeal Tribunals and Family Allowance Referees);
(3) Tribunals concerned with the National Health Service (e.g. the Medical Practices Committee, Services Committees and the National Health Service Tribunal);
(4) Tribunals concerned with Military Service (e.g. Military Service (Hardship) Committees and Reinstatement Committees, Conscientious Objectors Local and Appellate Tribunals and Pensions Appeal Tribunals);[15]

13. Report of the Committee on Administrative Tribunals and Enquiries, 1957. Cmnd 218, p. 8.
14. Ibid. p. 4.
15. Since the abolition of compulsory military service, no longer operative, with the important exception of the Pensions Appeal Tribunals.

(5) Tribunals concerned with Transport (e.g. Licensing Authorities for Public Service Vehicles and Goods Vehicles, and the Transport Tribunal).

In addition to these five main functional categories, the Commission found itself also confronted with what it described as a 'heterogeneous group', including the General and Special Commissioners of Income Tax, the Compensation Tribunal and the Independent Schools Tribunals. If it were re-doing its work today, the Committee might well wish to extend its categorization or broaden some of its categories to take in bodies such as the Monopolies and Restrictive Practices Court. It would also have to note, with special reference to the Prices and Incomes Board, that the distinction between advisory and judicial functions, never entirely clear at the edges, had become further blurred.

What emerges from any attempt at a classification of tribunals is that in Britain there is no system of administrative justice. Tribunals have been created as the need for them arose; their constitution and manner of appointment have varied widely, in accordance with no discoverable principle; and the right of appeal from their decisions to higher authority (i.e. to a Court of Law, a Minister or a superior tribunal) has – in those instances where it exists – been subject to equally unpredictable and inexplicable variations. Even the names of the various bodies concerned – tribunals, commissions, courts, committees, referees – reflect the heterogeneous circumstances of their origin.

However, the *reasons* for confiding a particular jurisdiction to a tribunal, instead of to an ordinary court of law, are clear enough. The most obvious one is that, in the absence of such specialized bodies, most of which employ comparatively simple and expeditious procedures, the burden on the courts, which work slowly as a result of their devotion to time-honoured procedural precedents, would soon become intolerable. For many cases, such as the thousands that come before the National Insurance Tribunals (most of them concerned with entitlement to benefit) a procedure that disposes of a claim rapidly, and with the minimum of expense, is essential. Another advantage is the expertness that a specialized tribunal soon develops, as a result of dealing with a series of cases all of the same kind. Although Sir Cecil Carr once said that no issue was too technical for a court, there can be no doubt that specialization helps to promote a desirable degree of uniformity, as opposed to diversity, in the decision-making process. Conversely, but equally usefully, an administrative tribunal, not being formally bound by precedent, can more easily correct its own previous error of judgment and develop more rapidly and freely than can the more traditional forms of jurisdiction a series of decision-taking criteria well adapted to the matters with which it is concerned. Its freedom from the curb of 'old father antique', the common law, also enables it to respond more readily to new developments in public policy and to play a more significant part in the evolution of the higher standards of provision (in matters such as health, education, housing, physical planning etc.) demanded by public opinion in the twentieth century. These advantages, of course, do not apply equally to all kinds of tribunals; many, such as the National Insurance Tribunals, are mainly occupied with more or less routine work involving the application of fairly specific rules to individual cases rather than with responding to new conceptions of public policy or participating in the development of new standards. But in general, it can be safely said that the 'tribunal' device has not only speeded up and cheapened, but imparted a new degree of flexibility to the processes of judicial decision. As Professor William Robson, Britain's most distinguished pioneer in the study of these new jurisdictions, has truly said, 'administrative law is law in the making'.

The Committee on Ministers' Powers (1929–32) believed that there were *some* circumstances that might justify the conferment of judicial functions on an administrative tribunal, rather than a court of law, but it hoped that they would prove exceptional. This hope, as we have seen, has proved quite ill-founded. It also made a distinction, which has befogged discussion of the subject ever since, between the judicial and the quasi-judicial. The latter category, it considered, was distinguished from the former by the lack of any strict relationship between the ultimate disposition of the case under consideration and the evidence adduced during the course of the enquiry. Whereas a judicial decision involved the strict application of a known body of law to the facts of the case, a quasi-judicial decision might contain a very considerable element of administrative discretion, based on considerations of public policy. In its recommendations based upon this distinction – which, as Professor Robson pointed out at the time, was the product of a misconception of the nature of the judicial process – the Committee opined that whereas quasi-judicial decisions should normally be entrusted to Ministers (subject to certain stringent procedural safeguards), 'truly' judicial decisions should normally be made by courts of law and exceptionally by administrative tribunals. Here, again, the Committee's hopes were falsified. The distinction that it made proved difficult to maintain, and, during the period that has elapsed since the publication of its report, an enormous number of decisions which, despite the element of discretion entering into them, are clearly within the 'judicial' category have been confided, not to courts of law or even administrative tribunals, but to Ministers of the Crown.

Ministers of the Crown, in fact, today possess a very large number of judicial responsibilities, both original and appellate. The Home Secretary, for instance, decides disputes about naturalization; the Minister of Social Security pronounces on questions relating to the classification, qualifications and contribution conditions of persons insured under the National Insurance Acts, the Minister of Health on the superannuation entitlements of NHSA officers, and the Minister of Education on those of teachers; while various Ministers wield very important appellate powers in respect of decisions made by local authorities in the field of planning, development, slum clearance, housing and school attendance. Powers such as these have been criticized even more strongly than those wielded by administrative tribunals; for an administrative tribunal, although normally appointed by the Minister within whose sphere of responsibility its jurisdiction lies, enjoys an independence which, although less than that possessed by a court of law, is normally respected, whereas a Minister all too frequently appears to be exercising judgment, if not in his own cause, at least on a matter on which he has already taken up an identifiable position. Moreover, it has been normal for the 'Minister's' decision to be made anonymously by a civil servant appointed for the purpose, without adequate procedural safeguards and without reasons given.

Another target for criticism – some of it admittedly not so firmly based – was the manner in which Ministers conducted the various enquiries which they were statutorily authorized to hold. As these frequently concerned property rights, as in the exercise of powers compulsorily to acquire land or to place restrictions on the manner in which it might be developed, powerful vested interests were inevitably brought into play. Although the powers conferred could not be strictly called 'judicial', since the freedom of the Minister to make what he regarded as the appropriate policy decision remained completely unrestricted, they necessarily involved certain judicial-type procedures. The normal procedure was to appoint an inspector to hold a local enquiry, at which the parties to the dispute – usually the local authority concerned and the property-owners affected – presented their respective cases, after which the inspector made a report to the Minister. The main demands of the critics of this procedure were that the enquiry should be subjected to more stringent rules, that the inspector's report should be published, and that the Minister, in the event of his making a decision which diverged from the inspector's recommendations, should state his specific reasons for so doing. These demands, and particularly the last two, were strongly resisted in the departments concerned on the grounds that they would involve harmful publicization of internal administrative processes and an invasion of the sacred principle of Ministerial responsibility to Parliament.

By the 1950s increasing dissatisfaction was being expressed with the chaotic collection of administrative tribunals, Ministerial jurisdiction and statutory enquiries which had been rather inappropriately lumped together under the heading of 'administrative law'. Critics alleged that, despite Britain's boasted adherence to the 'rule of law', the British actually provided far less effective safeguards to the citizen aggrieved by administrative action than did France, with its powerful and prestigious supreme administrative tribunal known as the *Conseil d'Etat*, through which the citizen, at small expense, although sometimes at the cost of long delays, could obtain a wide variety of remedies against arbitrariness, bad faith or maladministration on the part of public officials. Curiously enough, however, the incident which brought this dissatisfaction to a head and provoked a series of very important reforms in existing procedures, the famous 'Crichel Down' affair of 1953–54, did not involve any exercise of Ministerial jurisdiction, any action on the part of an administrative tribunal, or even the holding of a statutory enquiry (although there was an enquiry, 'internal' but public, into the circumstances of the affair itself).

The Crichel Down affair concerned the disposition of an area of land previously requisitioned by the Government for military purposes. Although its former owners wished to resume possession of it, officials of the Ministry of Agriculture had other ideas, in pursuit of which they behaved in a secretive, underhanded manner – although always entirely within the limits of the law. The persistence of the previous owners, who had the advantage of being extremely well-connected, made 'Crichel Down' into a *cause celèbre*, as a result of which the civil servants concerned were severely criticized in the report of a public inquiry, and the Minister of Agriculture, Sir Thomas Dugdale, was compelled to resign his office. In the public mind, these events were thought to have some responsibility for the appointment of the Committee on Administrative Tribunals and Enquiries in November 1955, and it can hardly be doubted that, in establishing the Committee, the Government was influenced by the excitement that 'Crichel Down' had generated. For these reasons the Committee itself was at pains to emphasize that 'the selected case of Crichel Down, . . . widely regarded as a principal reason' for its appointment, in fact fell outside the subjects with which it had been 'asked to deal'. For the exercise of ordinary administrative discretion, with which the Crichel Down affair was exclusively concerned, did not figure in the Committee's terms of reference. What it was instructed to consider were 'the cases in which the decision on objections' to particular decisions made by administrators was 'taken by a tribunal or by a Minister, after special procedure' had been followed.[16]

This did not mean, of course, that the Government had succeeded in by-passing the demand for a consideration of the methods by which ordinary administration decisions (many of which by their nature, required the adoption of a judicial attitude on the part of the responsible administrator) were in fact made. As we shall see, this was an issue which, because it affected so many people of so many different groups and classes, could not be put indefinitely in cold storage. Nevertheless, the fact that the Committee was authorized to enquire only into decisions that were taken by tribunals, as constituted by Statute, or by Ministers, 'after special procedure' of a judicial type, as authorized or required by Statute, had been followed, meant that 'administrative justice' in the rather formal sense that we have so far been using the phrase in the present chapter, received prior attention.[17]

The Committee found that there was much that required remedy or improvement. Tribunals often used unsuitable procedures; they were not invariably chaired by persons with legal

16. Report of the Committee on Administrative Tribunals and Enquiries, 1957. Cmnd 218, p. 3.

17. This was criticized by Professor H. W. R. Wade, who said that 'if everything had been done by the light of pure reason, it was the unjudicialized rather than the judicialized machinery which might have been investigated' (*Public Law*, Winter 1960).

qualifications; they did not always give appellants a fair hearing; too often they conducted their proceedings in secret when there was no real justification for doing so; in many cases they failed to publish the reasons for their decisions and in some there was no right of appeal, when such a right was obviously required, 'on fact, law and merits from a tribunal of first instance to an appellate tribunal'.[18] To rectify these deficiencies the Committee made appropriate recommendations, including the taking away of the 'relevant' Minister's power to appoint the chairman and members of tribunals. Chairmen, it considered, should be appointed by the Lord Chancellor (or in Scotland by the Lord President of the Court of Session or the Lord Advocate), members by one or other of the two standing *Councils on Tribunals* it proposed that the Government should constitute. These Councils, one for England and Wales and one for Scotland, 'should be set up to keep the constitution and working of tribunals under continuous review'.[19]

On Statutory Enquiries, the Committee came forward with analogous proposals to ensure what is called 'openness, fairness, and impartiality'. Objectors should be given the fullest possible prior knowledge of the case they had to meet; inspectors should be appointed, not by the relevant Minister but by the Lord Chancellor; suitable codes of procedure, 'simple and inexpensive but orderly'[20], should be formulated by the Council on Tribunals; proceedings should normally be in public; inspectors' reports should be published and open to correction on matters of fact; and the Minister's final decision should be a reasoned one.

Many of these recommendations – together with others which, for reasons of space, we have not been able to mention – were promptly implemented by departmental circular. Others, which required legislation, were fulfilled wholly or partly by a series of legislative measures, of which the most important was the Tribunals and Enquiries Act of 1958. This measure provided for the establishment of a single Council on Tribunals (with a Scottish Committee), consisting of thirteen members under a Chairman appointed jointly by the Lord Chancellor and the Secretary of State for Scotland. Its principal functions were – and are (1) to keep the constitution and working of specific classes of tribunals under review; (2) to report on any matter relating to a tribunal referred to it by its appointing Ministers; (3) to recommend, to

18. Report, p. 93, para. 25.
19. ibid. p. 91, para. 1.
20. ibid. p. 96, para. 72.

the appropriate Minister, what persons should be appointed to tribunals or to the panel of eligibles for Chairmanship maintained by the Lord Chancellor; (4) to be consulted before any exception was made to the rule that tribunals (and Ministers after Statutory Enquiries) should give reasons for their decisions; (5) to be consulted before the making of regulations for the procedures to be followed by tribunals or in statutory enquiries; (6) to express views, either at the request of the Lord Chancellor or Secretary for Scotland, or of its own volition, about particular questions of statutory enquiry procedure; and (7) to make annual reports to the Lord Chancellor and Secretary of State, who were to lay them, with such comments as they consider necessary, before Parliament.

In some respects, particularly as concerned Statutory Enquiries, these reforms went beyond the recommendations contained in the Franks Report. In others, the Government hesitated to go quite so far as the Committee had suggested, largely on the familiar but inappropriate grounds that Ministerial responsibility must at all costs be preserved. The relevant Minister, therefore, retained the right to appoint both members of tribunals and inspectors. The only concession to Franks here was that chairmen of tribunals had to be selected from panels maintained by the Lord Chancellor.

Undoubtedly, the establishment of the Council on Tribunals is the most important advance yet made towards the creation of a *system* of administrative law in Britain. It went a long way to meet the demands of such pioneers of reform as Professor William Robson and offered, for the first time, some formal guarantee to the applicant before an administrative tribunal or statutory enquiry that he would receive fair treatment. Admittedly, the courts of law, from time almost immemorial, had had at their disposal certain means to prevent the grossest perversions of administrative justice, in so far as they could use the doctrine of ultra vires to keep subordinate jurisdictions within their statutory powers, and the common law principles of 'natural justice' to ensure that at least a modicum of impartiality was maintained. The Franks Committee, far from proposing the abolition of recourse to the courts on these grounds, actually suggested that it should be widened and strengthened in certain respects. But more was obviously needed to ensure that the requirements of justice should be complied with as a matter of routine, and that the methods used by tribunals and enquiries should be as suitable as possible for the tasks confided to them. That 'more' has been provided, by no means perfectly but to a considerable measure, by the Tribunals and Enquiries Act of 1958.

Like the Statutory Instruments Committee, the Council on Tribunals has so far led a quietly useful life. Only once, in the famous 'Chalk Pit' case, has it hit the headlines. The most useful review of its achievements, to date, is the one made by J. F. Garner, Professor of Public Law in the University of Nottingham.[21] In his view, the Committee (which, as he reminds us, is a purely advisory body) has done comparatively little for the benefit of the individual complainants who have made representations to it. However, its revision of procedural rules has been 'extremely valuable'. These rules, writes Professor Garner, 'are now more clearly following a pattern and there is no real danger that the many points referred to in the Franks Report will be overlooked'. Quite as valuable, and perhaps more interesting to the student of British institutions, has been the bringing to bear by the Council of a 'novel influence' on the senior personnel of Government departments.

'The Council', writes Professor Garner, 'by its "consultative" function, for the first time has brought senior civil servants face to face with impartial and well-informed outsiders; it is not insignificant that consultation with representatives of the departments takes place not in the Ministries, but on the Council's own premises. This "confrontation" . . . is of great value and it may have in it the seed of future development.'

There is some exaggeration here; for it is difficult to see much qualitative difference between the civil servant's new 'confrontation' with the Council and his old one with parliamentary select committees – and particularly with those which, like the Public Accounts Committee, dispose of the services of an expert and impartial adviser. Nevertheless it may well be that the Council, in addition to its essential tidying-up functions, is contributing to the emergence of the civil servant from the 'comparatively cloistered official life' that Professor Garner alleges that he has 'traditionally' led.

That the work of the Council has received so little publicity – a fact which Professor Garner finds deplorable – may be evidence that the particular problems with which it is statutorily concerned are now well on the way to satisfactory solution. Be this as it may, the problems that have received most current attention since the passing of the Tribunals and Enquiries Act are those well outside

21. 'The Council on Tribunals' in *Public Law*, Winter 1965.

the Council's jurisdiction. Its concern, as we have seen, is with administrative tribunals and statutory enquiries. It does not investigate judicial or judicial-type powers confided, not to tribunals, but to Ministers – and therefore exercisable, within the limits set by natural justice, in whatever manner the Minister concerned may think fit; nor does it investigate the exercise of ordinary administrative discretion, which often involves the making of decisions which, to say the least, have a strong judicial flavour. These matters, the discussion of which, as we have seen, was powerfully stimulated by 'Crichel Down', were taken up by another committee – a private one appointed by the British Section of the International Committee of Jurists, and usually described, from the name of its chairman, as the Whyatt Committee.[22] Its terms of reference were 'to enquire into the adequacy of the existing means for investigating complaints against administrative acts or decisions of Government Departments and other public bodies, when there is no tribunal or other statutory procedure available for dealing with the complaints; and to consider possible improvements to such means with particular reference to the Scandinavian institution known as the ombudsman'.

The Committee found that whereas certain Government departments, such as the Ministry of Health, were highly 'tribunalized', others, such as the Ministry of Education and the Post Office, possessed the freedom to deal 'hierarchically' with many or most of the appeals made against their decisions, or against those of bodies over which they exercised ultimate control. Thus, in the Ministry of Education, it was the Minister himself (or, in practice, a civil servant acting on his behalf) who decided disputed questions relating to educational grants. Similarly it was the Postmaster General who awarded, or failed to award, compensation for loss of or damage to postal packets. In certain cases, the Minister might refer a dispute to an independent body appointed by himself, but such a body exercised advisory powers only. It was clear that the degree to which administration had become judicialized varied rather inconsequentially from one type of decision to another, displaying an almost total lack of principle. The question which the Committee had to consider was just *how far* it should become *further* judicialized – for no one could seriously propose that every conceivable decision made in a Government department should become subject to appeal before

22. 'Justice', *The Citizen and the Administration: the Redress of Grievances*, (Stevens 1961).

a supposedly impartial body. Judicialization works so thoroughly that, in the end, public satisfaction would be minimized rather than maximized.

The Committee's answer to this question was as follows:

'We think that . . . the guiding principle should be that the individual is entitled to have an impartial adjudication of his dispute with authority unless there are overriding considerations which make it necessary, in the public interest, that the Minister should retain responsibility for making the final decision.'[23]

The application of this principle would involve, in the Committee's view, 'the extension of the jurisdiction of existing tribunals or the creation of new tribunals'. As an indefinite multiplication of tribunals, however, would give rise to 'practical difficulties', it would be desirable to establish a '*General Tribunal*, on the Swedish model, . . . to deal with miscellaneous complaints against discretionary decisions where there is no specialized tribunal which can conveniently dispose of them'.[24] If 'the principle of impartial adjudication were applied to areas of discretion on the lines we have suggested,' said the Committee, 'it would do much to remove the sense of frustration and injustice felt by

23. ibid. p. 27, para. 56. Excellent examples of circumstances where formal judicialization would defeat the object of legislation conferring discretionary powers on Ministers are provided by Miss G. Ganz in her 'Control of Industry by Administrative Process' (*Public Law*, Summer 1967) which deals with the powers exercised under the Local Employment Act of 1960, the Control of Offices and Industrial Development Act of 1965, and the Industrial Development Act of 1966. In all these cases, the Government successfully resisted demands that refusal to issue licences, grant tax remissions or provide subsidies to individual applicants should be subject to appeal to a tribunal, on the very strong grounds that, had such demands been accepted 'an independent tribunal would . . . be dictating economic decisions to the Government'. In this area there has been, in Miss Ganz's view, a 'retreat from law', which is an 'inevitable outcome of increasing governmental control over industry which must be flexible and selective to achieve the desired results' (ibid. pp. 104, 106). She considers that this need not lead to a 'new despotism' so long as there are effective safeguards provided by (a) the development of suitable *administrative* conventions and (b) the possibility of ventilating grievances through the House of Commons. These requirements, she believes, are likely to be satisfied, particularly now that the office of Parliamentary Commissioner has been created. (See below, p. 267 passim.)

24. ibid. Set up in 1909 and called the Supreme Administrative Court, this Swedish body deals with a series of specifically enumerated types of discretionary decision, and has authority to 'substitute its own discretionary decision for the original decision'. (See *The Citizen and the Administration*, p. 32, paras 65–7.)

members of the public when faced with departmental decisions which they believe to be mistaken but which they have no effective means of challenging'.[25]

This, however, did not exhaust the reforms that the Committee wished to propose. The new tribunals (including the General Tribunal) would deal with the *substance* of decisions properly taken in accordance with the established rules. The complaint therefore, would be challenging a decision on the grounds that, although falling within the limits of statutory powers, arrived at by the following the prescribed procedures, and unsullied by bad faith, it was 'wrong' or 'unfair'. But further provision also needed to be made for the adjudication of 'complaints of official misconduct in the sense that the administrative authority' had 'failed to observe the proper standards of conduct and behaviour when exercising his administrative powers'.[26] He might, for instance, have acted oppressively, or shown unfair preference, or caused 'loss or damage to a citizen through inefficiency, negligence or error'. To such behaviour, the Committee gave the term 'maladministration'.[27] Although it recognized that some types of maladministration came clearly within the scope of the jurisdiction exercised by the ordinary courts of law, it held that the expense of litigation, together with the 'peculiar uncertainties and difficulties' attending much of it, made the remedies available from the courts the subject of a certain scepticism on the part of the ordinary person. Moreover, there was 'a wide field of maladministration outside the jurisdiction of the courts for which other methods of redress must be found'.[28]

Traditionally, such methods of redress were provided by Parliament, through the device of Ministerial responsibility. The practical limitations of this device, however, had become increasingly obvious. The only solution, in the Committee's view, was to introduce into Britain, in somewhat modified form, the well-known Scandinavian device of the Ombudsman, or 'grievance man'. In the Scandinavian countries, this parliamentary-

25. ibid. p. 28, para. 58.
26. ibid. p. 34, para. 72.
27. It recognized, as everyone is bound to recognize, that the dividing line between 'bad' decisions and 'maladministered' decisions might sometimes be difficult to draw. It suggested, for instance, that maladministration might cover – although rarely perhaps – 'a decision so harsh and unreasonable as to offend a sense of justice'. ibid. p. 35, para. 72.
28. ibid. p. 35, para. 73.

appointed official was authorized to receive and investigate complaints about maladministration. Where illegalities were revealed, he could initiate proceedings before a court of law; in cases of proven misbehaviour, inefficiency or negligence his main weapons were persuasion and publicity. His investigations were open, his reports public and his prestige high. Moreover, he was equipped with *full* investigatory powers, in that no officials could refuse to answer his questions and no department withhold from him any internal document he might wish to inspect.[29]

In delimiting the scope of the authority to be exercised by the proposed British Ombudsman, whom the Committee christened 'Parliamentary Commissioner', the Whyatt Report displayed what some critics regarded as undue caution. Initially, at least, he was to receive complaints only through Members of Parliament, and was to be subject to Ministerial veto on his proposed investigations. The bogey of Ministerial responsibility was responsible for the latter limitation; the former was intended to ensure that he should not be overwhelmed with business and that the traditional role of MPs, as vehicles for the remedy of grievances against the administration, should not be unduly disturbed. As a further sop to MPs, but also as a means of maintaining fruitful contact between the House of Commons and its new officer, the Report proposed that the Commissioner should work in association with a Select Committee (on the analogy of the association between the Public Accounts Committee and the Comptroller and Auditor General).

The Whyatt Committee's first proposal, for the establishment of a General Administrative Tribunal, has not yet been put into effect. As a major constitutional innovation, it encounters strong opposition from the more orthodox-minded members of the legal profession as well as from persons who shudder at anything that might disturb the placid grazing of that venerable animal, Ministerial Responsibility. However, Britain has now adopted the less radical device of the Ombudsman, having been preceded, among Commonwealth countries, by New Zealand in this sincerest form of flattery of Scandinavian institutions. The office of Parliamentary Commissioner was created by Statute in March 1967. He is authorized to investigate complaints of maladministration re-

29. These generalizations about the 'Scandinavian' Ombudsman, which are the authors' and not the Committee's, should not be taken as accurately describing the powers and duties of any *particular* Ombudsman. There are significant variations as between the different Scandinavian countries.

ferred to him by Members of the House of Commons, to report the results of his investigations to the Members requesting them and to the authorities involved and, in the event of his considering maladministration to have been committed and not subsequently remedied (or currently subject to remedial action), to lay a request before both Houses of Parliament. Limitations on his sphere of jurisdiction were, in the first years, rather severe – far too severe in the opinion of the more enthusiastic advocates of 'ombudsmanship'. He could not, for instance, deal with complaints arising from decisions made by local authorities, the nationalized industries, the hospital services or the police. However, under the terms of the National Health Service Reorganization Act 1973 and the National Health Service (Scotland) Act 1972, he has since assumed responsibilities as Health Service Commissioner for England, Wales and Scotland. While this is a welcome extension of the 'watchdog' principle it is nevertheless limited in that there is no investigation of complaints that in the Commissioner's opinion relate to the exercise of clinical judgment, no study of complaints for which statutory procedures already exist (e.g. general practitioners, dentists, pharmacists and opticians, who are still dealt with under the Service committee procedure), and no study of complaints which the Commissioner thinks could be reasonably pursued through the Courts or before a tribunal.[30]

The Parliamentary Commissioner, although not overwhelmed by the flood of cases which certain critics of the Act predicted would descend upon him, has not lacked occupation. Thus, over the four-year period 1970–73 he received 2,299 references. Of these, 1,260 were declared outside his jurisdiction, another 98 received partial investigation and 941 were fully investigated and reported back to the MPs who had forwarded the complaints. Of those pursued and eventually reported on in this period, the most noteworthy concerned the backdating of war pensions for a limited class of the former armed services and compensation for wrongful imprisonment, while from the early years of the Commissioner's work those concerning compensation payments to certain survivors of the Sachsenhausen Concentration Camp and the noise caused by air traffic using London Airport (Heathrow) stand out.

In evidence to the Select Committee with which he is associated,

30. We should also mention here that the Local Government Act of 1974 provides for the establishment of Commissions for the investigation of administrative action taken by or on behalf of local and other authorities.

Sir Edmund Compton, the first Parliamentary Commissioner, said that he had received 'excellent co-operation' from the Departments subject to his investigations, and that so far as the effect of his work on the process of administration was concerned, there were 'three credit items' and 'one debit item'. The 'credits' were (1) that the few cases of maladministration so far detected had been rectified; (2) that the complaints referred to him, which in former days might have been the subject of indefinite dispute, were 'finally disposed of'; and (3) that his investigations had had a 'tonic effect' on the Civil Service comparable with those resulting from the financial inquiries conducted by the Comptroller and Auditor General.

Sir Alan Marre, who succeeded Sir Edmund as Commissioner, added to this credit record when, in a report in 1973,[31] he listed nineteen examples affecting ten Departments where changes in administrative practices of benefit to the public could be shown to have been derived wholly or partly from the investigations of individual cases by his office. The debit item, in Sir Edmund's report, was the extent to which his office added 'to the coefficient of friction in the process of government', through increasing the amount of 'unproductive' work which departments had to do and making them less ready – for fear of being 'caught out' – to offer assistance to members of the public 'outside the limits of their statutory obligations'.[32] This was an important point which was well taken by the Select Committee. Controls of the type exercised by an ombudsman, and a fortiori by an administrative tribunal, do have a tendency (which may or may not be corrected) to make administrators more careful and meticulous in their behaviour at a time when the general demand (as expressed, for instance, in the Fulton Report on the Civil Service) is that they should be more bold and dynamic. Hence provisions intended to ensure that no injustice is done to individual clients of an administrative agency *may* also ensure that the general body of its clientele receive services which are less efficient than they would wish. There is

---

In June 1974 the first three local government commissioners were appointed to investigate complaints of maladministration against local authorities in England and Wales. Six weeks later a local commissioner for Wales was appointed.

31. HC 178.

32. Second Report from the Select Committee on the Parliamentary Commissioner for Administration, 17 July 1968. HC Paper 350, p. 9, para. 20; p. 55, Question 202, pp. 111–13, Question 673.

undoubtedly a potential contradiction here, too often disregarded by those who advocate a wide extension of the judicialization of the administrative process. Its reconciliation is clearly a matter of value-judgment, and the necessity for making such a judgment both generally and in specific contexts, must be overtly recognized.

There are certain distinguished students, of whom the most vocal is Professor J. D. B. Mitchell of Edinburgh, who are of the view that such a reconciliation can best be facilitated by root-and-branch reform of British administrative law, of a kind that would deal radically with 'the hard central problem of the judicial control of general administration'. In his view, the reforms that emanated from the Committee on Ministers' Powers, the Franks Committee and the Whyatt Committee, although beneficial in a limited way, are no more than 'tinkering'. His solution, which is similar to but wider in scope than that suggested by the Whyatt Committee in its proposals for a General Tribunal, is the establishment of an effective administrative jurisdiction after the style of the French Conseil d'Etat. It is only thus, he writes, 'that the courts can free themselves from the restricting legacies of the past in procedure and substantive law and the complacency with which this heritage is regarded. Only thus can the appropriate legal specialism be built up' – a specialism which understands the need for facilitating the administrative process while simultaneously offering adequate protection to the citizen against its abuses.[33]

For this purpose, he advocates the creation of a new court, recruited initially from high court judges, civil servants, and others who 'have studied administrative law seriously'. It should incorporate the Council on Tribunals, and the Parliamentary Commissioner for Administration might himself be given membership. It should cover both central and local government and be equipped with a 'threefold jurisdiction', viz. (1) the jurisdiction already exercised by the courts of common law (namely the doctrines of ultra vires, 'natural justice', etc.) over administrative tribunals; (2) 'a jurisdiction within a broad definition of the term' over 'the legality of general administrative acts'; and (3) 'a jurisdiction in public contracts and in reparation for administrative fault'. Essentially concerned with 'administrative morality', in effect it would say to the politicians and administrators, 'We care not what policies are adopted – that choice is for the political

33. 'Parliamentary Commissioner is the Wrong Answer' in *The Times*, 16 March 1967.

process; but what we will insist upon is that those policies are carried out with even-handedness and honesty.'[34] Such a compendious jurisdiction, presumably, would override the distinction, made in theory by the Whyatt Committee but difficult to maintain in practice, between decisions displaying procedural faults or bad faith and those that are defective in substance.[35] During the course of time, it would develop, like the French Conseil d'Etat, its own distinctive body of case law, known to the administrative agencies and well adapted to their own legitimate yet varying needs.

Should such a scheme be adopted, the need for having a Parliamentary Commissioner might well be questioned. It is true that Sweden has both an Ombudsman *and* a Supreme Administrative Court, but France has not chosen to supplement her Conseil d'Etat with any further device for the protection of her citizens against administrative arbitrariness, and a leading authority on French administrative law, Mme Questiaux (also a member of the Conseil) considered that a French version of the Ombudsman would be superfluous.[36] On the other hand, the important role traditionally played by the British Parliament in ventilating grievances and protecting liberties would seem to indicate the appropriateness of a new device, such as the Parliamentary Commissioner and his associated Select Committee would appear to provide, to enable the House to perform its duties in this field more effectively than it can perform them through the rather blunt instruments of Question and Debate.

34. J. D. B. Mitchell, 'Administrative Law and Parliamentary Control' in *Political Quarterly*, Vol. 38, no. 4, Oct.–Dec. 1967, pp. 370–1.

35. The Parliamentary Commissioner soon encountered this difficulty in the interpretation of his terms of reference. He considered that he was not authorized to 'extend his scope' to 'the class of case where the aggrieved person was found to sustain hardship and indeed injustice through the correct application in his case of an administrative rule'. The Select Committee, however, was of the view that 'it would be appropriate and consistent with the provisions of the Act for the Commissioner to extend his authority in such cases', but it immediately followed this up with the warning that 'it is not for the Commissioner to substitute his administrative decisions for the Government's, as also it is not for the Commissioner to re-write the Government's administrative rules'. (Second Report from the Select Committee on the Parliamentary Commissioner for Administration, Session 1967–68. HC Paper 350.)

36. See Nicole Questiaux: 'How Administrative Courts Meet the Need', in D. C. Rowat (ed): *The Ombudsman* (London, Allen & Unwin; Toronto and Stockholm 1965). This should be read in conjunction with Judge Holmgren's 'The Need for an Ombudsman Too' in the same symposium.

There, for the present, the controversy about administrative jurisdiction rests. The whole question is one of the most complex with which students of British government are confronted. Analytically, it can be reduced to the following elements. Starting with the initial administrative decision, one has to consider how far it embodies a judicial element, i.e. to what extent it involves an adjudication of a dispute, or potential dispute, between two parties, one of which, in most cases, is the administration itself. If the judicial element is strong and important, one has to ask whether the decision itself should be confided, not to an individual administrator or collegiate body of administrators, but to an independent tribunal or independent Commissioner with legal qualifications. If this is rejected, what provisions, if any, are to be made for an appeal against the decision either to a higher administrative authority or to an administrative tribunal, or perhaps to the former in the first instance and to the latter in the second? If the answer is 'a tribunal', there arises the further question of the grounds on which an appeal is to be allowed. Should it be based on defect of procedure, bad faith, or bad substance, or all three? What role, moreover, should be played by the courts, and how should they organize themselves for its performance? Are their present modes of controlling the acts of administrators and administrative tribunals, via the rather restrictive forms of jurisdiction which can be set in motion (and usually very slow motion) by means of special and rather complicated procedures to be maintained? Or is the solution to establish a supreme Administrative Court, enjoying a much wider field of jurisdiction and employing techniques of an inquisitory type, cheaper for the litigant and perhaps more effective in elucidating the truth? Finally, how is any scheme that may be devised to be reconciled, in case of *prima facie* contradiction, with the doctrine of Ministerial responsibility for administrative acts and with the role of the House of Commons as a forum for the ventilation of grievances?

These are not questions to which simple answers may be given. It may be that Professor Mitchell (whose proposals, in many respects, follow those of his pioneering predecessor, Professor Robson) has cut the Gordian Knot; but his solution has not as yet won more than limited support among politicians, administrators and lawyers. The urgency of finding solutions however, can hardly be underlined too strongly. As has so often been said, this is an age of big government, in which the powers of the bureaucracy to determine the shape of the citizens' lives have increased, are increasing and – despite Mr Enoch Powell – are not likely to be diminished. It is claimed that these powers exist and are exercised for the benefit of the citizen, and not even the most acid critic of bureaucracy would deny that this is so in at least *some* cases. How is it to be ensured that they are not exercised arbitrarily, unfairly or in bad faith? There is some guarantee – and a very important one – in the maintenance of the high qualities of the Civil Service to which tribute has so frequently been paid; but clearly one cannot have confidence that administrators will always do their best, never make mistakes and invariably act according to the highest standards of behaviour.[37] The discovery of appropriate forms of judicial control of administration is therefore important, as is that of the precise circumstances in which the processes of administration should themselves be exercised with the assistance of judicial-type procedures.

In the major part of this chapter, we have attempted, in the most general way, to define the issues and to describe the methods both adopted and proposed, for dealing with them. Our final emphasis must be on the fact – for fact it is – that Britain has by no means reached the end of her quest for a proper point of balance between the requirements of efficiency in administration and those of justice for the citizen. Indeed if the Law Commission's proposal[38] that a Royal Commission or 'Committee of comparable status' be appointed to enquire into the whole subject is accepted, a new stage in the search may be about to be inaugurated.

37. Nevertheless, as Miss Ganz has pointed out (see above, p. 270) considerable reliance has to be placed, in some of the most important fields where administrative discretion is exercised, on the development of suitable procedural conventions (unbuttressed by law) within the Government departments concerned. 'A country whose constitutional safeguards are embodied in conventions,' she writes, 'should not be afraid to apply similar checks to its administration' (*op. cit.* p. 106).

38. See the Law Commission, *Administrative Law* (May 1969). Cmnd 4059.

Part IV

Make or Break?

Chapter 12

The Future in the Present

(i)

This book was written at a time when there appeared to be far more dissatisfaction than satisfaction with the British political system and with the way that the country was governed. Such dissatisfaction was not confined to small groups of radicals, on both right and left; it was widespread among the more vocal middle-of-the-roaders and found expression in the sober columns of the quality press and in weighty books such as Mr Max Nicholson's *The System*. The burden of the familiar song was that Britain was ruled by an unimaginative 'establishment', incapable of dynamic leadership, mainly concerned with the perpetuation of its own privileges, and securely attached to a set of obsolete beliefs and prejudices.

It may be that Britain's comparatively poor economic performance in the 1950s and 1960s was sufficient explanation of this widespread uneasiness. Certainly, it would be surprising if economic stagnation were found to be devoid of effect on political attitudes. That distributable goods of all kinds did not flow freely enough to satisfy rising expectations, and that this disproportion has both stimulated political 'bloody-mindedness' among a minority and reinforced the political apathy of the majority may be taken for granted; and one could argue with some cogency that if the balance of payments situation should ever be put right, production start to rise again and unemployment reduced to its former extremely low level, political problems would be seen in truer perspective. One needs to bear in mind, however, the possibility that the revitalization of the economy may itself be dependent on the achievement of radical changes in both institutions and attitudes. More importantly, it would seem from foreign experience that relative prosperity by no means automatically dispels the sense of *alienation*, which indeed appears to be the child of affluence rather than of poverty. It was an economically buoyant France that underwent its 'days of May'; it was the richest country in the world, the United States, that was threatened with the kind of political chaos that we had previously regarded as more characteristic of the underdeveloped than of the developed countries.

(ii)

The word 'alienation', although rarely defined with any precision except by sociologists, may be fairly used to characterize a widespread attitude, by no means confined to any one class or section of the community, towards parliamentary politics. The frequently repeated assertion that Parliament has never sunk lower in public esteem may well be exaggerated – for the older generation of British citizens cannot remember a time when it was not being made. Nevertheless, the fact that it is now so rarely contradicted would seem to be indicative of a disenchantment that is unusually profound. Although no fully scientific survey of attitudes towards parliamentary government has been made, one may reasonably guess, from one's own experience, that it would reveal a great deal of indifference as well as of ignorance. What evidence we have about attitudes towards political parties points in the same direction. Intelligent enough to recognize that the differences between the two main political parties are of emphasis rather than of aim, the electorate is also disillusioned enough to care little about which of them currently occupies the seats of power.

If such disillusionment resulted in nothing more than an extension and deepening of the apathy that has always been characteristic of a substantial proportion of the British electorate, its effect on the modus operandi of the political system might not be of any great significance. The game, although arousing little interest among the spectators, could continue to be played in accordance with its well-established rules. It is possible, however, that beneath the apparent apathy there may be deep and dangerous frustrations, liable increasingly to express themselves in ways that bypass the normal political channels.

To what extent, therefore, may 'consensus' politics be regarded as seriously endangered? As we know, the very idea of consensus is always unacceptable to a minority of party activists. A party that labels itself 'socialist' for instance, inevitably draws into its ranks a number of enthusiasts for whom 'consensus' is equivalent to 'betrayal'. A whole series of left-wing groups in the Labour Party have consistently preached boldness in pursuit of socialist principles, primarily because they believe in them more firmly and dogmatically than their more cautious fellow-members, but also because they have come to the conclusion (in the face of a considerable body of contradictory evidence) that working people will respond positively and enthusiastically to a strong socialist lead. More surprising was the attempted takeover of the Liberal Party by the group of youngsters nicknamed the 'Red Guards', whose belief in the virtues of direct action seemed to equal that of the most extreme of the Labour rebels; but more serious is a certain hardening of opinion in and around the Conservative Party. If the measure of inter-party agreement which has hitherto facilitated the smooth working of democratic institutions is in danger of being broken, it is at least equally as possible that the break will come from the right as from the left; for the mood of the British people would seem to make them more susceptible to the impact of right-wing than of left-wing demagoguery.

How strong the consensus-breaking forces are, or are likely to become, is anybody's guess. What is certain is that the moderate politicians, on both sides, still have considerable reserves of strength, which they will deploy to the full. Both Labour and Conservative leaders are experienced in dealing with rebels, and are fortified by the fact that, at least up to now, it is the moderate rather than the extreme policy that has paid off electorally. But although the Labour leaders may have little to fear from the forces on their left, the Conservative leaders cannot so easily disregard those on their right. For as 'rightism' of a certain type could well prove an electoral asset to the Conservative Party, particularly among the working class, the moderate leaders of that party may be tempted to move towards the adoption of policies which might prove incompatible with the perpetuation of the present comparatively gentlemanly relationships between Conservative and Labour.

In contemporary Britain there is a pervasive feeling that new political alignments are in the course of formation; but it is impossible to foresee how these ill-defined trends will change the total pattern of politics. There is a possibility – although one could hardly describe it as a 'clear and present danger' – that the conflict between right and left, whatever organizational and institutional expression it may eventually assume, may overflow the bounds of constitutional convention and democratic consensus, in the manner that Harold Laski, in the 1930s, far too confidently predicted.[1] Alternatively, there is the possibility of a coming

1. See *Parliamentary Government in England*, and also Laski's subsequent retraction in *Reflections on the Constitution* (1951).

together of the moderates on both sides to form a coalition Government comparable with the 'National' Government of 1931–40, or even of their coalescence in a dominant centre party, similar in certain respects to the Indian National Congress. Such a coalition or coalescence could probably provide, at least temporarily, the 'strength' which, according to the opinion polls, most citizens look for in a political leadership, but one of its consequences could be to deprive the discontented and frustrated of the means of effective political action, with the result that 'anomic' political behaviour would undergo a sharp increase, and democratic political institutions thereby suffer further discredit.

If the preservation of democracy is the first priority, the 'ideal' political situation is one that displays a delicate balance. Party conflict must be sufficiently serious to appear significant, and sufficiently principled to deter the idealist from taking to the hills; yet it must not be so bitter as to undermine the preparedness of minorities to accept majority decisions, in the confidence of 'better luck next time'. To achieve this balance, for which Britain has long been famous, requires a combination of boldness and finesse on the part of politicians which they seem to be displaying less conspicuously than in former times.

Hence the cry of 'British democracy in danger' which now is raised with rather monotonous regularity. In assessing the justification for such alarms, which have been quite unnecessarily voiced on many past occasions, one must always remember that Britain possesses a remarkably tough political system which is certainly capable of withstanding far more serious assaults than have as yet been directed against it. To speak as if the moderates in both main political parties were at the end of their tether would be to repeat the error made by Sir Oswald Mosley in 1930, when he resigned from the Labour Party in disgust and decided to act the lone wolf, only to find himself being abandoned by his former political friends without acquiring any compensatory support from the great British public. The contrast between Mosley and Churchill, an infinitely wiser man, is significant. Churchill, too, had gone into the political wilderness, but, bowing to the strength of the 'system', he retained both his membership of the Conservative Party and the vantage point provided by a parliamentary seat. It was thus that he could rise to supreme office, amid popular and parliamentary acclaim, when events had convinced the Conservatives – and indeed the whole nation – that there was no alternative to his leadership. Although history does not repeat itself, one would be unwise to imagine that it has nothing to teach.

If the main contours of Britain's political system are to disappear, or be fundamentally changed, the most likely of possible causes are international conflict or economic crisis. Another world war, of course, would be incomparably more severe in its effects than any previous war in which Britain has been involved – indeed, sheer physical annihilation is the most likely outcome. But the impact of a major economic crisis is more problematical. The crisis of 1929–32 temporarily altered the shape of British party politics, but failed to generate tensions strong enough to destroy the consensus that maintains the parliamentary system. In the light of this experience, the 'leftist' and 'rightist' radicals who pin their hopes on a cataclysmic decline in production and employment may well be deluding themselves. However, circumstances of this kind would almost certainly raise the sense of political alienation to a level that it failed to reach in the 1930s, and would hence pose, perhaps more sharply than ever before, the question of how long a democratic set-up can continue to go through the familiar motions when people have ceased to feel any serious commitment to it. For Britain, the answer is probably 'quite a long time'; but it is certainly not 'for ever'.

(iii)

If Britain's democracy is to be preserved, in whatever form, an essential precondition is obviously the maintenance of civil liberties. Those, perhaps the most vital element in the British political tradition, are under attack – although not as yet dangerously so – by groups on both right and left which, while vociferously claiming the most complete freedom for themselves, would deny a similar freedom to their rivals. The reassertion and reinterpretation of the British tradition in this field has therefore become important.

Despite periods of regression, such as 1793–1821, or of voluntary and temporary sacrifice, such as 1939–45, Britain has enenjoyed a history of expanding liberties of the familiar liberal kind, such as freedom of movement, speech and association. These have been gradually extended, not without effort, to wider and wider sections of the population, through the repeal of restrictive laws (such as those that hampered the activities of trade unions) and the abolition of illiberal institutions (such as the recently-liquidated Lord Chamberlain's Office). One may readilv admit that, in an economically inegalitarian society, these liberties are more effectively available to the rich than to the poor. Nevertheless, the rise of mass interest groups, such as trade unions and professional associations, has tended to redress the balance, by enhancing the power of ordinary people both to exercise and protect what they regard as their rights.

The immediate danger is not that some dictatorially-minded politician will undermine or destroy these liberties, but that respect for them may be subtly eroded. Avoidance of such erosion cannot be accomplished by repeating the incantation to the effect that 'the price of liberty is eternal vigilance'. If civil liberties are to be preserved, they must be seen by the citizen as relevant, effective and useful. It is for this reason, among others, that 'libertarians' now place so much emphasis on the need for greater opportunities for participation in public affairs.

Admittedly, a part of this demand – although not a very significant one – is anarchistically utopian in character, and therefore incapable of satisfaction except at the unacceptable price of jettisoning the whole delicate machinery of public administration upon which people's welfare and ultimately their lives depend. Some of it, moreover, is irrelevant to the real problems with which Britain is confronted, as that uncomfortably perceptive Labour politician, Mr Anthony Crosland, has cogently argued. But a great deal of it is serious enough. The 'participation' for which the Liberal Party argues, for instance, is couched in clear, concrete, discussable proposals.

The question is how far countervailing forces, to offset the increasing bureaucratization of government, parties, pressure groups and a wide range of social and economic institutions, can be brought into existence or strengthened without reducing the functional efficiency of the whole system to an unacceptable level. The answer is by no means clear. We have suggested (Chapter 11) that the development of a properly-organized system of administrative law, capable of providing the citizen with readily-available remedies against bureaucratic arbitrariness and maladministration, would be of help. But the multiplication of *protective* devices cannot satisfy a demand for great *participation*. It is not without significance that France, despite her possession of one of the best systems of administrative law in the world, for so long hovered on the brink of political anarchy. Important as the protection of the citizen against oppressive, impudent or merely careless administrators may be, more than this is rather obviously needed if the sense of alienation is to be significantly diminished. Would the introduction of 'primary' elections and/or proportional representation help to build a bridge between 'them' and 'us'? Would it be helpful to devolve some of the powers now exercised by the Westminster Parliament on a series of regional assemblies, or to grant a substantial measure of political autonomy to Scotland and to Wales? Is it possible in any other way to strengthen the machinery of local government so as to give it a wider range of powers which it can exercise in response to the demands of the local electorate rather than to those of the so-called back seat drivers of Whitehall? How practicable is workers' participation in the management of the industries, both public and private, on which they depend for their livelihoods? What role can be played by students and by junior members of the staff in the running of universities and other institutions of higher education? Do the schools really need headmasters and headmistresses of the old autocratic type? What place is there for parents' associations? Questions of this kind are being posed more and more insistently.

(iv)

It would be unrealistic, however, to accept at its face value the demand for greater opportunities to 'participate'. Those who voice it are still few in number, while those who try to assess its implications or to embody it in specific institutional proposals are even fewer. One may suspect, moreover, that its apparently increasing popularity means little more than that it has become a 'with-it' manner of expressing a generalized discontent, rather than a genuine manifestation of what the Community Development people call a 'felt need'. For common experience tends to suggest that the number of citizens who feel a real urge to participate in public life and who find their opportunities to do so seriously frustrated is very small. Voluntary organizations are not normally faced with a superfluity of activists, and the calls on the time of those who are prepared to devote themselves to any form of public service are virtually unlimited.

Indeed, it can be argued that, for most of the people most of the time, political participation is either unwanted or impracticable. The desire to live a private life, devoted to non-political activities which are of inherent interest, is very widespread. The acquisition of an intellectual grasp of the major political issues is a burdensome exercise, beyond the capacity of the majority, even in a comparatively highly educated country. Moreover, any individual contribution that can be made to the total decision-taking process, except at the purely local level, is inevitably small in a country of more than 50 million inhabitants. What most people want, one may reliably guess, is simply more security, more income and more leisure – three *desiderata* which, incidentally, are not necessarily mutually compatible. If they believe that the 'authorities' are helping to make these things possible, general satisfaction with the behaviour of the politicians and their administrative agents will tend to increase, and active interest in politics as such will correspondingly decrease. If, on the other hand, there is a general belief that those who are placed in positions of authority are incompetent, negligent or selfish, mounting dissatisfaction may well express itself in the demand that 'the people' themselves should take over responsibility. There is little to suggest, however, that the satisfaction of this demand, even if it were politically practicable, would contribute anything of significance to the the felt needs which constitute its point of origin.

Any realistic analysis of Britain's present situation, moreover, leads inexorably to the conclusion that the British have entered a period, which will almost certainly be prolonged, during which demand for the good things of life will outstrip the possibilities of their supply, irrespective of the political, economic and social policies they decide to adopt. The consequence is an increase in tensions of a kind that cannot be *resolved*, whether by participation or by any other means, but only, on the most optimistic of assumptions, *contained*. For such containment of tensions Britain, as has often been pointed out in this book, possesses a capacity exceeding that of most other countries; but the maintenance of that capacity requires a readiness to adapt and innovate that, on any showing, exceeds any hitherto displayed. With the specific changes of policy and attitude that are needed this book is not concerned; for the focus of the authors' interest is institutional. In this field, we would suggest, emphasis on increasing the range of popular participation in the decision-making processes tends to evade the real problems. Whether increased participation is desirable per se, as a contribution to the realization of the concept of the good life, is a question that we leave to the political philosophers. There are those who would be satisfied with nothing less than a return to the spirit, if not the form, of the Greek polis; others, more interested in the preservation of political stability than in the raising of the level of political activity, see virtue in the prevalence of a fairly widespread *apathy* and cast doubt on the existence of any moral imperative even to exercise the right to vote. Our own emphasis is on the improvement both of the *efficiency* of the politico-administrative system and of its capacity to facilitate *communication* between governors and governed, upwards and downwards.

By 'efficient' institutions we mean institutions through which timely, consistent and well-informed decisions may be made and then put into effect with the minimum of cost and friction. Many of the proposals for the reform of Parliament, of the Cabinet, and of the administrative apparatus which we have discussed in previous chapters are aimed precisely at this. But efficiency, as everyone knows, is not an end in itself, but only a means to an end; and democracy is essentially about the method by which that end shall be determined. To say, as Schumpeter says, that democracy is nothing more than the periodical determination by popular vote of who shall govern is to empty it of most of its content. That comparatively small bodies of people have to accept the ultimate responsibility is obvious enough; it is also obvious, at least to the British, that they should be periodically accountable for their discharge of that responsibility to 'the people'. But there is more to it than this. The essence of democracy is a continuous dialogue between governors and governed, whereby a governor strives for understanding and acceptance by the governed, who, in their turn express to the governors their non-understanding and non-acceptance when the latter prove insufficiently persuasive. That is what we mean by 'communication'. Everyone admits that, in our modern governmental system, it is inadequately organized. That this should be so hardly surprises; for mass democracy is a comparatively new system, for which there is no historical parallel, and its advent has coincided with big government, which greatly aggravates the communicational difficulties inherent in a national constituency of many millions. Both the extension of the franchise and the expansion of governmental functions put a premium on attitudes and practices that we describe as bureaucratic when we are using that word in the pejorative sense. Hence the emphasis we have placed on proposals to unleash and even stimulate whatever countervailing forces may exist, so that the dialogue between governors and governed may become rather less one-sided. What one surely needs is an opportunity for ordinary people, whether as individuals or as members of groups, to communicate more effectively with the rulers, whenever they become aware of a need to do so. This does not imply continuous or persistent participation (for which there is, we repeat, no obvious demand), but the existence of better institutional means for the expression, at all levels, of what old-fashioned political scientists used to call 'public opinion'. How frequently and vigorously such means are actually used will depend on the state of public opinion itself. If they are comparatively neglected, this could indicate a degree of satisfaction which some might identify with political health, despite the comparative absence of overt participatory symptoms from the condition – or even *because* of their absence.

In short, we need a dialogue, whether continuous or intermittent; but it must be arranged in a way that permits the requirements of efficient government to be satisfied. If 'popular' government proves incompatible with efficiency it will very soon cease to be popular. This is an inescapable dilemma of democratic societies. As the preceding pages have shown, the more politically-articulate sections of the British people have become very conscious of its existence in the second half of the twentieth century. How successfully they will cope with it remains to be seen.

Further Reading

We have confined this Select Bibliography to the more obvious of the 'follow-up' books, excluding other general introductions to British government comparable in scope to our own. Students in need of a much fuller bibliography, including periodical articles, should consult that compiled by Mr Punnett in his *British Government and Politics* (London, Heinemann 1968).

1: The Heritage

BIRCH, A. H. *Representative and Responsible Government* (London, Allen & Unwin 1964)

BULMER-THOMAS, IVOR *The Growth of the British Party System* (2 Vols, London, John Baker 1965)

BUTLER, D. E. and STOKES *Political Change in Britain* (London, Macmillan 1969)

DICEY, A. V. *Introduction to the Study of the Law of the Constitution* (10th Edn – with an Introduction and Appendix by E. C. S. Wade: London, Macmillan 1959)

EMDEN, C. S. *The People and the Constitution* (2nd Edn, London, OUP 1956)

JENNINGS, SIR IVOR *The Law and the Constitution* (5th Edn, London, University of London Press 1961)

KEIR, SIR DAVID L. *The Constitutional History of Modern Britain since 1485* (6th Edn, London, Black 1960)

KINGSLEY, J. DONALD *Representative Bureaucracy, an Interpretation of the British Civil Service* (Yellow Springs, Ohio, Antioch Press 1944)

MACKINTOSH, J. P. *The British Cabinet* (2nd Edn, London, Stevens and Methuen 1968)

MAITLAND, F. W. *English Constitutional History* (London, CUP 1908)

MARSHALL, G. and MOODIE, G. *Some Problems of the Constitution* (2nd Edn, London, Hutchinson 1961)

MARTIN, KINGSLEY *The Crown and the Establishment* (Harmondsworth, Penguin Books 1963)

MORRAH, DERMOT, *The Work of the Queen* (London, Kimber 1958)

MURRAY-BROWN, JEREMY (ed.) *The Monarchy and its Future* (London, Allen & Unwin 1969)

NICOLSON, HAROLD *King George V* (London, Constable 1952)

ROSE, R. *Studies in British Politics* (London, Macmillan 1969)

SMELLIE, K. B. *A Hundred Years of English Government* (2nd Edn, London, Duckworth 1950)

WADE, E. C. S. and PHILLIPS, G. G. *Constitutional Law* (7th Edn by E. C. S. Wade and A. W. Bradley: London, Longmans 1965)

WHEELER-BENNETT, SIR JOHN *King George VI, His Life and Reign* (London, Macmillan 1958)

2: Electoral System

BENNEY, M. et al. *How People Vote* (London, Routledge 1956)

BIRCH, A. M. *Representation* (London, Macmillan 1972)

BLONDEL, J. *Voters, Parties & Leaders* (Harmondsworth, Penguin Books 1963)

BLUMLER, J. G. and MCQUAIL D. *Television in Politics* (London, Faber 1968)

BONHAM, J. *The Middle Class Vote* (London, Faber 1954)

BUTLER, D. E. *The British Electoral System since 1918* (London, OUP 1963)

BUTLER, D. E. *The British General Election of 1951* (London, Macmillan 1952)

BUTLER, D. E. *The British General Election of 1955* (London, Macmillan 1955)

BUTLER, D. E. and ROSE, R. *The British General Election of 1959* (London, Macmillan 1960)

BUTLER, D. E. and KING, A. *The British General Election of 1964* (London, Macmillan 1965)

BUTLER, D. E. and KING, A. *The British General Election of 1966* (London Macmillan 1966)

BUTLER, D. E. and PINTO-DUSCHINSKY *The British General Election of 1970* (London, Macmillan 1971)

FULFORD, R. *Votes for Women* (London, Faber 1957)

HODDER-WILLIAMS, R. *Public Opinion Polls and British Politics* (London, Routledge & Kegan Paul 1970)

JENNINGS, SIR W. I. *Party Politics I. Appeal to the People* (London, CUP 1960)

LAKEMAN, E. and LAMBERT, J. D. *Voting in Democracies* (London, Faber 1959)

LEONARD, R. *Elections in Britain* (London, Van Nostrand 1968)

MCKENZIE, R. T. and SILVER, A. *Angels in Marble* (London, Heinemann 1968)

MACKENZIE, W. J. M. *Free Elections* (London, Allen & Unwin 1958)

MILNE, R. S. and MACKENZIE, H. C. *Marginal Seat, 1955* (London, Hansard Society 1958)

MILNE, R. S. and MACKENZIE, H. C. *Straight Fight* (London, Hansard Society 1954)

NORDLINGER, E. A. *The Working Class Tories* (London, MacGibbon & Kee 1967)

PATERSON, P. *The Selectorate* (London, MacGibbon & Kee 1967)
PULZER, P. G. J. *Political Representation and Elections in Britain* London, Allen & Unwin 1967)
RANNEY, A. *Pathways to Parliament* (London, Macmillan 1965)
ROSE, R. *Influencing Voters* (London, Faber 1967)
ROSS, J. F. S. *Elections and Electors* (London, Eyre & Spottiswoode 1955)
RUSH, M. *The Selection of Parliamentary Candidates* (London, Nelson 1969)
TRENMAN, J. and MCQUAIL, D. *Television and the Political Image* (London Methuen 1961)

3: Political Parties

General

BAILEY, S. D. *The British Party System* (London, Hansard Society 1953)
BEATTIE, A. (ed.) *English Party Politics* (London, Weidenfeld & Nicolson 1971)
BEER, S. H. *Modern British Politics* (London, Faber 1965)
BRITTAN, S. *Left or Right: The Bogus Dilemma* (London, Secker & Warburg 1969)
BULMER-THOMAS, I. *The Growth of the British Party System* (2 Vols, London, John Baker 1965)
BULMER-THOMAS, I. *The Party System in Great Britain* (London, Phoenix House 1953)
COMFORT, G. O. *Professional Politicians: A Study of the British Party Agents* (Washington, Public Affairs Press 1958)
DUVERGER, M. *Political Parties* (London, Methuen 1964)
ELDERSVELD, S. J. *Political Parties* (Chicago, Rand McNally 1964)
LEES, J. D. and KIMBER, R. (eds.) *Political Parties in Modern Britain* (London, Routledge & Kegan Paul 1972)
LEISERSON, A. *Parties and Politics* (New York, Knopf 1958)
MCKENZIE, R. T. *British Political Parties* (Revised edn, London, Heinemann 1963)
MICHELS, R. *Political Parties* (London, Constable 1959 – first published in German in 1911)
NEUMANN, S. *Modern Political Parties* (London, CUP 1956)
OSTROGORSKI, M. *Democracy and the Organization of Political Parties* (London, Macmillan 1902)
ROSE, R. *Politics in England* (London, Faber 1965)

The Communist Party

KLUGMANN, JAMES *History of The Communist Party of Great Britain*, (Three volumes, London, Lawrence & Wishart 1968 & 1969)
MACFARLANE, L. J. *The British Communist Party* (London, MacGibbon & Kee 1966)

NEWTON, K. *The Sociology of British Communism* (London, Allen Lane 1970)
PELLING, H. *The British Communist Party* (London, Black 1958)

The Conservative Party

BOYD-CARPENTER, J. *The Conservative Case* (London, Wingate 1950)
CHURCHILL, R. S. *The Fight for the Tory Leadership* (London, Heinemann 1964)
HAILSHAM, SECOND VISCOUNT *The Conservative Case* (Harmondsworth, Penguin Books 1959)
HARRIS, N. *Competition and the Corporate Society: British Conservatives in the State and Industry, 1945-64* (University Paperbacks, Methuen 1973)
HOFFMAN, J. D. *The Conservative Party in Opposition, 1945–51* (London, MacGibbon & Kee 1964)
YOUNG, W. *The Profumo Affair: Aspects of Conservatism* (Harmondsworth, Penguin Books 1963)

The Labour Party

ATTLEE, FIRST EARL (C. R. Attlee) *The Labour Party in Perspective: and Twelve Years Later* (London, Gollancz 1949)
COLE, G. D. H. *A History of the Labour Party since 1914* (London, Routledge 1948)
COLE, G. D. H. *A Short History of the British Working Class Movement, 1789–1947* (London, Allen & Unwin 1948)
HARRISON, M. *Trade Unions and the Labour Party since 1945* (London, Allen & Unwin 1960)
HINDESS, B. *The Decline of Working Class Politics* (London, Paladin 1972)
JENKINS, R. *The Labour Case* (Harmondsworth, Penguin Books 1959)
LAPPING, B. *The Labour Government 1964–70* (Harmondsworth, Penguin Books 1970)
MILLIBRAND, R. *Parliamentary Socialism: A Study in the Politics of Labour* (London, Merlin Press 1961)
NORTHCOTT, J. *Why Labour?* (Harmondworth, Penguin Books 1964)
PELLING, H. *A Short History of the Labour Party* (London, Macmillan 1965)
PELLING, H. *A History of British Trade Unionism* (London, Macmillan 1963)
PRITT, D. N. *The Labour Government 1945–51* (London, Lawrence and Wishart 1963)
SMITH, B. G. and OSTERGAARD, G. N. *Constitutional Relations between the Labour and Cooperative Parties* (London, Hansard Society 1960)
WILLIAMS, F. *Fifty Years March: The Rise of the Labour Party* (London, Odhams 1949)

The Liberal Party

COWIE, H. *Why Liberal?* (Harmondsworth, Penguin Books 1964)
FULFORD, R. *The Liberal Case* (Harmondsworth, Penguin Books 1959)

GRIMOND, J. *The Liberal Future* (London, Faber 1959)
GRIMOND, J. *The Liberal Challenge* (London, Hollis & Carter 1963)
RASMUSSEN, J. *The Liberal Party: A Study of Retrenchment and Revival* (London, Constable 1965)
VINCENT, J. *The Formation of the Liberal Party 1857–68* (London, Constable 1966)
WATKINS, A. *The Liberal Dilemma* (London, MacGibbon & Kee 1961)

Other
BENEWICK, R. *Political Violence & Public Order* (London, Allen Lane The Penguin Press 1969)
CROSS, C. *The Fascists in Britain* (London, Barrie & Rockliff 1961)
KAUFMAN, C. *The Left* (London, Blond 1966)
THAYER, G. *The British Political Fringe* (London, Blond 1965)

4: Parliament

General
ABRAHAM, L. and HAWTREY, S. C. A. *A Parliamentary Dictionary* (London, Butterworth 1964)
FOOT, M. *Parliament in Danger* (London, Pall Mall Press 1959)
HANSON, A. H. and WEISEMAN, H. V. *Parliament at Work* (London, Stevens, 1962)
ILBERT, SIR C. *Parliament* (London, OUP 1960)
JENNINGS, SIR W. I. *Parliament* (London, CUP 1957)
LEONARD, D. and HERMAN *The Backbencher in Parliament* (London, Macmillan 1972)
MORRIS, A., et al. *The Growth of Parliamentary Scrutiny by Committee* (London, Pergamon 1970)
NICOLSON, N. *People & Parliament* (London, Weidenfeld & Nicolson 1958)
PUNNETT, R. M. *Front Bench Opposition* (London, Heinemann Education, 1973)
RICHARDS, P. G. *The Backbenchers* (London, Faber 1972)
RICHARDS, P. G. *Parliament and Conscience* (London, Allen & Unwin 1970)
STRATHEARN, G. *Our Parliament* (London, Hansard Society 1958)
WALKLAND, S. A. *The Legislative Process in Great Britain* (London, Allen & Unwin 1968)
WHEARE, K. C. *Legislatures* (London, OUP 1963)

Members
BERRINGTON, H. *Backbench Opinion in the House of Commons 1945–55* (London, Pergammon 1973)
BUCK, W. P. *Amateurs and Professionals in British Politics 1918–59* (London and Chicago, Chicago University Press 1963)

FINER, S. E., BERRINGTON, H. B. and BARTHOLOMEW, D. J. *Backbench Opinon in the House of Commons 1955–9* (London, Pergamon Press 1961)

FULFORD, R. *The Member and his Constituency* (London, Ramsay Muir Trust 1957)

HERBERT, A. P. *Independent Member* (London, Methuen 1958)

RICHARDS, P. G. *Honourable Members* (London, Faber 1959)

ROTH, A. *Business Background of M.P.s* (London, Parliamentary Profiles 1967)

Law, Procedure & Privileges

BROMHEAD, P. *Private Members' Bills in the British Parliament* (London, Routledge 1956)

CHESTER, D. N. and BOWRING, N. *Questions in Parliament* (London, OUP 1962)

HERBERT, SIR A. P. *The Ayes Have it* (London, Methuen 1937)

HOWARTH, P. *Questions in the House* (London, Lane 1956)

HUGHES, E. *Parliament and Mumbo-Jumbo* (London, Allen & Unwin 1966)

MAY, SIR T. E. *The Law, Privileges, Proceedings & Usage of Parliament* (London, Butterworth 1964)

TAYLOR, E. *The House of Commons at Work* (Harmondsworth, Penguin Books 1965)

Parliamentary Control

BRITAIN, SIR H. *The British Budgetary System* (London, Allen & Unwin 1959)

CHUBB, B. *The Control of Public Expenditure* (London, OUP 1952)

COOMBES, D. *The M.P. & the Administration* (London, Allen & Unwin 1966)

EINZIG, P. *Parliament's Financial Control* (London, Secker & Warburg 1959)

HANSON, A. H. *Parliament and Public Ownership* (London, Cassell 1961)

JOHNSON, N. *Parliament & Administration* (London, Allen & Unwin 1966)

KERSELL, J. E. *Parliamentary Supervision of Delegated Legislation* (London, Stevens 1960)

REID, G. *The Politics of Financial Control* (London, Hutchinson 1967)

Reform

CRICK, B. *The Reform of Parliament* (London, Weidenfeld & Nicolson 1964)

HANSARD SOCIETY *Parliamentary Reform* (London, Cassell 1967)

HILL, A. and WHICHELOW, A. *What's Wrong with Parliament?* (Harmondsworth, Penguin Books 1964)

HOLLIS, C. *Can Parliament Survive?* (London, Hollis & Carter 1949)

House of Lords
BAILEY, S. D. *The Future of the House of Lords* (London, Hansard Society 1954)
BENN, A. WEDGWOOD *The Privy Council as a Second Chamber* (London, Fabian Society, Tract No. 305, 1957)
BROMHEAD, P. *The House of Lords and Contemporary Politics* (London, Routledge 1958)
PIKE, L. O. *Constitutional History of the House of Lords from Original Sources* (London, Macmillan 1894)
WESTON, C. C. *English Constitutional Theory and the House of Lords* (London, Routledge 1965)

5: The Cabinet

ALDERMAN, R. K. and CROSS, J. A. *The Tactics of Resignation* (London, Routledge 1967)
AMERY, L. S. *Thoughts on the Constitution* (London, OUP 1964)
BERKELEY, H. *The Power of the Prime Minister* (London, Allen & Unwin 1968)
CARTER, B. E. *The Office of the Prime Minister* (London, Faber 1965)
DAALDER, H. *Cabinet Reform in Britain 1914–63* (London, OUP 1964)
EHRMANN, J. *Cabinet Government and War 1890–1940* (London, CUP 1958)
HANKEY, LORD *Government Control in War* (London, CUP 1945)
HOWARD, A. and WEST, R. *The Making of a Prime Minister* (London, Cape 1965)
JENNINGS, SIR W. I. *Cabinet Government* (London, CUP 1959)
JOHNSON, F. A. *Defence by Committee* (London, OUP 1960)
LASKI, H. J. *Reflections on the Constitution* (London, Manchester University Press 1962)
LOEWENSTEIN, K. *British Cabinet Government* (London, OUP 1967)
MACKINTOSH, J. P. *The British Cabinet* (2nd edn, London, Stevens and Methuen 1968)
MORRISON, LORD *Government and Parliament* (3rd Edn, London OUP 1964)
MOSLEY, R. K. *The Story of the Cabinet Office* (London, Routledge & Kegan Paul 1969)
OGILVY-WEBB, M. *The Government Explains* (London, Allen & Unwin 1965)
RICHARDS, P. G. *Patronage in British Government* (London, Allen & Unwin 1963)
SMITH, B. C. *Advising Ministers* (London, Routledge & Kegan Paul 1969)
WALKER, P. G. *The Cabinet* (London, Fontana 1972)

6: Central Administration

BEER, S. H. *Treasury Control* (London, OUP 1957)
BRIDGES, LORD *The Treasury* (London, Allen & Unwin 1964)
BRITTAN, S. *The Treasury under the Tories 1951–64* (Harmondsworth, Penguin Books 1964)
CAMPION, LORD et al. *British Government since 1918* (London, Allen & Unwin 1950)
CHAPMAN, B. *British Government Observed* (London, Allen & Unwin 1963)
THE CIVIL SERVICE *Report of the Committee 1966–68*, Vol. I (London, HMSO Cmnd 3638, 1968, with 5 volumes of Evidence)
COHEN, E. *The Growth of the British Civil Service 1780–1939* (London, Cass 1965)
DAALDER, HANS *Cabinet Reform in Britain 1916–1963* (London, OUP 1964)
DALE, H. E. *The Higher Civil Service of Great Britain* (London, OUP 1941)
DUNNILL, FRANK *The Civil Service, Some Human Aspects* (London, Allen & Unwin 1956)
FINER, S. E. *A Primer of Public Administration* (London, Muller 1950)
FRY, G. K. *Statesmen in Disguise: the Changing Role of the Administrative Class of the British Home Civil Service 1853–1966* (London, Macmillan 1969)
GARRETT, J. *The Management of Government* (London, Penguin Books 1972)
JENNINGS, SIR IVOR *Cabinet Government* (3rd Edn, London, CUP 1959)
KELSALL, R. K. *Higher Civil Servants in Britain* (London, Routledge 1955)
KINGSLEY, DONALD J. *Representative Bureaucracy* (Yellow Springs Ohio, Antioch Press 1944)
MACKENZIE, W. J. M. and GROVE, J. W. *Central Administration in Britain* (London, Longmans 1957)
MACKINTOSH, J. P. *The British Cabinet* (2nd Edn, London, Stevens and Methuen 1968)
MINISTRY OF RECONSTRUCTION *Report on the Machinery of Government Committee* (London, HMSO Cd 9230, 1918)
NICHOLSON, MAX *The System* (London, Hodder & Stoughton 1967)
REID, G. *The Politics of Financial Control* (London, Hutchinson 1967)
ROBSON, W. A. (ed.) *The Civil Service in Britain and France* (London, Hogarth Press 1956)
ROSEVEARE, H. *The Treasury* (Harmondsworth, Penguin Books 1969)
WILLSON, F. M. G. (ed.) *The Organisation of British Central Government* (2nd Edn, London, Allen & Unwin 1968)

7: Group Activity

ALLEN, V. L. *Trade Unions and the Government* (London, Longmans 1960)
BLANK, S. *Government and Industry in Britain: The Federation of British Industries in Politics 1945–65* (London, Saxon House 1973)
BEER, S. H. *Modern British Politics* (London, Faber 1965)
CHRISTOPH, J. B. *Capital Punishment and British Politics* (London, Allen & Unwin 1962)
COATES, R. D. *Teachers' Unions and Interest Group Politics* (London, CUP 1972)
DRIVER, C. *The Disarmers* (London, Hodder & Stoughton 1964)
ECKSTEIN, H. *Pressure Group Politics* (London, Allen & Unwin 1960)
EHRMANN, H. W. *Interest Groups on Four Continents* (Pittsburgh University Press 1958)
FINER, S. E. *Anonymous Empire* (2nd Edn, London, Pall Mall 1965)
GROVE, J. W. *Government and Industry in Britain* (London, Longmans 1962)
GUTTSMAN, W. L. *The British Political Elite* (London, MacGibbon & Kee 1963)
MACKINTOSH, J. P. *The British Cabinet* (2nd Edn, London, Stevens and Methuen 1968)
MANZER, R. A. *Teachers and Politics* (Manchester U.P. 1970)
POLITICAL AND ECONOMIC PLANNING *Advisory Committees in British Government* (London, Allen & Unwin 1960)
POTTER, A. M. *Organised Groups in British National Politics* (London, Faber 1961)
ROBERTS, G. K. *Political Parties and Pressure Groups in Britain* (London, Weidenfeld & Nicolson 1970)
ROSE, G. *The Struggle for Penal Reform* (London, Stevens, 1962)
ROTH, A. *Business Background of M.P.s'* (London, Parliamentary Profiles 1967)
SELF, P. and STORING H. *The State and the Farmer* (London, Allen & Unwin 1962)
STEWART, J. D. *British Pressure Groups* (London, OUP 1958)
WHEARE, K. C. *Government by Committee* (London, OUP 1955)
WILSON, H. H. *Pressure Group* (London, Secker & Warburg 1961)
WOOTTON, G. *The Politics of Influence* (London, Routledge 1966)

8: Ad hoc Agencies

ACTON SOCIETY TRUST, *Hospitals and the State: the Organisation and Administration of Hospitals under the National Health Service*, a series of six Reports (London 1957)
BARRY, E. ELDON *Nationalisation in British Politics* (London, Cape 1965)
CAMPION, LORD et al. *British Government since 1918* (London, Allen & Unwin 1950)

COOMBES, D. *The Member of Parliament and the Administration* (London, Allen & Unwin 1966)
GROVE, J. W. *Government and Industry in Britain* (London, Longmans 1962)
HANSON, A. H. (ed.) *Nationalisation* (London, Allen & Unwin 1963)
HANSON, A. H. *Parliament and Public Ownership* (London, Cassell 1961)
KELF-COHEN, R. *Twenty Years of Nationalisation* (London, Macmillan 1969)
MACKENZIE, W. J. M. and GROVE, J. W. *Central Administration in Britain* (London, Longmans 1957)
MINISTRY OF RECONSTRUCTION *Report of the Machinery of Government Committee* (London, HMSO Cd 9320, 1918)
REID, G. L. & ALLEN, K. *Nationalised Industries* (Harmondsworth, Penguin Books 1970)
SELECT COMMITTEE ON NATIONALISED INDUSTRIES *First Report, Session 1967–68. Ministerial Control of the Nationalised Industries* (HC Paper 371–1)
SHANKS, M. (ed.) *Lessons of Public Enterprise* (London, Cape 1963)
TIVEY, LEONARD *Nationalisation in British Industry* (London, Cape 1966)
TIVEY, LEONARD (ed.) *The Nationalized Industries since 1960: A Book of Readings* (London, Allen & Unwin 1974)
THORNHILL, W. *The Nationalised Industries* (London, Nelson 1968)
WEINER, H. E. *British Labour and Public Ownership* (London, Stevens 1960)
WILLSON, F. M. G. (ed.) *The Organisation of British Central Government* (2nd Edn, London, Allen & Unwin 1968)

9: The Management of the Economy

BAUER, R. and GERGEN, K. (eds.) *The Study of Policy Formation* (New York, Free Press 1968)
BRIDGES, LORD *The Treasury* (London, Allen & Unwin 1964)
BRITTAN, S. *The Treasury under the Tories 1951–64* (Harmondsworth, Penguin Books 1964)
CHAPMAN, R. A. *Decision Making* (London, Routledge & Kegan Paul 1969)
CHESTER, D. N. (ed.) *Lessons of the British War Economy* (London, CUP 1951)
DENTON, GEOFFREY, FORSYTH, MURRAY and MACLENNAN, MALCOLM *Economic Planning and Policies in Britain, France and Germany* (London, Allen & Unwin 1968)
DOW, J. C. R. *The Management of the British Economy* (London, CUP 1964)
FLORENCE, P. SARGENT *Industry and the State* (London, Hutchinson 1957)

FRANKS, SIR OLIVER *Central Planning and Control in War and Peace* (London, Longmans Green 1947)
GROVE, J. W. *Government and Industry in Britain* (London, Longmans 1962)
HANSON, A. H. *Planning and the Politicians* (London, Routledge & Kegan Paul 1969)
JONES, G. P. and POOL, A. G. *A Hundred Years of Economic Development in Great Britain 1840–1940* (2nd Edn, London, Duckworth 1948)
MITCHELL, J. *Groundwork of Economic Planning* (London, Secker & Warburg 1966)
NORMANTON, E. L. *The Accountability and Audit of Governments* (Manchester, Manchester University Press 1967)
PEACOCK, A. T. and ROBERTSON, P. J. *Public Expenditure, Appraisal and Control* (London, Oliver & Boyd 1963)
P.E.P. *Government and Industry* (London, Allen & Unwin 1952)
P.E.P. *Inquest on Planning in Britain* (London, 1967)
RICHARDSON, J. J. *The Policy-Making Process* (London, Routledge & Kegan Paul 1969)
ROGOW, A. A. and SHORE, P. *The Labour Government and British Industry 1945–51* (Oxford, Blackwell 1955)
ROSE, R. *Policy-Making in Britain* (London, Macmillan 1969)
ROWLEY, CHARLES K. *The British Monopolies Commission* (London, Allen & Unwin 1966)
SAMPSON, A. *Anatomy of Britain* (London, Hodder & Stoughton 1962)
SELF, P. and STORING, H. *The State and the Farmer* (London, Allen & Unwin 1962)
SHONFIELD, ANDREW *Modern Capitalism* (London, OUP 1965)
STEVENS, B. and YAMEY, B. S. *The Restrictive Practices Court* (London, Weidenfeld & Nicolson 1965)
WILLSON, F. M. G. (ed.) *The Organisation of British Central Government* (2nd Edn, London, Allen & Unwin 1968)
WORSWICK, G. D. N. and ADY, P. H. *The British Economy in the Nineteen-Fifties* (London, OUP 1962)

10: Regionalism and Decentralization

BARRITT, D. P. and CARTER, C. F. *The Northern Ireland Problem* (London, OUP 1962)
CHESTER, D. N. *Central and Local Government* (London, Macmillan 1951)
DENTON, GEOFFREY, FORSYTH, MURRAY and MACLENNAN, MALCOLM *Economic Planning and Policies in Britain, France and Germany* (London, Allen & Unwin 1968)
DICKINSON, R. E. *City and Region* (London, Routledge 1964)
FEDERATION OF BRITISH INDUSTRIES *The Regional Problem* (London 1963)

FREEMAN, T. W. *The Conurbations of Great Britain* (Manchester, Manchester University Press 1959)

FREEMAN, T. W. *Geography and Regional Administration* (London, Hutchinson 1968)

GREEN, L. P. *Provincial Metropolis, The Future of Local Government* (London, Allen & Unwin 1959)

GRIFFITH, J. A. G. *Central Departments and Local Authorities* (London, Allen & Unwin 1966)

HANHAM, H. J. *Scottish Nationalism* (London, Faber 1969)

JACKSON, R. M. *The Machinery of Local Government* (London, Macmillan 1958)

KELLAS, J. G. *The Scottish Political System* (CUP 1974)

LAWRENCE, R. J. *The Government of Northern Ireland* (London, OUP 1965)

LIPMAN, V. D. *Local Government Areas 1834–1945* (Oxford, Blackwell 1949)

MACKENZIE, W. J. M. and GROVE, J. W. *Central Administration in Britain* (London, Longmans 1957)

MACKENZIE, W. J. M. *Regionalism and Local Government* (London, Institute of Municipal Treasurers and Accountants 1963)

MACKINTOSH, JOHN P. *The Devolution of Power* (London, Penguin and Chatto & Windus 1968)

MILNE, D. *The Scottish Office* (London, Allen & Unwin 1957)

PRYDE, G. S. *Scotland* (London, Benn 1956)

RHODES, G. R. and RUCK S. K. *The Government of Greater London* (London, Allen & Unwin 1970)

RICHARDS, P. G. *The Reformed Local Government System* (London, Allen & Unwin 1973)

ROBSON, W. A. *The Development of Local Government* (3rd Edn, London, Allen & Unwin 1954)

ROBSON, W. A. *Local Government in Crisis* (2nd Edn, London, Allen & Unwin 1969)

SELF, P. J. *Regionalism* (London, Fabian Society 1949)

SENIOR, D. (ed.) *The Regional City, an Anglo-American Discussion of Metropolitan Planning* (London, 1966)

SMITH, BRIAN C. *Advising Ministers* (London, Routledge 1969)

SMITH, BRIAN C. *Field Administration* (London, Routledge 1967)

SMITH, BRIAN C. *Regionalism in England* (3 Vols, London, Acton Society Trust 1966)

STEELE, D. *More Power to the Regions* (London, Fabian Society 1964)

WEST MIDLAND GROUP *Local Government and Central Control* (London, Routledge 1956)

WOLFE, J. N. (ed.) *Government and Nationalism in Scotland* (Edinburgh University Press 1969)

11: Delegated Legislation and Administrative Tribunals

ALLEN, SIR C. K. *Law and Orders* (London, Stevens 1965)
BROWN, R. D. *The Battle of Crichel Down* London, Bodley Head 1955)
CARR, SIR CECIL *Concerning English Administrative Law* (London, OUP 1941)
ELCOCK, H. J. *Administrative Justice* (London, Longmans 1969)
GELLHORN, W. *Ombudsmen and Others* (London, OUP 1967)
GRIFFITH, J. A. G. and STREET, H. *Principles of Administrative Law* (London, Pitman 1967)
HAMSON, C. J. *Executive Discretion and Judicial Control* (London, Stevens 1954)
'JUSTICE' *The Citizen and the Administration, The Redress of Grievances* (London, Stevens 1961)
KERSELL, J. E. *Parliamentary Supervision of Delegated Legislation* (London, Stevens 1960)
ROBSON, W. A. *Justice and Administrative Law* (3rd Edn, London, Stevens 1951)
Report of the Committee on Administrative Tribunals and Enquiries (London, HMSO Cmnd 218, 1957)
Report of the Committee on Ministers' Powers (London, HMSO Cmd 4060, 1932)
ROWAT, D. C. (ed.) *The Ombudsman* (London, Allen & Unwin 1965)
SAWER, G. *Ombudsmen* (London, CUP 1964)
SELF, P. *Administrative Theories and Practice* (London, Allen & Unwin 1972)
STACEY, F. *The British Ombudsman* (London, OUP 1971)
WADE, H. W. R. *Administrative Law* (3rd Edn, London, OUP 1971)
WADE, H. W. R. *Towards Administrative Justice* (Ann Arbor, University of Michigan Press 1963)
WHEARE, K. C. *Maladministration and its Remedies* (Hamlyn Lecture No. 25, Stevens 1973)
WRAITH, R. E., & HUTCHESSON, P. G. *Administrative Tribunals* (London, Allen & Unwin 1973)

12: Make or Break?

ALMOND, G. and VERBA, S. *The Civic Culture* (Revised Edn, Boston, Mass, Little, Brown 1965)
BEER, S. H. *Modern British Politics* (London, Faber 1965)
BUTT, RONALD *The Power of Parliament* (London, Constable 1967)
CHAPMAN, B. *British Government Observed* (London, Allen & Unwin 1963)
CRICK, BERNARD *The Reform of Parliament* (London, Weidenfeld & Nicolson 1964)

DRIVER, CHRISTOPHER *The Disarmers, a Study in Protest* (London, Hodder & Stoughton 1964)

LAPPING, BRIAN and RADICE, GILES (eds.) *More Power to the People* (London, Longmans 1968)

NICHOLSON, MAX *The System* (London, Hodder & Stoughton 1967)

NEWTON, KENNETH *The Sociology of British Communism* (London, Allen Lane The Penguin Press 1969)

PARKIN, T. E. *Middle Class Radicalism* (Manchester, Manchester University Press 1968)

ROSE, RICHARD *Influencing Voters* (London, Faber 1967)

ROSE, RICHARD *Politics in England* (London, Faber 1965)

SHANKS, MICHAEL *The Stagnant Society* (Harmondsworth, Penguin Books 1961)

STREET, HARRY *Freedom, the Individual and the Law* (Harmondsworth, Penguin Books 1963)

THAYER, GEORGE *The British Political Fringe* (London, Blond 1965)

THOMAS, HUGH (ed.) *The Establishment* (London, Blond 1959, New English Library Ltd 1962)

WILLIAMS, RAYMOND (ed.) *May Day Manifesto 1968* (Harmondsworth, Penguin Books 1968)

WINDLESHAM, LORD *Communication and Political Power* (London, Cape 1966)

Index

Fontana Politics

The English Constitution Walter Bagehot
edited by R. H. S. Crossman

Problems of Knowledge and Freedom Noam Chomsky

Understanding American Politics R. V. Denenberg

Marx and Engels: Basic Writings
edited by Lewis S. Feuer

Governing Britain A. H. Hanson and Malcolm Walles

Edmund Burke on Government, Politics and Society
edited by Brian Hill

Machiavelli: Selections
edited by John Plamenatz

Mao Ninian Smart

Lenin and the Bolsheviks Adam B. Ulam

The National Front Martin Walker

The Commons in the Seventies
edited by S. A. Walkland and Michael Ryle

John Stuart Mill on Politics and Society
Geraint Williams

To the Finland Station Edmund Wilson

The Anarchist Reader
edited by George Woodcock

Fontana History

Fontana History includes the well known series History of Europe, edited by J. H. Plumb, and Economic History of Europe, edited by Carlo Cipolla. Other books available include:

Lectures on Modern History Lord Acton

The English Constitution Walter Bagehot

The Conservative Party from Peel to Churchill Robert Blake

The Shield and the Sword Ernle Bradford

The Mediterranean and the Mediterranean World in the Age of Philip II (2 vols) Fernand Braudel

The English Reformation A. G. Dickens

The Practice of History G. R. Elton

History of Europe (2 vols) H. A. L. Fisher

Debates with Historians Pieter Geyl

A Short History of Socialism George Lichtheim

Ireland Since the Famine F. S. L. Lyons

The Elizabethan House of Commons J. E. Neale

Hitler: the Fuhrer and the People J. P. Stern

The King's Peace C. V. Wedgwood

The King's War C. V. Wedgwood

Fontana Social Science

Books available include:

African Genesis Robert Ardrey

The Territorial Imperative Robert Ardrey

The Social Contract Robert Ardrey

Racial Minorities Michael Banton

Ideology in Social Science
Edited by Robin Blackburn

The Sociology of Modern Britain
Edited by Eric Butterworth and David Weir

Social Problems of Modern Britain
Edited by Eric Butterworth and David Weir

Men and Work in Modern Britain
Edited by David Weir

Strikes Richard Hyman

The Dominant Man H. Knipe and G. Maclay

Strike at Pilkingtons Tony Lane and Kenneth Roberts

Figuring Out Society Ronald Meek

Drugs, Science and Society Alan Norton

Dockers David Wilson